"The enduring influence of what G  gelical-ism' is critical for the health and v rightly looks to the greatest intellectual fi m, Carl Henry, as a mentor and guide. At it book, directed at the most crucial issues fa. his is an important work by a leading evangelical scholar. We can only hope ... this book becomes widely influential."

R. Albert Mohler Jr., President and Joseph Emerson Brown Professor of Christian Theology, The Southern Baptist Theological Seminary

"This is the best book on Carl F. H. Henry published to date. Greg Thornbury shows why Henry is too important to be forgotten. Closely argued and well researched, this book can lead the way to a Henrician revival—one that can strengthen the fibers of faith within the evangelical soul."

Timothy George, Founding Dean, Beeson Divinity School; General Editor, *Reformation Commentary on Scripture*

"Greg Thornbury clearly understands the theological genius of Carl Henry. This marvelously written volume brilliantly captures the essence of Henry's massive writings for a new generation of students, thinkers, and leaders. Seeking to reclaim and recover Henry's primary theological commitments, his vision for shaping evangelicalism, and his strategic and irenic approach to engaging both academy and culture, Thornbury superbly interprets and applies Henry's writings in a persuasive and winsome manner. Those who have already learned much from Henry, those who have rejected or misunderstood Henry, and those who have yet to be introduced to the dean of twentieth-century evangelical theologians will benefit from this significant work. *Recovering Classic Evangelicalism*, simply stated, is an extraordinary contribution."

David S. Dockery, President, Union University

"Greg Thornbury is an exceptional emerging scholar, and his *Recovering Classic Evangelicalism* is an important, erudite work that should be read by anyone who longs for a return to a robust, vital evangelicalism. At a time when Protestant Christianity in the West is on the decline, and evangelicalism is ever more fractured, Thornbury has something important to say—imploring us to re-form an evangelicalism with sturdy foundations, a confident connection to our doctrinal heritage, and a winsome engagement with the broader world. With characteristic clarity and conviction, Thornbury suggests that evangelicalism need not reinvent the wheel in order to remain relevant; rather, it must reclaim the essentials of its Protestant heritage and immerse itself in the beautiful basics that once made it great."

Barry H. Corey, President, Biola University

"The witness of Carl Henry and classic evangelicalism to absolute truth and objective knowledge; the critical importance of theology in life and ministry; the total truthfulness of Scripture and biblical inerrancy; a churchly, faithful, and Christian engagement with culture; and a vision of what evangelicalism could and should be are all things that we need to hear or recover today. Every chapter of this book instructed, challenged, and encouraged me personally and prompted me to want evangelicals of this generation to read and heed the lessons from the story that Greg Thornbury tells so well."

**J. Ligon Duncan,** John E. Richards Professor of Systematic and Historical Theology, Reformed Theological Seminary; Senior Minister, First Presbyterian Church, Jackson, Mississippi

# RECOVERING
# CLASSIC
# EVANGELICALISM

# RECOVERING
# CLASSIC
# EVANGELICALISM

## APPLYING THE WISDOM AND VISION
## OF CARL F. H. HENRY

*Gregory Alan Thornbury*

CROSSWAY
WHEATON, ILLINOIS

*Recovering Classic Evangelicalism: Applying the Wisdom and Vision of Carl F. H. Henry*

Published by Crossway
         1300 Crescent Street
         Wheaton, Illinois 60187

Cover design: Dual Identity inc.
Cover image: Courtesy of Billy Graham Center Archives

First printing 2013

Printed in the United States of America

Unless otherwise indicated, Scripture quotations are from the ESV® Bible (*The Holy Bible, English Standard Version®*), copyright © 2001 by Crossway. 2011 Text Edition. Used by permission. All rights reserved.

Scripture references marked NIV are taken from The Holy Bible, New International Version®, NIV®. Copyright © 1973, 1978, 1984 by Biblica, Inc.™ Used by permission. All rights reserved worldwide.

Scripture quotations marked KJV are from the King James Version of the Bible.

Trade paperback ISBN: 978-1-4335-3062-3
PDF ISBN: 978-1-4335-3063-0
Mobipocket ISBN: 978-1-4335-3064-7
ePub ISBN: 978-1-4335-3065-4

**Library of Congress Cataloging-in-Publication Data**
Thornbury, Gregory Alan.
    Recovering classic evangelicalism : applying the wisdom and vision of Carl F. H. Henry / Gregory Alan Thornbury.
        p. cm.
    Includes bibliographical references and index.
    ISBN 978-1-4335-3062-3
    1. Evangelicalism. 2. Theology, Doctrinal. I. Henry, Carl F. H. (Carl Ferdinand Howard), 1913–2003. II. Title.
BR1640.T49 2013
230'.04624—dc23                                        2012035468

Crossway is a publishing ministry of Good News Publishers.

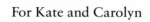

For Kate and Carolyn

# Contents

# Preface

I have always been one to appreciate odd juxtapositions in life, and that sentiment isn't lost upon me as I write the preface to this volume. I am sitting here at Lennon Studios in San Francisco waiting on a friend to finish up rehearsals for a highly anticipated reunion performance of the glam-rock band he played in back in the '80s. Seems like the perfect place to pause and reflect about finishing up a project on Carl F. H. Henry, right? For reasons I will explain in this book, there are those who see Henry's thought as a relic of a bygone era. I beg to differ, but if Carl becomes an antihero of a new orthodox generation, a dream will have come true!

Several years ago, I raised the possibility of doing this book with a prominent pastor, and he didn't exactly encourage me. "I loved Carl," he said, pausing for a moment, "but would anybody care about him now?" Since that conversation, all of the conversations I have had on the question have pointed in the other direction. Perhaps now, one decade removed from Henry's passing, the timing is right for this project.

For the past fifteen years, my context has been Union University in Tennessee, and it really is hard to imagine a community more supportive of a book with a subject such as this one. In 2000, Dr. Henry gave his name to a new center, which I had just been given responsibility to lead. It was a vote of confidence in our work at Union as a place committed to the great Christian intellectual tradition, and it boosted the commonweal. As the dean of the School of Theology and Missions at Union, I count it an immense privilege to be surrounded by the greatest team of colleagues, who are some of the leading scholars in their respective fields, but who are also deeply committed to "classic evangelicalism." Among those colleagues a few in particular really helped me "power through" this volume toward completion: Taylor Worley, Gene Fant, Hunter Baker, Hal Poe, Jim Patterson, and C. Ben Mitchell.

More than other colleagues, however, no one has been more enthusiastic about my work on Henry than David S. Dockery, president of Union University, friend, mentor, and my systematic theology teacher. No one is more a living embodiment of the best of the Henry legacy than he.

My staff at Union during this time has been pure gold. Corey Taylor tracked down bibliography and helped me comb through *God, Revelation and Authority*. Christy Young ran interference for me on many occasions when people were puzzled why they had to wait for days to get an appointment to see the dean. Special thanks though is due to Andrew Norman, who helped me manage my classes at Union and worked long hours reading, editing, fixing references, compiling material, and just being relentlessly helpful.

Beyond the campus of Union, so many other colleagues have offered fresh supplies of support and insight. Paul R. House has been subjected to numerous multihour conversations about the Henry legacy, and his thoughts have been formative and indispensable. Russell D. Moore, as always, has been an inspiration.

Other dear friends, some who have never read a word of Henry, have cared that their friend, "the professor," gets his book done. Among these are Jonathan Paul Gillette, Richard Bailey, Charles and Kristin Norman, Jeff and Shelly Colvin, Amy Mesecher, and last but not least, the Diogenes Club.

In addition, I would like to thank Lane Dennis and Crossway profusely not only for their willingness to publish this work, but also for their long-standing commitment to the Henry vision. Also, if there is a better acquisitions editor who "gets it" more than Justin Taylor, I certainly don't know of one. His patience while he awaited the arrival of this book is the stuff of legend.

Most of all, the lion's share of thanks goes to Kimberly, Kate, and Carolyn, my little family, who endured a number of Saturdays at state parks, outings, and Civil War battlefields without Daddy so he could write. My parents, John and Reta Thornbury, prayed faithfully for me during this project. And Kimberly's parents, John and Carolyn Carmichael, were extremely generous in helping underwrite some research assistance for me throughout the writing of this manuscript.

For all of these, I am exceedingly grateful.

# CHAPTER 1

# The Lost World of Classic Evangelicalism

Everyone loves a good opening sequence in a film, and one of my favorites has to be the first fifteen minutes of *Jurassic Park*, the adaptation of Michael Crichton's novel. The story introduces the audience to Dr. Alan Grant, a paleontologist who spends his days on archeological digs looking for dinosaur bones, when he is sought out by John Hammond, an underwriter of Grant's research and owner of a genetics lab. Hammond invites Grant and his graduate student Dr. Ellie Sattler to come with him to review his latest project, situated on Isla Nublar, about one hundred miles off Costa Rica. Upon arriving at the island via helicopter, Grant and his colleagues are taken on their first tour of Jurassic Park. As they make their way through the gates, Grant's jeep pulls up the side of a hill, and what he sees leaves him speechless: a brontosaurus goes lumbering past them. When Hammond tells Grant that the park has a live T. rex, the paleontologist gets light-headed and has to sit down. For years he has been studying dry bones and fantasizing about a world in which these magnificent creatures actually lived and moved about in power on the earth. Now, he is confronted with the reality before him: "Dinosaurs aren't just an object of study anymore—they are standing here right in front of me, confronting me with their strange and powerful ways."

It may seem strange to begin a book on Carl F. H. Henry's legacy by comparing him to a dinosaur. We live, however, in unstable days, and somehow the juxtaposition seems strangely apt, as I hope to show. For if we were going to press the Jurassic Park analogy further, we might note that the dinosaurs still have some fight left in them.

I grew up in the Northeast, where my father pastored a village church just outside of Lewisburg, Pennsylvania. Our congregation at the time was aligned with the American Baptist Churches (USA). Throughout his time serving as a minister, my father was actively involved in evangelical renewal projects, which proved to be a discouraging, if not impossible, task. But I remember his attending a denominational meeting in which Carl Henry spoke about recovering confidence in biblical authority. The presentation buoyed his spirits, so he wrote Henry to thank him. Several weeks later, he received a very gracious and thoughtful reply from the great theologian. My friend and colleague Owen Strachan, who worked in the extensive Henry archive at Trinity Evangelical Divinity School, sent me a copy of the letter, which was on file. It reminded me of the debt that I personally, and I believe all of us corporately, owe to this great man.

My own sense of gratitude to Henry is reflected in my own biography. In my freshman year of college, I was exposed to a high dose of the historical-critical method of biblical study from a very kind, brilliant, and influential professor. Our freshman biblical survey textbook was Marcus J. Borg's *Jesus: A New Vision*. My mind reeled as I read through its contents. I had been brought up with the conviction that the Bible was God's very word, that it had a supernatural, objective origin, and that it was wholly trustworthy. And yet, in the classroom I was being confronted by a well-studied and persuasive scholar with an Oxford DPhil who was teaching us about form and redaction criticism, and the all-too-human manner in which the Scriptures came together. I came within a whisker of losing my evangelical confidence in the authority of Scripture. I called former mentors and consulted the authors I had read in high school, but none of these answered my doubts. Then, remembering my father's high esteem for the theology of Carl F. H. Henry, I went to the library. Taking up nearly a whole shelf on its own was *God, Revelation and Authority*. As an undergraduate student engaged in both philosophy and biblical studies, I immediately identified with Henry's approach and scholarship. Here was a philosopher-theologian of astonishing erudition and a titanic intellect. I remember thinking, "If this guy could believe in biblical inerrancy, then I can too." It proved to be the turning point for me.

I must make one other confession at the outset before proceeding any further. During my PhD work at The Southern Baptist Theological Seminary in Louisville, Kentucky, several friends and I gathered in the office of the newly engaged *Southern Baptist Journal of Theology*, where it soon became apparent that each and every one of us had the legacy of Carl Henry running through our veins. Paul R. House wrote Carl to ask him whether he had the rights to his masterwork *God, Revelation and Authority* (GRA), and whether he had any interest in seeing it republished. Henry wrote back, answering in the affirmative, and four of us—Paul House, C. Ben Mitchell, Richard Bailey, and I—journeyed to meet Carl, who seemed exiled in Watertown, Wisconsin. During that visit, we were all transformed into official Henry protégés of a sort, and I had the good fortune of beginning a correspondence with Carl and his wife, Helga, over a period of time. In fact, one of the greatest privileges of my academic career was to travel to Trinity Evangelical Divinity School to present on Hans Frei and postliberalism at one of Henry's last graduate seminars. In time, and with the enthusiastic support of R. Albert Mohler, president of Southern Seminary, and Lane Dennis from Crossway, *GRA* was reissued as a complete set in 1999. So, in the interest of full disclosure, I confess up front that I am no unbiased bystander or scholar of the Henry corpus. I feel like Dr. Grant in *Jurassic Park*. I have seen a time in which giants roamed the land, and like all travelers who sojourn in magical places, I long for myself and my fellow evangelicals to return to the world of Henry—where the promise and power of evangelicalism seemed to be just within reach.

## Evangelicalism: A Suicide Death Cult

Throughout its relatively brief and checkered history, evangelicalism has been given many definitions. The question, who are we? bedevils any family, culture, or religious group. Likewise, the question, who am I? is the fundamental query of human existence. It was, after all, the thorny matter at hand when Descartes began searching for his Archimedean point in epistemology. During this quest to discover the indubitable foundations for thought, Descartes realized that such issues are inextricably bound up with personhood. His program of methodological doubt—supposing that everything he saw or experienced was a chimera and illusory—plunged him into a deep melancholy—if his *Meditations on First Philosophy* are taken as memoir as much as description of his approach to achieving truth. Descartes supposed that some malicious demon might be controlling his senses, causing him to believe that which was spurious. But it was precisely this moment of despair, the French philosopher believed, that occasioned his greatest discovery: that if he was being deceived, then he most certainly existed.

> And let this [deceiver of supreme power and cunning] deceive as much as he can, he will never bring it about that I am nothing so long as I think that I am something. So after considering everything very thoroughly, I must finally conclude that this proposition, *I am, I exist*, is necessarily true whenever it is put forward by me or conceived in my mind.[1]

Descartes's *cogito* stands as an archetype of the "who am I?" interrogative. For him, it was crucial to know who we are in order to get to the question of what we can be, or what can be known. One need not be a Cartesian to appreciate his contribution to the history of self-definition. Discovering one's identity—both as an individual and as part of culture—is important to a person's internal sense of purpose and prerogatives. For their part, evangelicals have in the past almost fetishized the business of self-examination. In the 1980s and 1990s it was the subject of seemingly endless discussion, with more conferences, essays, monographs, confessions, and salvos than any other comparable movement. This is not to gainsay such discussions

---

[1]René Descartes, *Meditations on First Philosophy* (*Meditationes de prima philosophia*, 1641), rev. ed., trans. John Cottingham (Cambridge: Cambridge University Press, 1996), 17 (meditation 1 and part of 2).

by any means, for the book you are reading is a kind of alternative memoir of evangelicalism: its past, present, and future.

While lecturing in Norway recently, I was asked to define evangelicalism. "It is," said I, "a suicide death cult." I got the quizzical look I was anticipating, so I went on to explain. Evangelicals are a people who are constantly second-guessing themselves and constantly reimagining their project(s) along those lines. Stated differently, we are an editorial people, or, put more precisely, a self-editorializing people. Like most core traits of a collective, this attribute of evangelicalism expresses itself in a bipolar manner. First, the penchant for editing has made evangelicals a dynamic, forward-thinking movement. As Joel Carpenter has demonstrated in his helpful history *Revive Us Again*, this impulse to change sometimes served in positive ways, with revivalism helping the movement break free of the shackles of fundamentalism.[2] Timothy George built on this point in his work on William Carey[3] and D. L. Moody,[4] arguing that fresh gospel resources are always available to each successive generation. Similarly, *A God-Sized Vision*, by John Woodbridge and Collin Hansen, has detailed the sort of *esprit de corps* that inspired great movements of missional advance for the evangelical cause in America, from the First Great Awakening through the 1950s and the reinvigoration that the ministry of Billy Graham brought to believers around the globe.[5] In addition to this willingness to leave behind certain practices and traditions in order to make room for renewal and growth, evangelicals have inherited the virtue of self-critique from their Protestant forebears and their insistence on *semper ecclesia reformanda*. To admit error, to declare *mea culpa* and attempt to square with even the hardest truths, is a Christian virtue setting us apart from other religious traditions, say, cults that must lay claim to the infallibility of their

---

[2]Joel Carpenter, *Revive Us Again: The Reawakening of American Fundamentalism* (New York: Oxford University Press, 1999).

[3]Timothy George, *Faithful Witness: The Life and Mission of William Carey* (Birmingham, AL: New Hope, 1991).

[4]Timothy George, *Mr. Moody and the Evangelical Tradition: The Legacy of D. L. Moody* (Edinburgh: T&T Clark, 2004).

[5]Collin Hansen and John Woodbridge, *A God-Sized Vision: Revival Stories That Stretch and Stir* (Grand Rapids: Zondervan, 2010).

leaders, or even other world religions like Islam that are wary of admitting shortcomings in the reception of their tradition.

There is, however, another side to this penchant for internal critique. Left to themselves, evangelicals will criticize themselves to death, or at the very least, to the point of exhaustion. We have a self-image problem, and there is a veritable cottage industry for this analysis. Much of the navel gazing is welcome, entertaining, and precisely on target. Stephanie Drury's blog, "Stuff Christian Culture Likes," hits close to home. Her tagline—"Christian culture is funny because it doesn't have much (if anything) to do with Christ himself"—rings true.[6] Then there is the string of volumes assessing our condition, from Os Guinness's *Fit Bodies, Fat Minds*[7] to Brett McCracken's *Hipster Christianity*,[8] to virtually anything Randall Balmer has written in the past ten years.

Several years ago, while I was reading Brian McLaren's *A Generous Orthodoxy*, I found myself wondering how much of this could have been avoided if Brian as a little boy had not been made to wear clip-on ties and shoes with slick soles to church.[9] And just to show that I am being evenhanded with my analysis, consider David Wells's series of apocalyptic books about evangelical decline: *No Place for Truth*,[10] *God in the Wasteland*,[11] *Losing Our Virtue*,[12] and *Above All Earthly Pow'rs: Christ in a Postmodern World*.[13] What really strikes you about those volumes is that they are a systematic theology *via negativa* but read through a quasi-sociological lens. The primary mode of discourse is lament.

---

[6]Stephanie Drury, "Stuff Christian Culture Likes," http://www.stuffchristianculturelikes.com.
[7]Os Guinness, *Fit Bodies, Fat Minds: Why Evangelicals Don't Think and What to Do About It* (Grand Rapids: Hourglass, 1994).
[8]Brett McCracken, *Hipster Christianity: When Church and Cool Collide* (Grand Rapids: Baker, 2010).
[9]Brian A. McLaren, *A Generous Orthodoxy* (Grand Rapids: Zondervan, 2004), 20.
[10]David F. Wells, *No Place for Truth, or, Whatever Happened to Evangelical Theology?* (Grand Rapids: Eerdmans, 1993).
[11]David F. Wells, *God in the Wasteland: The Reality of Truth in a World of Fading Dreams* (Grand Rapids: Eerdmans, 1994).
[12]David F. Wells, *Losing Our Virtue: Why the Church Must Recover Its Moral Vision* (Grand Rapids: Eerdmans, 1998).
[13]David F. Wells, *Above All Earthly Pow'rs: Christ in a Postmodern World* (Grand Rapids: Eerdmans, 2005.)

What is ironic about all of these books is that the hand-wringing is actually quite justified. But what I want to point out is that you never really see conservative Roman Catholics heaping the self-criticism on the curia, the papacy, or the canon law by way of contrast. Instead, they are keen to protect their milieu. I was reminded of this recently when some friends of mine in Oregon attended an event at a local Roman Catholic church on the life of G. K. Chesterton. Initially, they had been invited to remain afterward for a conclave of local priests and dignitaries. However, when they raised questions about Chesterton's views on women and evangelicals, they were politely informed that they had been disinvited from the post-Chesterton-event festivities. They were not upset about it, but I'm fairly certain that had this been an event sponsored by evangelicals on one of our heroes, we would have invited, even relished the criticism. Because that is who we are—it's just how we roll. This is also one of the reasons why evangelicalism struggles to maintain its shape or to adopt a different image, why it splinters so easily. We either cannot bear the burden of being right or, even if we can, we're sure the term *faithful* is an adjective modifying the noun *few*.

## Killing the Father

In either case, we feel compelled to undermine or move away from the people who got evangelicals where they are today. Keeping in mind George Marsden's definition from nearly twenty years ago that an evangelical is "someone who likes Billy Graham," we will exclude the famous evangelist from the picture for a moment.[14] That leaves out a few of the seminal figures who were present and active when the foundations were laid for the movement. We might include individuals such as J. I. Packer and the late John R. W. Stott in this list because, let us be honest with ourselves, who among us of age in the 1970s and 1980s was not influenced by books like *"Fundamentalism"*

---

[14]George Marsden, "Contemporary American Evangelicalism," in *Southern Baptists and American Evangelicals: The Conversation Continues*, ed. David S. Dockery (Nashville, TN: Broadman & Holman, 1993), 27.

*and the* Word of God,[15] Knowing God,[16] Basic Christianity,[17] *and*
Christ the Controversialist,[18] respectively? But here again I think we
have another exception to the rule. Both Packer and Stott were British, and American evangelicals are hopeless Anglophiles—so these
figures each tend to escape criticism on the whole. No, if you want
to witness the tendency to demolish our own evangelical heroes, you
need look no further than Francis Schaeffer or Carl F. H. Henry. The
former has been raked over the coals by his own son, Frank, first in
the novel *Portofino*[19] and more explicitly in Frank's memoir *Crazy
for God*,[20] as well as his *Sex, Mom, and God*.[21] Certainly no one
can dispute Frank's own experiences and perceptions, but he almost
seems to revel in recounting what he sees as his father's shortcomings
as a hot-tempered, petulant, miserable man who felt miscast in the
role of an evangelist, and of his mother as a sexual-revolutionary
wannabe miscast as an evangelist's wife.

With respect to Henry, the critiques have rolled in for the past
fifteen years or so. Although we will turn to the specifics of these
concerns later in the book, it is a fair summary to say that figures
associated with what might be considered the postmodern turn in
evangelical theology have been unhappy with the Henry legacy.
Although the moment for the most trenchant critiques seems to
have passed, it is safe to say that the Henry legacy has taken a sound
drubbing for the past twenty years or so. It began somewhat auspi-
ciously with George Marsden's landmark history of the early years
of Fuller Seminary, *Reforming Fundamentalism*.[22] In Marsden's

[15] J. I. Packer, *"Fundamentalism" and the Word of God: Some Evangelical Principles* (Grand Rapids: Eerdmans, 1990).
[16] J. I. Packer, *Knowing God* (Downers Grove, IL: InterVarsity, 1973).
[17] John R. W. Stott, *Basic Christianity* (London: Inter-Varsity, 1958; repr., Grand Rapids: Eerdmans, 1971).
[18] John R. W. Stott, *Christ the Controversialist: A Study in Some Essentials of Evangelical Religion* (Downers Grove, IL: InterVarsity, 1970).
[19] Frank Schaeffer, *Portofino: A Novel* (New York: Macmillan, 1992).
[20] Frank Schaeffer, *Crazy for God: How I Grew Up as One of the Elect, Helped Found the Religious Right, and Lived to Take All (or Almost All) of It Back* (New York: Carroll & Graf, 2007).
[21] Frank Schaeffer, *Sex, Mom, and God: How the Bible's Strange Take on Sex Led to Crazy Politics and How I Learned to Love Women (and Jesus) Anyway* (Cambridge, MA: Da Capo, 2011).
[22] George Marsden, *Reforming Fundamentalism: Fuller Seminary and the New Evangelicalism* (Grand Rapids: Eerdmans, 1987).

work, Henry comes across looking something akin to an out-of-place snow miser from New York living in sunny California. He is caricatured as the patron saint of lost causes, trying to hold the line on the doctrine of inerrancy at an institution that has already capitulated on the issue. In correspondence with Henry, Marsden claimed that Carl had mistaken Marsden's historical analysis as critique; Marsden went so far as to state that his own theological position was sympathetic with Henry's. While Marsden's criticism of Henry was more oblique, individuals such as the late Stanley J. Grenz,[23] John Franke,[24] and Kevin Vanhoozer[25] have been more pointed in their cavils of Henry. In sum, they view the epistemology Henry spent the better part of his career cultivating as the philosophical relic of a bygone era.

Slovenian philosopher Slavoj Žižek has observed that from the perspective of Freudian psychology the one truly obscene thought is that the father lives. One of the themes of the present book is that evangelicals are in danger of theological patricide. Our attempts to avoid unnecessary rigidity or morbidity have brought us to the threshold of dispensing with certain convictions that once inspired and animated evangelicals toward greatness. These commonplaces, if they are exchanged for unworthy alternatives, will carry our traditions and institutions in a direction that may feel new and exciting, but will no longer be what I am calling "classic evangelicalism." To be fair, the innovative impulse of evangelicalism is simultaneously its greatest strength and weakness. But if we are honest with ourselves, we have never been very good at staying ahead of the curve. We became fascinated with neoorthodoxy at precisely the moment it was going out of style in mainline Protestantism. We turned to models like speech-act theory to explain the phenomena of divine

---

[23]Stanley J. Grenz and Roger E. Olson, *20th Century Theology: God and the World in a Transitional Age* (Downers Grove, IL: InterVarsity, 1992).
[24]John Franke, *The Character of Theology: An Introduction to Its Nature, Task, and Purpose* (Grand Rapids: Baker Academic, 2005).
[25]Kevin Vanhoozer, "Lost in Interpretation: Truth, Scripture, and Hermeneutics," *Journal of the Evangelical Theological Society* 48, no. 1 (2005): 89–114.

revelation even though John Searle himself believes that value judgments of any sort are epistemically subjective.[26]

Remember my Norwegian interlocutor who asked me to define what an evangelical is? Well, I also gave him a slogan that I think nicely defines what evangelicals have become in the early twenty-first century: "Anything you can do, we can do later. We can do anything later than you." We seem ready to accept trends just after the sell-by date of the rest of the academy. We are adopting postmodern forms of inquiry just as the broader world of theory seems to be going back to Hegel. We cannot keep up. By way of contrast, the post–World War II neoevangelicals started out during that period with high hopes and big dreams for their movement as they emerged from the shackles of fundamentalism. They dreamed of an evangelistic program that would see America and Europe turn to Jesus Christ as Savior and Lord. They envisioned a body of thought consistent with historic Christian orthodoxy that would appeal to the intellectual class of the day and spawn new work across the disciplines of human inquiry in the arts, psychology, science, and politics. In the main, the spirit was hopeful, upbeat, and progressive, which I intend to demonstrate in the following chapters. During this critical period, it would be fair to say that if Billy Graham was the heart of evangelicalism, Carl F. H. Henry was its head. It was a time in which young evangelicals could look to a figure like Henry, the man with the massive brain, a journalist's pen, and Athanasian fortitude.

Times have changed. Nowadays, nothing seems so positively square and yesteryear as Henry. In such a clime, I propose something seemingly impossible in this moment in evangelicalism's biography. I want to make Carl Henry cool again. This does not mean that what follows here is some kind of hagiography. In recent conversations with my colleague Paul House, we have agreed upon some core weaknesses of Henry the man. What follows is by no means an exhaustive list, but here are some:

---

[26] John R. Searle, Daniel C. Dennett, and David J. Chalmers, *The Mystery of Consciousness* (New York: New York Review of Books, 1997), 122. Vanhoozer is the chief offender here, but Erickson argues this as well.

For all of his brilliance and ability, Carl Henry was certainly not a perfect man. First, he was not a good public speaker, as either a preacher or extemporaneous lecturer, and lacked a powerful preaching ministry. Even so, former disciples of Henry have praised his prayerful attitude toward students. According to evangelical philosopher Win Corduan, Henry told his charges there are two kinds of teachers: those you hate during the course for being too hard, and those you hate after the class for being too easy. He wished to be counted among the former.

Second, while it is probably the case that *Christianity Today* did not deal forthrightly with Carl despite his honesty with them, he never did quite see how saying he could resign at any moment led to the *CT* board's finally making a move when they got political pressure from J. Howard Pew. Henry tended to treat *CT* involvement like a one-year academic contract, and the board wanted a long-term commitment. In other words, he was not all that politically astute.

Third, though Carl cited a lot of Bible verses in his work, context for those references was not always provided, which, coupled with his relatively weak command of Hebrew, may have limited his exegesis. Fourth, he did have a temper and could be curt and harsh with people at times. Fifth, his standards were high, perhaps unreasonably so, such that he often pushed people toward goals and ends they were incapable of achieving. This probably made them better than they would have been (e.g., *CT*), but it must have rankled his colleagues nonetheless. Sixth, he placed too much confidence in big-event and big-organization evangelicalism and could have benefitted from thinking more organically and ecclesially. This tendency probably resulted from his own experience and ministry.

Seventh, he linked the United States and democracy too closely to godliness, though during the Soviet era one could sympathize with that temptation. Eighth, he did not stand as he knew later he should have for civil rights. He pushed hard at *CT* and was proud of his track record there, but Nelson Bell pushed harder, and the magazine lacked the prophetic edge it might have had during the Civil Rights era, a feature noted by Peter Goodwin Heltzel in *Jesus and Justice: Evangelicals, Race, and American Politics.*[27] Ninth, he overstated the potential of evangelicalism as he conceived it, even while he rightly understood the unending potential of the gospel message itself. Tenth, he did not always think strategically with his own writings, as demonstrated by the fact that he never wrote a single-volume or dual-volume theology text, which would have led people to the six volumes of *GRA*. Eleventh, he was too dependent on Billy Graham until 1968. Twelfth, he admitted later that he was better suited for working at a university than at a seminary.

In sum, Henry had his foibles and his blind spots. He probably wrote one too many jeremiads. He felt like an outsider in a world of insiders and good old boys, and was embittered about the way in which the evangelical project developed away from his original vision.[28] He had difficulty keeping teams together, whether at Fuller Seminary or at *Christianity Today*, and with respect to his theological output, it is fair to submit his work to scrutiny. But if I don't miss my guess, one of the problems that has most hindered Henry's reception in recent years comes from the fact that people have read more of his cultural essays than his serious theological work. And that certainly makes sense. *God, Revelation and Authority* is a dense, sometimes unapproachable six-volume work of philosophical and theological analysis on the concept of epistemology from a theistic point of view. Millard Erickson, knowing that I kept in touch with Carl, once inquired as to how he was doing. After I told him of Carl's battles with spinal stenosis over the previous months, Millard asked me to convey greetings to Carl the next time we spoke. And then his eyes twinkled and he quipped, "You know I love Carl Henry's work. It's extremely important. I hope someday that it is translated into English." He was, of course, right. Henry was an English-speaking theologian whose agenda was to write a German *Wissenschaft* for evangelicalism. And I would argue that he was the first and last person who really made a serious attempt at that enterprise.

---

[27]Peter Goodwin Heltzel, *Jesus and Justice: Evangelicals, Race, and American Politics* (New Haven, CT: Yale University Press), esp. 71–72, 82–88.

[28]See, for example, the panel discussion with Richard Mouw, Russell Moore, Craig Mitchell, and Peter Heltzel, moderated by Michael White, at the annual meeting of the Evangelical Theological Society, 2009, New Orleans.

## A Thumbnail Biographical Sketch

Several years ago, I was approached by a publisher to write a biography of Henry. I declined, not from any lack of interest, but because
I am, first and foremost, a philosopher and theologian, not a biog-
rapher. But second, I think it is relatively difficult to improve upon
the currently available assessments, beginning with Henry's own
inimitable memoir, *Confessions of a Theologian*.[29] This is really
the place to begin if you want to hear Henry in his own voice. In
addition to this source, the best summaries of Henry's career can be
found in Albert Mohler's chapter in *Baptist Theologians*[30] and Paul
House's thematic tribute, "Remaking the Modern Mind: Revisiting
Carl F. H. Henry's Theological Vision."[31] With this caveat in mind,
it might be helpful here to survey the basic features of his career
and life, which overlapped so consistently with many of the central
institutions and movements in the history of evangelicalism: Wheaton
College, Fuller Seminary, *Christianity Today*, the Lausanne Congress on World Evangelism and its corresponding statement of faith,
Prison Fellowship, World Vision, and his institutional connections
with Trinity Evangelical Divinity School, and, toward the end of his
career, Southern Seminary and Union University.[32]

Henry (b. 1913) enjoyed a distinguished ninety years on planet
Earth. A New York City public-school kid cum boy-genius editor of
the Suffolk county *Smithtown Star*, the young journalist could as well
have been a real life Tintin as the philosopher-theologian he became.
But everything changed for Henry when, as he used to say repeatedly,
he encountered "the risen Lord." Thanks to the evangelistic efforts of
an outreach to leaders called "the Oxford Group," he understood the

---

[29]Carl F. H. Henry, *Confessions of a Theologian: An Autobiography* (Waco, TX: Word, 1986).
[30]Albert Mohler, "Carl F. H. Henry," in *Baptist Theologians*, ed. Timothy George and David S.
Dockery (Nashville, TN: Broadman, 1990).
[31]Paul R. House, "Remaking the Modern Mind: Revisiting Carl F. H. Henry's Theological
Vision," *Southern Baptist Journal of Theology* 8, no. 4 (2004).
[32]In 2003, Union University named its center for Christian leadership the Carl F. H. Henry
Institute for Intellectual Discipleship in honor of Henry shortly after he died. Likewise, in
2004, The Southern Baptist Theological Seminary in Louisville, Kentucky, established its own
Carl F. H. Henry Center for Science and Theology, with Trinity Evangelical Divinity School
following suit in 2005, renaming its Center for Theological Understanding the Carl F. H. Henry
Center for Theological Understanding in honor of the former TEDS alumnus.

importance of regeneration through personal faith in Jesus Christ. Despite having been confirmed into the Episcopal Church at the age of twelve, in which he was pronounced "an inheritor of the promises of the Kingdom of God," he later reflected, "I was, in fact, no more regenerate than the Long Island phone directory."[33] The miracle of conversion never wore off for him, and he took the matter of personal evangelism very seriously from that point forward.

As Henry made his way through Wheaton College, he was struck by the robust emphasis on the cognitive dimension of the Christian faith that was modeled by the institution's president, J. Oliver Buswell, but especially his main philosophy professor, Gordon H. Clark. Despite any caricature to the contrary, Henry certainly lived a life of vibrant piety and sensitivity to the work of the Holy Spirit, a conviction he constantly emphasized and for which he was well known by the students of Trinity Evangelical Divinity School, who regarded him as a professor who made it a priority to pray personally with his students. But it was the idea that Christianity is the most intellectually satisfying account of reality that energized him the most. This theme defined his written work from that point on. He was not a charismatic or outgoing personality, but it seemed that his Lord did the networking for him, for it was during his days at Wheaton that Carl formed friendships with Billy Graham and Harold Lindsell, and most importantly, that was where he met Helga Bender, who would become his lifelong wife and faithful companion, and to whom he gave the affectionate German pet name "Shatzie" ("my love").

After completing graduate degrees at Wheaton and Northern Baptist Theological Seminary, Henry joined the faculty of Northern as professor of systematic theology and philosophy of religion in 1942. He went on to complete a PhD in philosophy at Boston University, where he examined the impact of Edgar Brightman's personal idealism on the theological development of the preeminent Baptist theologian Augustus Hopkins Strong at the turn of the twentieth century. Although Henry considered himself a Northern Baptist, he understood the kingdom of God as being much larger than eccle-

---

[33]Henry, *Confessions of a Theologian*, 26.

siastically focused Christianity. It was perhaps this orientation that prompted Henry to associate with organizations that transcended denominational lines—associations that made him a central figure in the development of evangelicalism. In addition to being one of the younger leaders involved in the start of the National Association of Evangelicals, Henry went on to participate in the formation of many of the key institutions that would shape orthodox Protestant Christianity for the rest of the century: Fuller Seminary, *Christianity Today*, the Lausanne Congress, World Vision, and Prison Fellowship.[34]

In a letter to Billy Graham about the prospects for a "new evangelical magazine" that would provide an orthodox counterpart to *The Christian Century*, Henry replied that, if done right, what was to become *Christianity Today* could be: "(a) transcontinental, (b) interdenominational, (c) theologically affirmative, (d) socially aggressive and (e) irenic." And there you have it. That is Carl F. H. Henry. That is who he was.

In sum, what was most important about Henry's life and work was this: Carl F. H. Henry was born, he wrote *The Uneasy Conscience of Modern Fundamentalism*, the massive six-volume *God, Revelation and Authority*, contended for evangelical epistemological priorities, and he died. Reductionism indeed. What I am trying to say, however, is that what made Henry unique was his mind, his pen, and the methods by which he deployed his enormous intellect to help evangelicals introduce people to Jesus of Nazareth, the Christ, the risen Lord. Because he operated from this prime directive, Henry also made distinctive contributions to central concerns of the evangelical community: the grounds for Christian theism, the importance of reaching contemporary culture, the need for a transdenominational evangelical witness, and the preservation of faithful evangelical institutions. So this book is simultaneously about and not about Carl F. H. Henry. It is about the survival of the cherished subject of his career, an idea that some both explicitly

---

[34]Henry's relationships with these institutions is a mixed legacy and, in certain cases, the stuff of legend.

and tacitly have concluded is little more than a wish-dream and fantasy: evangelicalism.

In the later years of his career, Henry moved away from his primary calling as the leading thinker expounding the philosophical gravitas of divine revelation to become more a defender of the faith. He assailed missiological proposals that seemed in his mind to prioritize dubious understandings of contextualization at the expense of fixed patterns of gospel presentation.[35] By convening the Evangelical Affirmations conference in 1989, he advanced the cause of the communion of saints, reasserting verities while trying to reach common ground with a wide variety of biblical, theological, philosophical, and sociological thinkers.[36] Assessing the reappraisal of Karl Barth via postliberalism through the work of Hans Frei, Paul Holmer, and the New Yale school, Henry critiqued their understanding of narrative coherence as an adequate basis for constructive theological formulation. And long before the furor broke out in evangelicalism over justification, Henry wrote a prescient review article on the topic in the *Journal of the Evangelical Theological Society*, outlining his concern that attempts for new understandings of the doctrine could undo the evangelical project. "The modern ecumenical effort to reconcile long-standing Protestant-Catholic differences has not met with spectacular success," he wrote in 1995. "Justification is God's declaration and implementation of his eternal will giving sovereign assurance in a divine verdict that we otherwise doomed sinners are by faith now acquitted."[37] He went on to voice his concern over attempts to return to the Thomistic notion of infused righteousness or the conviction of Karl Barth that the mere confession of Christ as Lord could supersede the grounds of acceptance and forgiveness with God. Still, Henry emphasized the importance

[35]Carl F. H. Henry, "The Cultural Revitalization of Revelation," *Trinity Journal* 1, no. 2 (1980): 81–84.

[36]Kenneth S. Kantzer and Carl F. H. Henry, *Evangelical Affirmations* (Grand Rapids: Zondervan, 1990).

[37]Carl F. H. Henry, "Justification: A Doctrine in Crisis," *Journal of the Evangelical Theological Society* 38, no. 1 (1995): 57–65.

of justification as God's power for righteousness in the believer, striking a balanced tone.[38]

Over the years, evangelicals counted on their dean of theologians to help them navigate the thorny issues that arose in the academy but inevitably found their way into the preaching and teaching of church leaders. In essence, we could then afford to live like contented Hobbits in the Shire, often blissfully ignorant of the encroachments of Mordor into the surrounding territory, because there were Dúnedain like Henry, Packer, Kantzer, and company, who ranged about protecting the evangelical borders. These were men who were convictional without being pugilistic, and who responded in a theologically astute way without devolving into mere punditry. What made Henry even more remarkable was that his defense of the central axioms of evangelical conviction was not born out of some sort of provincial concern to protect an institution, coterie of colleagues, or denominational tribe. He truly believed that the gospel transcends such divisions and that evangelicals should be known more by what we are for than what we are against.

## Prospectus

In his later years, Carl Henry routinely recounted to his associates how he had read that Albrecht Ritschl's influence did not take effect until a generation after his death, when Wilhelm Hermann and Adolf von Harnack took up his mantle. Henry longed for a similar reception and hoped that he might eventually receive a new hearing after he passed away. Shortly before his passing, I organized a conference at Union University to consider the Henry legacy and invited a panoply of different voices to help interpret that legacy, including Millard Erickson, Stanley Grenz, Paul House, Albert Mohler, and among others, even Anthony Thiselton, who provided an outsider's perspective. While Carl could not attend the conference in person, owing to the spinal stenosis that kept him homebound in his final year

---

[38]For a concise overview of Henry's life and contribution, see House, "Remaking the Modern Mind"; Mohler, "Carl F. H. Henry"; or G. Wright Doyle, *Carl Henry—Theologian for All Seasons: An Introduction and Guide to* God, Revelation, and Authority (Eugene, OR: Pickwick, 2010).

of life, he was gratified to see such an august gathering of scholars convene to discuss his work in light of contemporary debates in evangelicalism. At that meeting, Paul House attempted to summarize the Henry legacy as an ambitious effort to provide a basis for a preferred evangelical future based upon prerogatives implicit in divine revelation. House argued that Henry's objective was every bit as bold as the title of his 1946 monograph *Remaking the Modern Mind*. House writes:

> [His] vision was comprehensive in that it considered the proposed evangelical worldview as the hope of the world, not just the way to reform straying American denominations affected negatively by modernism. This vision was a sustained one in that it remained amazingly consistent over fifty years. It deepened and broadened, especially as it was shared in several cultural contexts, yet retained its basic shape. . . .
>
> Stated simply, Henry's vision for theology was that it be epistemologically viable, methodologically coherent, biblically accurate, socially responsible, evangelistically oriented and universally applied. In this way theology will thereby serve the church universal, which was the view of the church most important to him. Henry's vision was that evangelical theology be nothing less than God's means of remaking modern and postmodern minds.[39]

Such a program in the midst of today's evangelical muddles seems almost naive or even romantic in light of all the divisions in evangelicalism, the compromises in doctrine, the surprisingly positive reception of Barth's theological method in evangelical circles, and the linguistic turn in philosophy. "Remaking the modern mind" seems fantastic, perhaps even messianic for an era in which some of our key leaders cannot compose differences on basic doctrines like justification by faith, the role of the church in society, and the exclusivity of the gospel. Indeed, I fear that we may have passed beyond the point of no return, that we are stuck in Oz without the possibility of a path home to Kansas, and that in Oz we fear there

---

[39]House, "Remaking the Modern Mind," 5.

might actually be some truth to the suspicion that there was nothing magical behind the curtain of evangelicalism to begin with. Any endeavor that would seek to recover classic evangelicalism must face this prospect squarely.

But I am not ready to give up quite yet because I have come to the conclusion that I am not alone. As I have told friends and colleagues about undertaking a book whose purpose is to reset the relevance of the legacy of Carl F. H. Henry for the current situation, they have invariably cheered on the project, affirming that such a book is long overdue. More than a decade ago, Carl Trueman penned an homage to Henry that began with the following commendation/attestation by the narrative theologian Gabriel Fackre: "If the twentieth century 'evangelical renaissance' in North America has produced a Michelangelo, that exemplar is surely Carl Henry."[40] Trueman, in typical good form, goes on to liken the work of Henry to the Sistine Chapel, and commends a reappraisal of Henry's insistence on propositional theology as the sine qua non of evangelical authenticity. While Trueman rightly acknowledges that Henry's work must be evaluated in the light of more recent developments in the field of hermeneutics, he points to the crucial issue at hand with which we must deal and to which Henry so directly pointed us: "Who God is, how he has revealed himself, and how we appropriate that revelation are not really three discrete issues, but three aspects of the one great problem of revelation—and all three aspects must be dealt with in any theology which aspires to the title of 'Christian.'"[41] *God, Revelation and Authority*, Trueman avers, "was intended to serve as a rallying call for evangelicals to think about their faith commitments in the same way that Henry's ethical works served as a call for evangelicals to act upon those same commitments."[42]

So it seems as though there may still be enough of us left who believe that Carl Henry, a key to evangelicalism's past, may in fact be a cipher to its future. It is a relatively small group, those of us

---

[40]Gabriel Fackre, *Ecumenical Faith in Evangelical Perspective* (Grand Rapids: Eerdmans, 1993).
[41]Carl R. Trueman, "Admiring the Sistine Chapel: Reflections on Carl F. H. Henry's *God, Revelation and Authority*," *Themelios* 25, no. 2 (2000): 48–58.
[42]Ibid., 51–52.

who have this intuition. To return to the analogy of the Shire, the admirers of Henry form a fellowship of sorts who felt better during the days when figures like Kantzer, Schaeffer, Packer, and Henry were the mainstream. To restate the relevance of works like *God, Revelation and Authority* and the cultural program of works like *Uneasy Conscience* and *Remaking the Modern Mind* for our time has become for me something of a quest. Like Frodo taking the ring to Mount Doom and realizing there is no return to the Shire as it once was, I have wondered if the journey might reveal to me something that I do not want to know, something I fear: perhaps the evangelicalism I "signed up for" is gone forever. Worse yet, perhaps it never even existed. But every time I feel this way, I stop and think that there really was once a Shire. Once upon a time, evangelicalism was a countercultural upstart movement. Positioned in between mainline denominational liberalism and reactionary fundamentalism, the evangelicals saw themselves as evangelists to all of culture. Billy Graham was reaching the masses with his Crusades, Francis Schaeffer was reaching artists and university students at L'Abri, Larry Norman was recording Jesus music on secular record labels and touring with Janis Joplin and the Doors, and Carl F. H. Henry was reaching the intellectuals through *Christianity Today*. It was "classic evangelicalism." Surveying the current evangelical landscape, one gets the feeling that we're backpedaling quickly. We are more theologically diffuse, culturally gun-shy, and balkanized than ever before. What happened? And how do we find our way back?

I originally wanted to title this book *Lost Propositions*, as a pun on the fact that the animating theses behind Henry's work have been neglected in favor of other pursuits among American evangelicals. Wisely, my editors thought better of the negative title and suggested the more positive moniker *Recovering Classic Evangelicalism*. Recovery can mean many things, including "retrieval." But recovery is also a term that is juxtaposed to patients who are ill, suffering, and perhaps even dying. Perhaps most poignantly for our context, recovery indicates the path one must travel to emerge from psychosis. So in that spirit, let us head to the infirmary and see whether the leading features of Carl F. H. Henry's life and thought are good for what ails us.

## The Approach of This Volume

In a Q&A after a public lecture several years ago, Slavoj Žižek received a critical query from the floor charging him with reading Derrida through a dogmatic Lacanian lens.[43] Rather than responding defensively, Žižek remarked that his interlocutor was knocking on an open door. He was a dogmatic Lacanian: guilty as charged. He went on, however, to say that this is the trajectory of anyone who engages in analysis with theory in view (e.g., commentators on Derrida need not be ironic or critical to appropriate the author's theoretical resources). It was a good point. In this volume, I intend to reengage Henry as a theorist of classic evangelicalism unapologetically through the lens of key texts in his written corpus. While many of Henry's writings will be referenced, my emphasis will admittedly be, at times, a paraphrase of three volumes in particular: volumes 2 and 4 of *God, Revelation and Authority*, and *The Uneasy Conscience of Modern Fundamentalism*. In my opinion, if these works are recovered for their force of argument, albeit paraphrastically, you the reader will be better positioned to draw your own conclusion as to whether you would like to become, like this author, a dogmatic Henrynian as well.

---

[43] http://www.youtube.com/watch?v=p36NeCAucRI.

# CHAPTER 2

# Epistemology Matters

## The Missing Mark of Current Evangelical Theology

In the previous chapter, I reviewed what I called the "lost world" of classic evangelicalism, a world in which Carl F. H. Henry was the leading thinker among a cadre of theologians such as Bernard Ramm, E. J. Carnell, Kenneth Kantzer, Colin Brown, Donald Bloesch, Gordon Lewis, Bruce Demarest, Norman Geisler, and Millard Erickson. The common trait among all these figures is that their work was fundamentally philosophical in orientation. When Henry took his post at Fuller Seminary, he assumed the position of professor of philosophy of religion. He and his colleagues were of the opinion that the future of evangelical theology would never rise above its foundations. A survey of the early works of the figures listed above shows a lineup of classic evangelical thinkers devoted to demonstrating that a biblically rooted Protestant worldview could not only compete in the broader world of ideas but actually flourish.

For various reasons, this philosophical conscience now appears careworn and out of fashion, especially in light of the leading evangelical theologians today. I remember how disappointed I felt at the release of the first edition of Wayne Grudem's *Systematic Theology* when I cracked open the volume to discover that there was virtually no traditional prolegomena to theology in the work. The entire basis for doing evangelical theology was missing. Gone was a discussion of definitions of theology, philosophical criteria, considerations of arguments for the existence of God, and so forth. Of course, systematic theologies have different approaches, but the vast popularity of Grudem's work as a textbook in colleges, seminaries, and churches got me thinking that the times had definitely changed. As time wore on, I wondered if it was merely a phase through which Reformed theology was moving. But a similar, if not identical, pattern obtained in other prominent Reformed thinkers. Other proposals appeared that confirmed my hypothesis. In *Covenant and Eschatology*, Michael Horton actually argued that, in effect, theology needs to operate confessionally, not epistemologically.[1] While I could certainly appreciate the presupposition that theology needs to possess the unique resources of an ecclesial tradition or confessional subscription (a topic that, admittedly, interested figures like Henry very little), I could not shake the impression that the new emphasis was found wanting. Where the matter of theological method was raised, as in Robert Reymond's *New Systematic Theology of the Christian Faith*,[2] philosophical issues were dealt with in a more cursory fashion, perhaps out of obligation, rather than as a fundamental stage upon which the grandeur of the evangelical enterprise was to be engaged. The notion of "Christian philosophy" seemed increasingly implausible to Reformed thinkers. One leader in theological education proudly reported to me that his school did not teach courses in philosophy or ethics, focusing instead on biblical theology, church history, and tradition.

I asked myself whether or not I had simply been wrong to expect theologians from the Reformed tradition to care about theological method and how Christian doctrine proposes to answer the awesome challenges presented by both modern and postmodern philosophers. Ultimately, I decided that this was not necessarily the case, especially if one considers the work of figures in the tradition such as Bavinck, Ames, Edwards, Turretin, and, arguably, Calvin. Although this debate could easily devolve into some sort of internecine squabble, my only contention here is that for twentieth-century neoevangelicalism after fundamentalism, the following dictum prevailed: epistemology matters in theological formulation.

At the same time that Reformed theologians began debating the value of prolegomena, those following in the train of the New Yale school, with its hope for a second naiveté in hermeneutics, began to

---

[1] Michael S. Horton, *Covenant and Eschatology: The Divine Drama* (Louisville, KY: Westminster John Knox, 2002).

[2] Robert L. Reymond, *A New Systematic Theology of the Christian Faith* (Nashville, TN: Nelson, 1998).

capture the imagination of more creative evangelical theologians. The publication of Alister McGrath's 1990 Bampton Lectures as *The Genesis of Doctrine* showed that evangelicals were ready to shift gears away from the epistemologically oriented and propositionally serious method of theologians like Henry.[3] For McGrath, "while some writers of the Reformation period treated Scripture as a doctrinal sourcebook—*doctrinae Christianae compendium* (Melanchthon)—there has been a recent and entirely justified tendency to stress the narrative character of the scriptural material."[4] Reflecting the influence of such figures as Hans Frei and George Lindbeck, McGrath redefined theology in communitarian terms: "Doctrine is . . . an 'insider' phenomenon, reflecting the specific perspectives of the community of faith."[5] Ever the vigilant watchman, Carl Henry immediately recognized the underlying impulse of this move and expressed concern about McGrath's train of thought. Reviewing *The Genesis of Doctrine* for the *Journal of the Evangelical Theological Society*, Henry wrote:

> When McGrath tells us that "in the end, Christian doctrine stands or falls in relation to scripture, not a particular set of concepts" (p. 65), we can join his protest against the imposition of alien conceptualities. But one is left wondering about the role of objective Scriptural truths. The Scriptural narrative, we are told must be allowed "to generate its own framework of conceptualities." But what then is the role of logical consistency and of Scriptural verification in the identification of revelation? Doctrines define God, we are told, "not in order that God might be comprehended" but that "the believer may relate to God in faith" (p. 78). "'Reason' and 'Revelation' are both subject to the limitations of historicity" (p. 90).
>
> [For McGrath] The revelatory Christ-event does not take conceptual form (p. 176). . . . Yes "the quest for a universal framework of rationality, independent of the vexatious contingencies of

---

[3] Alister E. McGrath, *The Genesis of Doctrine: A Study in the Foundations of Doctrinal Criticism* (Oxford, UK: Blackwell, 1990).
[4] Ibid., 4.
[5] Ibid., 12.

history remains frustratingly unresolved" (p. 191). One wonders whether McGrath rejects the universal applicability of the laws of logic in theological affirmation and, if so, what alternative he would propose.

. . . We are told that "outside the community of faith Jesus of Nazareth will continue to be interpreted according to rival theories of truth and reason; within the community of faith, however, Jesus of Nazareth remains the central object of worship, adoration, and wonder" (p. 193). But what has happened here to objective truth? And can McGrath seal off from the universal historical location doctrinal formulations of his own preferred option? What are the implications for evangelism and apologetics of the thesis that "only by standing within the Christian tradition" can the "full depth and meaning of its symbols and doctrines be understood" (p. 199)?[6]

If Henry were still with us, one wonders what he would make of McGrath's recent attempts to construct a "scientific theology" based upon the verities of rational discourse into nature and the elegant ways of God in the cosmos. Although I will return at the end of the next chapter to Henry's poor reception among evangelicals currently involved in the field of hermeneutics, what I intend to indicate by drawing attention to Henry's review of McGrath's *Genesis of Doctrine* is that the leading evangelical theologian of the time was always interrogating the matter of epistemology—the grounds for belief and knowledge. Although I believe discourse on philosophical hermeneutics is essential for theological method in our time, my fundamental concern stems from the fact that those who would in general agree with Henry's approach will not engage the issue. Today's evangelical thinkers are interested in many things: defining the gospel, defending a view of justification affirmed by the Protestant Reformers, thinking carefully about the practicalities of church order and structure, surveying missional strategies, and critiquing extant cultural mores. And although there has been quite a bit of interest in popular skirmishes such as responding to the new atheists or to skeptics like Bart Ehrman, the tone is less constructive than it

[6]Carl. F. H. Henry, review of *The Genesis of Doctrine*, by Alister McGrath, *Journal of the Evangelical Theological Society* 38, no. 1 (1995): 101–3.

is reactionary. Further, the current conversation wherein traditional ethical norms are questioned seems to accept as a forgone conclusion that one can appeal to divine revelation as a basis for acquiring objective truth. Carl Henry wrote some six volumes to this effect. Today, our appeals to the Bible are at best sheepish and apologetic in the wrong sense of the term. We attempt to establish our positions on some variation on Lewis's Tao, or some iteration of Thomism.

In a similar fashion, seminarians from a generation ago took active interest in philosophy of religion and apologetics. They took sides in the epistemological debates extant among the tribes: there were evidentialists and presuppositionalists. Within both camps, people drew even further distinctions between themselves. One took cues variously from Van Til, Clark, Dooyeweerd, Montgomery, or Geisler. Suspicions regarding the view of Scripture advocated by Karl Barth generated a thread of unity among evangelicals: they fundamentally rejected the key axiom of neoorthodox theology that faith is disassociated from reason, history, and science. God is not wholly other—he has revealed himself through the verities of divine revelation. Belief can interrogate unbelief—regardless of whether you come from an Augustinian or Thomistic predisposition. One could listen to the classic debate between Greg Bahnsen and Gordon Stein, or to William Lane Craig taking on John Dominic Crossan, note the differences in methodology, but see the common goal: to convince skeptics that the Christian world-and-life view operates from a position of genuine philosophical credibility. Stated differently, it was understood that there is a pattern to truth.

These days, countless conferences attract pastors, church leaders, parents, and college students to a wide range of crucial theological, social, and ministry agendas. But they all run the risk of an elephant-in-the-room dilemma. Is this stuff actually true? How would we know? Influential pastors and theologians say it is so, and say it with passion and zeal. They offer various and sundry prudential arguments for accepting the gospel and why it is the best way to live. There are screeds and there is hand-wringing about the fact that secularism is advancing and that people increasingly no longer defer de facto to church officials and the theologians. There are also romantic appeals to block out the objections of the modern and postmodern world and simply return to the way things once were when the church set the cultural agenda.[7] There are organizations that promote, discuss, and disseminate wonderful websites, conferences, and material about the gospel in general, and preaching and church life in particular. All of these can and should be supported and celebrated. What seems to be missing, however, is a substantive milieu—an epistemological backdrop against which the drama of redemption and the work of the church are played out. And if Carl F. H. Henry were still with us, my guess is that he would most likely agree with this assessment.

In the era of the twenty-first century, we have entered a period that bears the hallmarks of what Dietrich Bonhoeffer foresaw in *Letters and Papers from Prison*, wherein he described a religionless age being thrust upon the world in the post–World War II environment. Writing to Eberhard Bethge from Tegel Prison, Bonhoeffer states:

> I consider the attack by Christian apologetics on the world's coming of age as first of all pointless, second ignoble, and third, unchristian. Pointless, because it appears to me like trying to put a person who has become an adult back into puberty, that is, to make people dependent on a lot of things on which they in fact no longer depend, to shove them into problems that are, in fact, no longer problems for them. Ignoble, because an attempt is being made here to exploit people's weaknesses for alien purposes to which they have not freely consented. Unchristian, because it confuses Christ with a particular stage in man's religiousness, i.e. with a human law.[8]

Bonhoeffer continues in this trajectory, tracing out the theology of Karl Barth, who sought to disrupt the project of liberal theology by bringing "in against religion the God of Jesus Christ, '*pneuma* against *sarx*.' That remains his greatest service (his Epistle to the Romans, second edition, in spite of all the neo-Kantian eggshells)."[9]

---

[7]Cf. Peter Leithart, *Deep Exegesis: The Mystery of Reading Scripture* (Waco, TX: Baylor University Press, 2009); James Jordan, *Reconstruction of the Church* (Tyler, TX: Geneva Ministries, 1986); and Gary North and Gary DeMar, *Christian Reconstruction: What It Is, What It Isn't* (Tyler, TX: Institute for Christian Economics, 1991).

[8]Dietrich Bonhoeffer, *Letters and Papers from Prison* (Minneapolis: Fortress, 1996), 427.

[9]Ibid., 429.

Barth's failure, Bonhoeffer maintains, was that he could not translate the gospel into the epistemological vernacular of the age: "It was that in the non-religious interpretation of theological concepts he gave no concrete guidance, either in dogmatics or ethics. There lies his limitation, and because of it, his theology of revelation has become positivist, a 'positivism of revelation,' as I put it."[10] In this, Bonhoeffer critiques the venture of merely setting forth dogmatics without hermeneutics and thereby gradually "exhausting itself." We cannot merely assert the verities of theology and expect the world to "eat it." Although Bonhoeffer is notoriously evasive about the way forward (e.g., he cannot see a return to classical apologetics), his theological method in the rest of his work betrays him. Works such as *Sanctorum Communio*[11] and *Act and Being*[12] reveal a profound epistemological and ontological foundation rooted in the life and work of the local Christian church. In the end, Bonhoeffer's life and theology do not provide by themselves an adequate roadmap for precisely how the church is to engage in a religionless age.

My concern here is that current evangelical movements, although rightly emphasizing the centrality of a proper view of soteriology and the role of the church as a foretaste of the kingdom, are in danger of their own "positivism of revelation." Classic evangelicalism saw itself in continuity with the Reformers not only in terms of defining the gospel, but also in terms of an approach to truth that leads to faithful theological expression. Their leading theologians, with Henry at the vanguard, concerned themselves not only with right doctrine, but also with establishing how the concept of the reliability and authority of the Scriptures could be established and maintained in the modern world. This involved more than a mere commitment to defending biblical authority and inerrancy, although that is important, as a forthcoming chapter in this volume will argue.

In other words, classic evangelical thinkers once dared to set forth a prolegomena for evangelicalism that stood in continuity with the

---

[10]Ibid.

[11]Dietrich Bonhoeffer, *Santorum Communio* (Minneapolis: Fortress, 1996).

[12]Dietrich Bonhoeffer, *Act and Being* (Minneapolis: Fortress: 1996).

Reformers. They were followed by a formidable host of scholars—thinkers like Erickson, Carson, and Groothuis—who understand that the gospel necessarily rests upon an articulable theory of truth. In the last few years, however, evangelicals seem to have slaked their thirst for such efforts. More than any other theorist, Henry sought to stake out the territory for this effort in *God, Revelation and Authority*, along with numerous other lesser-known works such as *Toward a Recovery of Christian Belief*.[13] The success of such an undertaking demanded an authentic and truly Protestant conviction, one that refused to bow to the philosophical controls of Roman Catholic theorizing. For his part, Henry set the stage for a generation by taking his place as an heir of Reformation epistemology.

## "Incommensurable Qualities"?

As I mentioned at the outset of this book, it has recently become somewhat *en vogue* for evangelicals to engage in an increasing amount of self-deprecation. James Nuechterlein, editor of the magazine *First Things*, reflected on the penchant that evangelicals seem to have for lament and self-criticism. Although the review of Mark Noll's recent book on evangelicalism by Ralph Wood was specifically in view, Nuechterlein's comments were likewise aimed at evangelicals in general. According to Nuechterlein, Ralph Wood, professor of English at Baylor University, bemoaned evangelicals' inability "to embrace the ecclesial virtues of other Christian bodies, especially those of the [Roman] Catholic Church."[14] Nuechterlein, himself obviously sympathetic to much of Wood's critique, nonetheless observed:

> The problem is that [Wood's] prescriptions call for, in effect, a squaring of the theological and ecclesial circle. But all systems of thought, religious or otherwise, are partial. They are also all package deals. Their distinctive strengths come together with distinctive weaknesses. Neither in theology or anywhere else can we maximize all good things at once.

---

[13]Carl F. H. Henry, *Toward a Recovery of Christian Belief: The Rutherford Lectures* (Wheaton, IL: Crossway, 1990).

[14]James Nuechterlein, "Evangelical and Catholic Together?," *First Things*, October 2001, 8.

Prof. Wood wants an evangelicalism that will be at once individual and communal, fully engaged with the culture, and yet
distinct from it, authentically Protestant and authentically Catholic. He wants, in short, an evangelicalism that will no longer be
distinctly evangelical—even as he wants a Billy Graham who would
no longer be Billy Graham. We cannot blend incommensurable
qualities.[15]

Nuechterlein's observations hit the mark. And they stung. They
revealed so much about the identity crisis within evangelicalism, and
about the ways in which evangelicals are constantly looking over
their collective shoulders, doubting themselves and their theological
tradition. Now, at times, lament is certainly an appropriate theme,
and clearly it can be done well. But such persistent self-critical navel-
gazing discourages a new generation of young evangelicals about the
resources of their own intellectual tradition and leaves them especially
susceptible to any other thoughtful alternative. And so in the last
two decades evangelicals have witnessed a steady stream of defections from the camp to other groups within the broader Christian
communion. In the mid-1980s, evangelicals lost Peter Gilchrist and
a cadre of former Campus Crusade workers who sought the myster-
ies and compelling liturgy of Eastern Orthodoxy. Many evangelicals
expressed sadness or befuddlement when they lost from their ranks,
variously, filmmaker and author Franky Schaeffer (son of Francis!),
writer Frederica Mathewes-Green, and journalist Terry Mattingly to
Eastern Orthodoxy. Additionally, theologian Robert Webber informed
his audience that many Wheaton students were leaving the thorough-
fare of evangelicalism to merge onto the Canterbury trail.[16] And then,
of course, there was the string of converts to Roman Catholicism,
beginning, most notably of course, with Richard John Neuhaus, who
was subsequently followed by Thomas Howard, Michael P. Shea,
Scott Hahn, J. Budziszewski, Francis Beckwith, and many others.

---

[15]Ibid., 9.
[16]Robert Webber, *Evangelicals on the Canterbury Trail: Why Evangelicals Are Attracted to the
Liturgical Church* (Waco, TX: Word, 1985).

This is not to say that there are not severe theological crises within the evangelical communion. Both Open Theism and a late-to-the-cultural-dance but unabashed embrace of postmodernism have recently enthused certain self-proclaimed evangelicals, thus sobering even the most upbeat boosters of the cause. The lack of resolve in other quarters to respond clearly and convictionally to crises such as same-gender marriage shows just how deep the problems go. A cottage industry of books now consumes itself with various screeds about the current state of affairs within evangelical churches on matters both theoretical and practical. Trenchant critique certainly has a place in intra-ecclesial apologetics. But the various dirges may be offering, however unwittingly, a better critique of Protestantism than even the *New Oxford Review* could mount.

Especially in this environment, evangelicals must remind themselves of the glorious advances that were secured as a result of the Reformation and its heirs. Our shortcomings are often the result of an abandonment of the presuppositions that once made evangelicalism great. As Os Guinness accurately observed:

> At the heart of the Reformation was an insistence on the utter dependability of God and an unrelenting protest against any abso-lutizing of the created, the relative, and the purely human. . . . Protestant and evangelical are two faces of the same truth. Protestant is the critical stance of evangelicalism, just as evangelical is the positive content of Protestantism.[17]

Unfortunately, as Guinness concludes, "yet the Protestant principle is weak in American evangelicalism today."[18] The church certainly needs reform. The very name evangelical is derived from the work of the Protestant Reformers; for it was they who challenged the medieval abuses of the church, both theological and practical, by urging a return to the Word of God alone.

---

[17] Os Guinness, "Introduction," in *No God but God*, ed. Os Guinness and John Seel (Chicago: Moody, 1992), 25.
[18] Ibid.

## The Unwitting Reformation?

In addition to the more overt self-deprecations, another kind of inter-necine brow-beating persists among evangelicals. This kind comes from their own evangelical cultural analysts who, in their attempt to explain what has gone wrong with the modern world, lay much blame (albeit without much fanfare) at the doorstep of Renaissance humanism in general, and the Protestant Reformation in particular. Here is how the story is generally told. During the High Middle Ages, scholastic theology achieved a glorious philosophical and cultural hegemony, serving as the glue that held Christendom together. At the center of this hegemony lay the philosophy of Aristotle, as interpreted by Saint Thomas, with its inherently teleological structure. This teleology gave the universe, and particularly human beings, a sense of place and an interpretive scheme for understanding the world, a great chain of being into which everything fit. This epistemology was known as the *via antiqua* (i.e., old path; read also here scholasticism and Aristotelian reason), and under its pedagogical gaze Christendom flourished and all was right with the world. With trusty guides such as Aristotle and Thomas, one could glory in a culture produced by and for the church.

But one day, a philosophical disruption ruined Christendom's cultural paradise when the scholastic theologian William of Occam (cue the villain music here) began questioning the medieval philosophical synthesis and suggested a different course, subsequently dubbed the *via moderna* or nominalism. Contra Duns Scotus, Occam dissented from Thomism and basically claimed that Saint Thomas had actually misunderstood Aristotle. One need not, Occam allowed, divine some inherent teleological structure within the physical world to understand it. Rather, one could go to the particular things themselves and learn how each thing, in fact, worked. As a result, early modern thinkers like Francis Bacon, influenced by Occam, eventually said that if you wanted to understand what makes a frog tick, you need not locate where the frog fits in a universal scale of perfection—the frog's position in the great chain of being—thus completing the investigative task. No, to understand the frog and its systems, you dissect the frog.

The world is made up of particulars, Occam observed, and particulars alone. Occam believed, contrary to Thomas's interpretation, that he had rightly understood Aristotle by privileging epistemological particularity, a claim with which modern commentators largely agree. As Luther scholar Bernhard Lohse concludes, "Occam has often been charged with epistemological skepticism. But he merely applied the Aristotelian scientific principle more critically than other thinkers."[19]

Furthermore, Occam taught that understanding of the universe comes not by speculating at some mysterious teleology behind things that is somehow simply given and necessary. Rather, things are as they are simply because God has willed them to be that way, a truth that has come to be known as voluntarism. Based on this voluntaristic assumption, the universe can be studied and understood on its own merits without constantly giving reference to all of the complexities of Aristotelian physics. Hence, Occam developed his law of parsimony, most commonly referred to as the "razor," which states that entities should not be multiplied beyond necessity. Occam's razor effectively made possible the method of modern scientific inquiry as we know it and precipitated huge advances in our understanding of the natural world. Jacques Barzun offers an application of Occam's razor:

> William of Occam's principle of economy, that the best explanation is the one that calls for the least number of assumptions, was an argument against Ptolemy, in addition to the awkward facts. It impelled Copernicus to revise—not destroy—the system, by supposing the sun to be the center instead of the Earth. He was thereby able to reduce the epicycles from 84 to 30.[20]

Occam's epistemological developments effected an essential schism within medieval scholarship and precipitated a new school of philosophy that emphasized the freedom of the will of God in creation more than its predecessors. In other words, the nominalists/voluntarists claimed that the universe exists in its present form simply because God wills it so, in accordance with his own nature.

[19]Bernard Lohse, *Martin Luther's Theology* (Minneapolis: Fortress, 1999), 18.
[20]Jacques Barzun, *From Dawn to Decadence* (New York: HarperCollins, 2000), 192.

And it was this idea that caught the attention of a young Augustinian monk named Martin Luther and, perhaps less directly, a French humanist named John Calvin. How do we know what the world is all about? We must go to the will of God. And how do we know the will of God? By reading Aristotle? The church fathers? Saint Thomas? On the contrary, God reveals his will to those whom he wills, and he does this most preeminently through his Word. Only by the grace of God do we understand the full truth about ourselves and about the world. In the spirit of Paul's words to the Corinthians, the Christian worldview seems like foolishness to the worldly wise and nonsense to religionists (1 Cor. 1:18–25). As Luther declaimed in his own inimitable way at the Heidelberg Disputation, "One cannot philosophize well unless he is a fool, that is, a Christian." And "he who wishes to philosophize by using Aristotle without danger to his soul must first become thoroughly foolish in Christ."[21]

For his part, Calvin headed off the notion that the particulars could be studied as ends in and of themselves. The creation should be studied in consonance with what is revealed in Scripture if we want to understand the world in which we live. For as Calvin commented, "However fitting it may be for man seriously to turn his eyes to contemplate God's works, since he has been placed in this most glorious theater to be a spectator of them, it is fitting that he prick up his ears to the Word, the better to profit."[22] Calvin also elsewhere depreciated the notion that Christianity could make sense apart from a central epistemological axiom rooted in divine revelation. In the *Institutes of the Christian Religion*, the Genevan Reformer wrote that the greatest insights of the philosophers cannot begin to approach the epistemological power of the Scriptures. He surmised that the "human writings" of the philosophers, "however artfully polished," are not

> capable of affecting us at all comparably. Read Demosthenes or
> Cicero; read Plato, Aristotle, and other of that tribe. They will, I

[21]Martin Luther, *Luther's Basic Theological Writings*, ed. Timothy F. Lull (Minneapolis: Fortress, 1989), 32.
[22]John Calvin, *Institutes of the Christian Religion*, ed. John T. McNeill, trans. Ford Lewis Battles (Philadelphia: Westminster, 1960), 1.6.2.

admit, allure you, delight you, move you, enrapture you in wonderful measure. But betake yourself from them to this sacred reading. Then, in spite of yourself, so deeply will it affect you, so penetrate your heart, so fix itself in your very marrow, that, compared with its deep impression, such vigor as the orators and philosophers have will nearly vanish. Consequently, it is easy to see that the Sacred Scriptures, which so far surpass all gifts and graces of human endeavor, breathe something Divine.[23]

Understandably, Thomists expressed displeasure at the new configuration of the post-Reformation philosophical landscape, and have been understandably complaining about it ever since. Unfortunately for Occam and the Reformers, their critics have only increased in number in recent years. In addition to his Thomist and Roman Catholic detractors, Occam and the residua of voluntarism within the Reformation draw the fire and ire of evangelical philosophers and those who have inspired recent evangelical philosophy. The list includes many admirable writers, including, variously, Richard Weaver, Arthur Holmes, A. J. Conyers, Craig Gay, William Dembski, D. G. Hart, and others.[24] All of these point to Occam and the Reformers as the witting or unwitting fountainhead for all of the subsequent problems of modern (and now postmodern) philosophy. As Richard Weaver breathlessly (and quite peremptorily) concludes in *Ideas Have Consequences*:

> It was William of Occam who propounded the fateful doctrine of nominalism, which denies that universals have a real existence. . . . The practical result of nominalist philosophy is to banish the reality which is perceived by the intellect and to posit as reality that which is perceived by the senses.[25]

---

[23]Ibid., 1.8.1.
[24]See for example, William A. Dembski, *Intelligent Design* (Downers Grove, IL: InterVarsity, 1999), 110ff.; Craig Gay, *The Way of the Modern World* (Grand Rapids: Eerdmans, 1998), 65ff., 237–70; Arthur Holmes, *Fact, Value, and God* (Grand Rapids: Eerdmans, 1997), 68ff.; and D. G. Hart, *The Lost Soul of American Protestantism* (Lanham, MD: Rowman and Littlefield, 2003).
[25]Richard Weaver, *Ideas Have Consequences* (Chicago: University of Chicago Press, 1984), 3.

By focusing on the particulars apart from the traditional medieval synthesis, Occam, or so Weaver and others charge, precipitated an unhelpful empirical turn in philosophy that gave birth to the subjective turn in philosophy with whose bitter fruit we are still dealing today. Furthermore, these authors intimate that because the Protestant Reformers broadly followed the *via moderna* (i.e., nominalism as opposed to the old medieval realism), they are unwitting accomplices in the demise of the West. If only the poor Reformers had known better, perhaps we may have avoided Nietzsche. Prolific Thomist Ralph McInerny condemns the Reformation, casting it into the philosophical ash heap of history with the following observation: "It is not just a well-turned phrase that modern philosophy is the Reformation carried on by other means. Most of the major figures are Protestant or apostate or both. Luther's attack on reason and his Manichean split between nature and grace poisoned the well of thinking."[26]

There is, no doubt, some explanatory power to this analysis. Clearly something went wrong in the modern period. Modernity gave way to modernism. To offer a biblical allusion, the Thomist, the Calvinist, and the postmodernist can all lie down and let a little child lead them together on that issue. But to suggest that the blame and bane of modernism as we now know it is to be laid at the feet of an unwitting group of Reformers is nothing short of ludicrous. The notion lacks any serious measure of perspective and two-dimensionalizes intellectual history. Although it lies beyond the purview of the present discussion to offer a thoroughgoing counter to these charges, three observations serve to begin the task.

First, as far as Occam himself is concerned, careful attention must be given to the nuance of his argument. Occam did not deny the existence of universals quite in the way he is often believed to have done. Rather, as far as I can deduce, Occam feared positing universals in a way similar to Platonism, wherein universal ideas superseded even God. In other words, Occam wanted the biblical God who creates *ex nihilo*, not the demiurge-like craftsman Plato

---

[26]Ralph McInerny, *A Student's Guide to Philosophy* (Wilmington, DE: ISI, 1999), 25.

suggests in the *Timaeus*.[27] This is why, for instance, Occam claimed to be the true heir of Aristotle. Occam did not deny the objectivity of truth; he simply cautioned against adding a fourth transcendental or hypostasis, or possibly more, beyond the one God in three persons. To do that would be to commit heresy. As philosopher Ernest A. Moody stated,

> Insofar as Ockham is called a nominalist, his doctrine is not to be construed as a rejection of any ontological determination of meaning and truth, but rather as an extreme economy of ontological commitment in which abstract or intensional [*sic*] extralinguistic entities are systematically eliminated by logical analysis.[28]

A second rebuttal to the charges against Occam and the Reformation points out that Luther and Calvin were hardly faithful or slavish followers of nominalism as it developed throughout the remainder of the scholastic period. Luther's *Disputation Against Scholastic Theology*, for example, is replete with references to his significant and sizable disagreements with Occam and Gabriel Biel, ostensibly Occam's most famous disciple.[29] Specifically, Luther and Calvin chafed at the Pelagianism of the writings of the scholastics in general and Occam in particular. Still, the Reformers certainly appreciated Occam's work insofar as it emphasized the sovereignty of God over his creation. Stated differently, the Reformers focused on the concept of voluntarism (i.e., the creative power of God's will) as an appropriate critique of the medieval synthesis over and against nominalism, a philosophy that certainly took an unexpected, modern turn. The truth of voluntarism points humanity to our absolute dependence

---

[27]Plato's cosmology and theology are contained in his dialogue *Timaeus*, available in *The Dialogues of Plato*, vol. 2, trans. B. Jowett (New York: Random House, 1937), 3–70.

[28]Ernest A. Moody, "William of Ockham," in *The Encyclopedia of Philosophy*, vol. 8, ed. Paul Edwards (New York: Macmillan/The Free Press, 1967), 307, emphasis mine. The idea of eternal, uncreated metaphysical entities that exist alongside God himself leaves the impression that God is not independent from reason. This Aristotelian notion has concerned philosophers such as Herman Dooyeweerd, who worried that if God is not sovereign over all his created order, including reason, then he is not God and reason has become an idol.

[29]For example, thesis 56 reads, "It is not true that God can accept man without his justifying grace. This is in opposition to Ockham." Cf. Luther, *Luther's Basic Theological Writings*, 17.

upon divine revelation for true understanding about both God and the created order. The world as we know it is so because God, who never changes, declares it to be so. In his brilliant introduction to Luther's *Bondage of the Will*, J. I. Packer beautifully sums up the ethos of Reformation epistemology:

> [Luther's] unflagging polemic against the abuse of reason has often been construed as an assault on the very idea of rational coherence in theology, whereas in fact it is aimed only at the ideal of rational autonomy and self sufficiency in theology—the ideal of philosophers and scholastic theologians, to find out and know God by the use of their own unaided reason. It was in her capacity as the prompter and agent of natural theology that "Mistress Reason" was in Luther's eyes, the Devil's whore; for natural theology is, he held, blasphemous in principle, and bankrupt in practice. It is blasphemous in principle, because it seeks to snatch from God a knowledge of Himself which is not his gift, but man's achievement—a triumph of human brain power; thus it would feed man's pride, and exalt him above his Creator, as one who could know God at pleasure, whether or not God willed to be known by him. Thus natural theology appears as one more attempt on man's part to implement the programme which he espoused in his original sin—to deny his creaturehood, and deify himself, and deal with God henceforth on an independent footing. But natural theology is bankrupt in practice, for it never brings devotees [to] God; instead it leaves them stranded in a quaking morass of insubstantial speculation. Natural theology leads men away from the Divine Christ, and from Scripture, the cradle in which he lies, and from the *theologia crucis*, the gospel doctrine which Christ sets forth. But it is only through Christ that God wills to be known and gives saving knowledge of himself.[30]

A third response rejecting the criticism that the Reformation is the fulcrum upon which modernism pivoted bears in mind that Renaissance humanism and late medieval scholasticism contributed

---

[30] J. I. Packer, "Historical and Theological Introduction," in Martin Luther, *The Bondage of the Will*, trans. J. I. Packer and O. R. Johnston (Grand Rapids: Revell, 1957), 45–46.

as much to the rise of modernity as did the Reformation, if not more, and it did so largely under the auspices of Rome's blessing and supervision. History is not so easily compartmentalized. The collective results of humanism, the Reformation, and the Counter-Reformation were intrinsic to the initiation of modern science as we know it today. The change was inevitable. Fourteenth- and fifteenth-century intellects realized increasingly that certain crucial elements of Aristotelianism could not be rehabilitated. Craig Gay of Regent College, who supports, at least in part, the "Reformation opened a modernistic Pandora's box" theory, nonetheless qualifies his discussion with the following candid observation:

> It is important to stress . . . that, quite apart from the actual impossibility of turning the clock back, the attempt to repristinate the medieval social order would not be a very good idea. . . . In the first place Aristotelian science is simply not believable any more. Even more significantly, attempting to revitalize Aristotelian teleology by way of Aquinas would not really solve the problem of human individuality and creativity. Whatever the Aristotelian "god" is, it is not personal, and the Aristotelian system does not permit any real space for human freedom and creativity. Indeed, even modern scientific nominalism allows more latitude for personal agency than medieval (Aristotelian) science did.[31]

## Carl F. H. Henry: Heir of Reformation Epistemology

James Nuechterlein's query to evangelicals concerning whether we can find our way and remain authentically evangelical in our theological method can be answered with an emphatic yes. But to do this, one must begin with the epistemology of the Reformers and their dogged, untiring insistence that human beings rely, as Luther once put it, "upon the poor tokens of the Word of God alone." But evangelicals seem to have lost their way, both philosophically and theologically, since the Reformation. Furthermore, the Reformers never faced the skepticism

---

[31] Craig Gay, *The Way of the Modern World* (Grand Rapids: Eerdmans, 1998), 278–79. The context for Gay's comments here relates to a theology of personhood. His consideration of the *imago Dei* includes an ontological definition of person I find compelling.

of modernity as do their successors in the twenty-first century. To whom can one turn for guidance? Although many worthies might be offered, evangelicals should turn once more to the model set forth by Carl F. H. Henry, a man who inherited the epistemology of the Reformers and faithfully applied it to the challenges of modernity.

Henry not only found the respective trajectories of fundamentalism, liberal theology, and neo-Thomism unstintingly wanting in the light of a Reformed theological perspective historically, but also lacking theologically in the gaze of a distinctly Hebrew-Christian worldview. To Henry's level of vision and engagement we would do well to return again, specifically taking into account his full corpus of written work. Henry's early work especially is impressive in its scope and consideration of the issues. Let me encourage those who have not done so to read such early Henry volumes as *The Uneasy Conscience of Modern Fundamentalism*, *Remaking the Modern Mind*, *The Protestant Dilemma*, and *The Drift of Western Thought*, which deftly engage then contemporary scholarship and demonstrate why early neoevangelicals gained the attention and respect of the broader culture as well as the religious academy.

Henry espoused a Reformation-inspired voluntarism in the best sense of the term. He stressed the absolute dependence of human knowledge upon divine disclosure, whether natural or particular. In other words, according to Henry, we know what we know because God wills both the possibility and the content of that knowledge. Henry came to these views early on in his theological career and never wavered. Defining "the Christian Revelation-Claim," Henry wrote:

> In a sense, all knowledge may be viewed as revelational, since meaning is not imposed upon things by the human knower alone, but rather is made possible because mankind and the universe are the work of a rational Deity, who fashioned an intelligible creation. Human knowledge is not a source of knowledge to be contrasted with revelation, but is a means of comprehending revelation.
>
> Thus God, by his immanence, sustains the human knower, even in his moral and cognitive revolt, and without that divine preservation, ironically enough, man could not even rebel against God, for he would not exist. Augustine, early in the Christian centuries, detected

what was implied in this conviction that human reason is not the creator of its own object; neither the external world of sensation nor the internal world of ideas is rooted in subjectivistic factors alone.[32]

Thus, God circumscribes and determines what can be known. Nonetheless, the world remains knowable because God himself is an intelligent Deity. Contrary to the trajectory of rationalism, no autonomous standard for reason can be offered since reason itself loses meaning apart from the divine character. Since the divine discloses himself as a person, revelation is personal in nature and can therefore speak to all of humanity. Consequently, revelation both coheres and corresponds to reality because God is one. It is not a truism to say, therefore, that divine revelation is communication that we can trust. Thus, as Henry declares, "Only the fact that the one sovereign God, the Creator and Lord of all, stands at the center of divine disclosure, guarantees a unified divine revelation."[33]

Every condition of knowledge (i.e., justified true belief), therefore, stems from an allowance of either common or particular grace to the end that we live in the world God has actually created, and glorify the agent of said creation, even Jesus Christ. In an address before an emerging evangelical audience at Soongsil University in Seoul, South Korea, in 1987, Henry summarized his views thus:

> The Christian ontological axiom is the living, self-revealed God. The Christian epistemological axiom is the intelligible divine revelation. All the essential doctrines of the Christian world-life view flow from these axioms: creation, sin, and the fall; redemption, by promise and fulfillment; the incarnation, substitutionary death and resurrection of the Logos; the church as the new society; the approaching divine consummation of history; the eschatological verities.[34]

---

[32]Carl F. H. Henry, *The Drift of Western Thought* (Grand Rapids: Eerdmans, 1951), 104.
[33]Carl F. H. Henry, *God, Revelation and Authority*, vol. 2, *God Who Speaks and Shows: Fifteen Theses, Part One* (Waco, TX: Word, 1976), 9.
[34]Carl F. H. Henry, *Gods of This Age, or God of the Ages?*, ed. R. Albert Mohler Jr. (Nashville TN: Broadman and Holman, 1994), 209.

Certainly the most programmatic exposition of Henry's Reformation-inspired epistemology comes from the panoramic *God, Revelation and Authority*, Henry's six-volume magnum opus, which is often alluded to but seldom read with patience. The fifteen theses spell out in brief what Henry delivers in detail throughout volumes 2 and 3. Particularly in thesis 5, Henry happily shows his voluntaristic colors:

> 5. Not only the occurrence of divine revelation, but also its very nature, content, and variety are exclusively of God's determination.
>
> God determines not only the if and why of divine disclosure, but also the when, where, what, how, and who. If there is to be a general revelation—a revelation universally given in nature, in history, and in the reason and conscience of every man—then that is God's decision. If there is to be a special or particular revelation, that, too, is God's decision and his alone. Only because God so wills it is there a cosmic-anthropological revelation. It is solely because of divine determination, Paul reminds us, that "that which may be known of God is manifest . . . for God hath showed it . . . . For the invisible things of him from the creation of the world are clearly seen, being understood by the things that are made, even his eternal power and Godhead" (Rom. 1:19–20, KJV). It is solely by God's own determination that he reveals himself universally in the history of the nations and in the ordinary course of human events. He is nowhere without a witness (Acts 14:17) and is everywhere active either in grace or judgment.[35]

With these words, Henry models a flowering of the Augustinian/Reformation perspective with a clarity unmatched in modern evangelical theology. What we know, Henry argues, we know because God wants us to know it. In this sense, then, Henry defies the foundationalist label that some have recently attempted to place upon him, a trend that began with Hans Frei's response to Henry's critique of narrative theology. Unfortunately for the Henry legacy, the impression stuck and has been repeated by other postliberal writers such

---

[35]Henry, *God, Revelation and Authority*, 2:9–10.

as George Hunsinger.[36] Certainly, evangelical neo-Thomists such as Norman Geisler and R. C. Sproul might be surprised, to say the least, at the notion that Henry is somehow a cobelligerent with them in the realm of foundationalist apologetics and epistemology. For Henry, there is no neutral, antiseptic path to knowledge. Knowledge, properly defined, is permitted, made accessible, and circumscribed by God himself.

In Kuyperian fashion, Henry averred that all knowledge owes its origin to the God who speaks and shows. Henry's doctrine of creation is not, therefore, deficient on the grounds that it does not appropriate natural theology. On the contrary, Henry distinguished between general revelation and natural theology. He gladly affirmed that God speaks in and through creation, but he rightly reminded his readers that general revelation remains precisely that—revelation. And yet for this very reason, Christians have a genuine and meaningful point of contact with the nonbelieving world simply because we all benefit, whether wittingly or unwittingly, from God's self-disclosure, whether in creation or most preeminently in his written Word. If anything, this principle explains simply Henry's longstanding gripe with the epistemology of Karl Barth. When Barth argued that the *imago Dei* was obliterated in the fall, Henry repeatedly retorted that Barth summarily closed off the conduit through which God speaks to human beings, whether regenerate or not. Recent attempts to rehabilitate Barth's legacy on this point in particular and on revelation in general have not yet explained to anyone still appreciative of Henry's withering critique of neoorthodoxy how Barth's acceptance of Kant's radical phenomenal-noumenal distinction can produce a worldview that simultaneously engages and yet challenges the prevailing secular culture.[37] In sum, as British evangelical theologian Peter Hicks concurs:

---

[36]For example, see, variously, Hans Frei, *Types of Christian Theology* (New Haven, CT: Yale University Press, 1992), 84; Carl F. H. Henry, "Narrative Theology: An Evangelical Appraisal," *Trinity Journal* 8, no. 1 (1987): 3–19; and George Hunsinger, "What Can Evangelicals and Postliberals Learn from Each Other? The Carl Henry–Hans Frei Exchange Reconsidered," in *The Nature of Confession: Evangelicals and Postliberals in Conversation*, ed. Timothy R. Phillips and Dennis Okholm (Downers Grove, IL: InterVarsity, 1996), 134–50.

[37]For example, see Bruce L. McCormack, "The Being of Holy Scripture Is in Becoming: Karl Barth in Conversation with American Evangelical Criticism," in *Evangelicals and Scripture: Tradition, Authority, and Hermeneutics*, ed. Dennis L. Okholm, Vincent Bacote, and Laura C.

Henry's central thesis is that God reveals and speaks. There is no reason why we should limit God to one form of revelation (through either a person or a book, through either encounter or concept). God reveals and speaks in a number of ways, in his creation, in general revelation, and supremely in Christ, the incarnate Word. But, additionally and foundationally, he is able to formulate and communicate truth in an epistemic word, in which he articulates truth verbally through "intelligible disclosure"; and this, in sovereign grace, he has chosen to do.[38]

Recently, in a spate of books on the future of evangelical theology, an array of authors have criticized Henry's emphasis and insistence upon propositional revelation in verbal-conceptual form. Although a thorough consideration of the relative merits of Henry's contribution in that area lie beyond the purview of this chapter, a passing word might note that some of the treatments of Henry's work border on caricature. In *Evangelical Futures*, for example, Alister McGrath condemns Henry's understanding of revelation, calling it "purely propositional" and slavish to Enlightenment rationalism.[39] While Henry certainly took the position that cognitive thought is not possible without words, McGrath's statement overlooks Henry's own words and clear position that "in both general and special revelation—in nature and in history, in the mind and conscience of man, in written Scriptures, and in Jesus of Nazareth, God has disclosed himself."[40] Such sentiments seem, at least in my estimation, perfectly consistent with McGrath's own recent emphasis on the history of redemption and the story of Jesus Christ.

When considering Henry's contribution, evangelicals run the following risk: in the rush to dismiss the particular subtleties of Henry's understanding of revelation as the epistemological engine of his theology, something important about Henry's disposition toward

Miguelez (Downers Grove: InterVarsity, 2004), 55–75. To a lesser extent, a similar approach is undertaken by Stanley Hauerwas in *With the Grain of the Universe* (Grand Rapids: Brazos, 2001).

[38]Peter Hicks, *Evangelicals and Truth* (Leicester, UK: Apollos, 1998), 89–90.

[39]Alister McGrath, "Engaging the Great Tradition," in *Evangelical Futures*, ed. John G. Stackhouse Jr. (Grand Rapids: Baker, 2000), 150.

[40]Henry, *God, Revelation and Authority*, 2:10.

theology is lost—something that is distinctly Protestant. And that distinctive includes no less than the assertion that God, and God alone, is the source and arbiter of all wisdom and knowledge, and God himself determines the bounds and limits of all true knowledge. In some ways, one might say that Henry poses the following fundamental questions to evangelicals today: Is the truth the truth because God wills it to be the case? Is God a Deity who speaks in intelligible sentences and paragraphs? If the answer to those two questions is affirmative, then no other church tradition offers a better theological method than Protestant evangelicalism—a movement that at its origin radically committed itself to theological conclusions explicated in the Word of God alone.

## Conclusion

As recently as 1995, Carl Henry was still holding forth articulately for a Reformation worldview in the pages of *First Things* with his straightforward article, "Natural Law and a Nihilistic Culture." Essentially, Henry dropped a plumb line before his readers in a refreshingly direct way. Choose ye this day, he seemed to say, which epistemology you will serve: natural law or divine revelation. For his part, Henry cast his lot with the Reformation.

> The greatest appeal of natural law theory lies in the claim that it mirrors universally shared norms and moral principles that lift humanity above modern subjectivism and relativism. Yet the Reformers in principle questioned the epistemic viability of natural law theory, whether stated in pre-Christian Greco-Roman terms or on premises pursued by Thomas Aquinas. The Reformers do have a doctrine of transcendent and universal morality, but it is based upon different foundations. Upon the resolution of this conflict may well turn the moral fortunes of the Western world, and beyond that, ultimately, the planet.[41]

---

[41]Carl F. H. Henry, "Natural Law and a Nihilistic Culture," *First Things,* January 1995, 55–60, accessed February 26, 2002, http://www.firstthings. com/ftissues/ft9501/articles/henry.html.

Given *First Things'* primary audience, Henry's argument hardly won the award for "most beloved article of the year." Nevertheless, until his death in late 2003, Henry continued to serve on the editorial advisory board of the journal. The debate rages on as to whether or not the Reformation is over. Mark Noll and Carolyn Nystrom, writing for the optimistic majority, answer with a "not yet but getting there" in their monograph on that question.[42] But elsewhere the signs of continued deep differences are everywhere on display. Most of the attention focuses on the material principle of the Reformation, but where the cold war really still exists in a profound way is at the level of epistemology. As Brad Gregory's *The Unintended Reformation: How a Religious Revolution Secularized Society* posits, a change in views about authority, ushered in by the Protestant Reformers, unhinged Europe from its foundations and ushered in all of the ills we now experience in a post-Christian West.[43] Although Ephraim Radner, writing in *First Things*, has helpfully challenged Gregory's conclusions on the basis that the real problem of modernity is "love waxing cold," the fact is that Gregory has a very valid point: how one views authority frames one's view of the world.[44] Carl Henry would have disagreed with Gregory's conclusions, but affirmed the premise: epistemology shapes everything, and, generally speaking, one inhabits a view of the world that emanates from either of two worlds: Rome or Wittenberg/Geneva.[45]

---

[42]Mark Noll and Carolyn Nystrom, *Is the Reformation Over? An Evangelical Assessment of Contemporary Roman Catholicism* (Grand Rapids: Baker Academic, 2008).

[43]Brad Gregory, *The Unintended Reformation: How a Religious Revolution Secularized Society* (Cambridge, MA: Belknap Press of Harvard University Press, 2012).

[44]Ephraim Radner, *First Things*, June/July 2012, 47–52.

[45]A portion of this chapter draws on material from my chapter in *A Theology for the Church*, ed. Daniel L. Akin (Nashville, TN: B&H Academic 2007), 29–35, and is used here by permission.

# CHAPTER 3

# Theology Matters

## The Bold Vision of *God, Revelation and Authority*

One of the greatest obstacles frustrating the reception of Carl Henry's work by the current generation of theologians is expressed in the complaint that his magnum opus is densely philosophical and, often, written in seemingly inaccessible prose. This is a common and legitimate critique of *God, Revelation and Authority*, as well as other important works in the Henry corpus. Labeling his writing as obscure is an ironic and puzzling assessment, given Henry's background as a news writer and magazine editor who saw his task as reaching a general, albeit literate, evangelical public. One would not think that such features would intimidate academic theologians accessing Henry's theology. Still, I wonder. When I hear critiques of his theological method and his view of divine revelation, I am often left scratching my head: "Are these people reading the same Carl F. H. Henry that I am?" My suspicion is that Henry most often is read—or scratch that—raided, to sound as brittle, inflexible, and modernistic as possible, a tendency that the content of this book aims to attenuate.

To appreciate Henry authentically and fully, it really is best to *read* him. Throughout the formation of this volume, however, I thought that it may be constructive at various points to summarize key passages and texts from the Henry corpus. They are as follows: the fifteen theses he exposits in volume 2 of *GRA* (particularly the first seven, discussed in this chapter, and theses 11–14 in the next), his explication of the concept of biblical inerrancy in volume 4, and the cultural agenda set forth in his 1946 classic *The Uneasy Conscience of Modern Fundamentalism*. The collected writings of Henry are extensive, but in my estimation, these are the essential excerpts of the larger whole. Get these and you will get Henry. Having summarized Henry's theological method in his own words, we will then turn to the current critics of Henry, consider their objections, and draw a few conclusions about the way forward for the doctrine of revelation as it relates to theological exposition in the contemporary evangelical landscape.

Part of the limitation of *God, Revelation and Authority* is that Word Publishers released the volumes individually as they were completed, and thus they never appeared as a set. In fact, until Crossway reissued *GRA* in 1999, it was something of a challenge to assemble the entire collection. Further complicating matters was the fact that volume 1 (*Preliminary Considerations*) was a terrible leadoff batter. Esoteric and turgid, the book was extremely difficult to get through, and it read more like a Windows computer manual of insider theological and philosophical agenda than an introduction into the defining convictions of evangelical theology. What a shame. The best approach is to set aside volume 1 and dive right into volume 2, *God Who Speaks and Shows, Fifteen Theses, Part One*. Crack it open and this is what you read:

## Fifteen Theses

1. Revelation is a divinely initiated activity, God's free communication by which he alone turns his personal privacy into a deliberate disclosure of his reality.
2. Divine revelation is given for human benefit, offering us privileged communication with our Creator in the kingdom of God.
3. Divine revelation does not completely erase God's transcendent mystery, inasmuch as God the Revealer transcends his own revelation.
4. The very fact of disclosure by the one living God assures the comprehensive unity of divine revelation.
5. Not only the occurrence of divine revelation, but also its very nature, content, and variety are exclusively God's determination.
6. God's revelation is uniquely personal both in content and form.
7. God reveals himself not only universally in the history of the cosmos and of the nations, but also redemptively within this external history in unique saving acts.

8. The climax of God's special revelation is Jesus of Nazareth, the personal incarnation of God in the flesh; in Jesus Christ the source and content of revelation converge and coincide.

9. The mediating agent in all divine revelation is the Eternal Logos— preexistent, incarnate, and now glorified.

10. God's revelation is rational communication conveyed in intelligible ideas and meaningful words, that is, in conceptual-verbal form.

11. The Bible is the reservoir and conduit of divine truth, the authoritative written record and exposition of God's nature and will.

12. The Holy Spirit superintends the communication of divine revelation, first, by inspiring the prophetic-apostolic writings, and second, by illuminating and interpreting the scripturally given Word of God.

13. Bestower of spiritual life, the Holy Spirit enables individuals to appropriate God's truth savingly, and attests its power in their personal experience.

14. The church approximates God's kingdom in miniature, mirroring to each generation the power and joy of the appropriated realities of divine revelation.

15. The self-manifesting God will unveil his glory in a crowning revelation of power and judgment; in this disclosure at the consummation of the ages, God will vindicate righteousness and justice, finally subdue and subordinate evil, and bring into being a new heaven and earth.

## Thesis 1

What follows in volume 2 of *GRA* is nothing less than a magisterial explication of what makes evangelicals evangelical and what keeps them that way: the doctrine of divine revelation. In chapter 1, Henry sets forth the expectations we can have of "The Awesome Disclosure of God." His definition of revelation in thesis 1 is indeed classic and should be memorized by every pastor and seminarian: "Revelation is a divinely initiated activity, God's free communication by which he alone turns his personal privacy into a deliberate disclosure of his reality."[1] The very terms upon which God communicates are cause enough for his people to fall down and worship. Henry makes it clear

---

[1]Henry, *God, Revelation and Authority*, vol. 2, *God Who Speaks and Shows: Fifteen Theses, Part One* (Waco, TX: Word, 1976), 17.

that if God had insisted on not communicating with us, we would have no possibility of learning anything about him. Correlative to this assertion is its logical obverse: the Godhead is completely inaccessible to mere human reason.[2] Not only is this the conviction of theological reason; it is a well-founded historical fact. In primitive times, Henry states, cultures accessed the divine through mystical objects or sacred individuals under the assumption that human beings can comprehend the divine solely by their own intuition. The ancient Roman mystery cults likewise assumed that no intrinsic schism exists between the divine and humanity. For its part, Greek philosophy, trying to press beyond mere religious insight, sought to syncretize subjective and cosmic reason and attempted to master the universe through human reasoning. All of these approaches to apprehending divine revelation are incompatible with the Judeo-Christian view.[3]

Henry further grounds his view by appealing to the Bible's own meaning of divine self-disclosure. Scripture uses several specific words to describe the nature of divine revelation:

- *mystērion* ("mystery"; the root meaning is "closed" or "hidden"), signifying what God has made plain in his revelation
- *galah* ("to reveal"; the root idea is of nakedness or of the removal of barriers to perception)—Numbers 24:4; 1 Samuel 3:21; 2 Samuel 7:27; Daniel 2:47
- *apokalyptō* ("to uncover")
- *phaneroō* ("to manifest," "to show oneself")
- *gnōrizō* ("to make known")[4]

Simply put, philosophical speculation alone cannot compose theological verities. Divine self-disclosure is utterly central for any successful theological enterprise. And in light of God's Word, theology does not derive its claims from explorations into the human psyche, consciousness, the history of religion, or other reflections on nature or conjectures about the infinite and absolute.[5] Further,

---

[2]Ibid., 2:18.
[3]Ibid., 2:19–20.
[4]Ibid., 2:20–22.
[5]Ibid., 2:24–25.

if one rejects the Bible as the inspired word of God, he eventually begins to conceive of primitive religions as steps on the evolutionary ladder of religion, elevating developmental reality into an unalterable absolute.[6] Revealed religion does not find its strength in any sort of syncretism, Henry argues, as if the integration of Yahweh and Baal were possible. Quite the contrary, the prophets were clarion in their distinction and choice between Yahweh and Baal. For example, when Elijah massacred the priests of Baal, God mercifully demonstrated that "theological vacillation must be seen for what it is, namely, spiritual rebellion."[7]

## Thesis 2

In his second thesis, Henry asserts that "divine revelation is given for human benefit, offering us privileged communication with our Creator in the kingdom of God."[8] In other words, our ability to flourish in God's kingdom, which is operational even now and available in power to us, is directly linked to the life-giving affirmations of the Word of God. But, Henry explains, we are mistaken if we focus on the benefits afforded to humanity alone when speaking of the Scriptures. While revelation is ordained for human benefit, Henry affirms again and again that God reveals himself in sovereign freedom first and foremost for his own glory. The following tenet is thus central: God need not have revealed himself to man. He could very well have created other forms of life on other planets and revealed himself to them. Or, because of his displeasure at our sin, he could have ended his revelation with the wrath in the garden. He need not have continued his revelation until the present time, either. He could have unleashed his final wrath when Jesus was crucified. It is not a matter of either human deserving or divine obligation that God has continued to reveal himself to us and offer us forgiveness.[9] Stated simply, divine revelation is the concept that frames our notion of

---

[6] Ibid., 2:25.
[7] Ibid.
[8] Ibid., 2:30.
[9] Ibid., 2:30–31.

grace. This is Henry's most moving doctrine, and one for which he is often not well remembered.

Further, in stark contrast to the common tendencies of modern theologians, Henry does not oppose the meaning of the gospel with practices of living and fostering the kingdom. Instead, he combines them. In *GRA*, the kingdom is God's and God's alone, only as he bears the sovereignty, authority, wisdom, and freedom required to rule as the Creator. The universe is fashioned as intrinsically and vitally redemptive. Jesus is the Lamb "slain from the foundation of the world" (Rev. 13:8, KJV).[10] Even now, Jesus, who died and was raised for us, "pleads our cause" (see Rom. 8:34) before God in heaven. He died so that we might live with him (1 Thess. 5:10). God has offered us a place in his kingdom. He liberates us so that we will have faith in him.[11]

What is more, the theme of the kingdom pervades Jesus's life, from the prophecies foretelling his coming, to the present time, when he is seated at God's right hand.[12] During his ministry, Jesus proclaimed the felicity found of the kingdom for those who dwell within it—for the righteous, who obey God's will. Contrary to the "easy believism" that would later characterize some sectors of evangelicalism, Henry states that merely hearing God's good news is not automatically constitutive of redemption. The gospel can be either refused in unrepentant rebellion or received by repentant trust. "To spurn God's mercy is a double indignity." When that is done, not only is God's overt offering rejected, but the revelation God has given in conscience and in nature is suppressed. The New Testament is not merely preoccupied with the eschatological implications of faith and unbelief, but it speaks directly to present life, when God's eschatological action is already initiated by way of anticipation (John 3:18; 5:24–29; 6:54; 11:25–27; 12:31; 14:3, 18–20; Rom. 8:1; Eph. 1:14).[13]

Further, human beings within the created order must contend with the sobering theme of the Bible that God weighs people's actions

---

[10]Ibid., 2:32.
[11]Ibid., 2:33.
[12]Ibid., 2:38.
[13]Ibid., 2:39–40.

and judges them truly (1 Sam. 2:3; Rom. 2:2). Nothing could be further from the truth than the caricature of *GRA* as a text interested primarily in theoretical concerns. The central motif of the Christian tradition is not revelation in and of itself, but reconciliation. Knowledge of God's truth is by no means synonymous with salvation. The entrance of God's light into the world is far more than just the communication of information; it also resounds with God's plea for and requirement of personal reconciliation. Therefore, we must not confuse the comprehension of revelation with salvation.[14]

## Thesis 3

Henry's third thesis reads thus: "Divine revelation does not completely erase God's transcendent mystery, inasmuch as God the Revealer transcends his own revelation."[15] This statement is, without a doubt, the most ignored declaration in the entire body of Carl Henry's work. Unlike scholastic theologians, who believed that theology could in some way place the human mind on par with the divine essence, Henry clearly says that God transcends even his holy Word. It is a worshipful thought at this stage in the development of *GRA's* proposal. It insists that God's revelation does not exhaust his being and activity. He is still wholly incomprehensible and shrouded in mystery. There is more to God's plan and perfections than we presently know.[16] The God of the Bible differs notably from the pantheistic Absolute of speculative idealism, in which the whole universe is an exhaustive manifestation of the divine. God, however, is revealed by his creation and yet ontologically transcends his creation. Herein lies the decisive difference between biblical prophecy and Greek thought: in opposition to the Greeks, Hebrew-Christian thought excludes any and every possibility of human divinization.[17] This point provides a substantive evangelical critique of the concept of theosis in the Orthodox tradition, although Henry himself never offered a thoroughgoing extension of his thought on this matter. In every area of

[14]Ibid., 2:42–45.
[15]Ibid., 2:47.
[16]Ibid.
[17]Ibid., 2:47–48.

earthly life, man stands superior to the object of his study; however, with respect to God, man is always dependent on God's purposes and subject to the reality of his revelation.[18] Henry writes:

> If we take seriously the *prima facie* data of biblical prophets who set forth their own deep self-understanding of divine disclosure, there can be no doubt that these spokesmen deny that the message they convey is of their own making. We are left with a choice between dismissing them as self-deceived psychotics who were victims of auditory or visual hallucinations, or men for whom transcendent divine revelation was a striking reality. Any attempt to reduce the content of their message to a studied exposition of their religious convictions is excluded by the testimony they bear.[19]

The Bible distinctly differentiates between true and false prophets: true prophets are known by their initial resistance to God's revealed call on their lives, "almost like a draft-resister."[20] Examples include Moses, Isaiah, Jeremiah, Jonah, and Paul. This quality was so common in the Old Testament as to almost be a hallmark of the true prophet. False prophets, on the other hand, all boasted a self-grasped revelation, which was therefore not true revelation at all. The conclusion is that human beings have no native ability or resourcefulness for delineating God's nature and will.[21] God's revelation does not dignify inspired prophets or apostles with divine status precisely because they are still utterly dependent on God and his divine revelation. Thus, humility is as becoming to the Christian theologian, who depends on the prophetic-apostolic revelation for his work, as to the secular scientist, who must vet his findings against external reality.[22]

Henry accurately notes that the New Testament writers use the term *mystery* with connotations of awe and wonder, but its context is always one of imminent disclosure (1 Cor. 15:51; 1 Tim. 3:9).[23]

---

[18]Ibid., 2:49.
[19]Ibid.
[20]Ibid., 2:50.
[21]Ibid.
[22]Ibid., 2:52.
[23]Ibid., 2:53.

Even though our knowledge of God is not exhaustive, we are not rendered silent or incapable of describing God faithfully; the Word that we have is trustworthy.[24] It is thus impossible to take either *Deus absconditus* or *Deus revelatus* and construct a speculative system that expounds upon God's nature in a way that falls into either rationalism or agnosticism. But at the same time, Scripture is permeated by the insistence that humanity only penetrates the mystery surrounding God insofar as God chooses to reveal himself. The present finitude of human knowledge does not therefore necessitate theories of divine incognito or of God's hiddenness beyond all knowability.[25] In other words, the divine mystery should not terminate into apophatism.

Taking this understanding of divine revelation as a precondition, Henry moves to confront contemporary theology in its attempt to bypass the doctrine of divine revelation. He argues that recent theological systems misconstrue the *imago Dei* as the human capacity for self-transcendence; they assert the radical transcendence of man with equal fervor as the transcendence of God. Human imagination, thus, is the exemplar of the divine spark, the apospasma. This emphasis is self-defeating, even if one relies on the neoorthodox appeal to a noncognitive divine encounter or on a humanistic appeal to the internal experience of the inherently unintelligible.[26] These theories are problematized by the nature of human experience itself, which shows no discernible boundary between where selfhood ends and otherness begins. The concept of self-transcendence is nonsensical and fallacious precisely because the self cannot be an object in the same way that nature is an object of thought; grasping the nature of consciousness continues to elude us. One can transcend nature to make it an object of thought, but to transcend oneself in the same way seems, even on first glance, to be schizophrenic. By way of contrast, "The great watershed between the biblical and nonbiblical religions is the self-revealing God who, in contrast with the static gods of other religions, speaks and acts intelligibly. Judeo-Christian

---

[24]Ibid., 2:54.
[25]Ibid., 2:54–55.
[26]Ibid., 2:58–61.

religion worships the God who takes initiative—who plans, creates, judges, reveals and redeems."[27]

At this point, Henry contrasts Christian meditation with Eastern meditative practices. While Eastern modes of prayer focus on emptying the mind and the repetition of mantras, Christian meditation focuses on the Mediator and his Word—on rational statements instead of devotional chants.[28] The popularity of Eastern thought exposes the inherent egoism of the modern religious conscience. Such a divinized conceit obscures the transcendent Creator God, and in so doing, obscures the *imago Dei* within humanity itself. In sum, modern man seeks to desensitize his conscience, dismiss universal morality, and discard any supernatural source of objective truth.[29] In light of this extant reality, "only the shock of divine confrontation, of God's revelation in his Word, can remove the terrible deformity of the human psyche and fully overcome the illusion of an amputated invisible transcendent world."[30]

## Thesis 4

Henry's fourth thesis in *GRA* addresses the integrity of biblical theology: "The very fact of disclosure by the one living God assures the comprehensive unity of divine revelation." This is followed by the memorable lines: "The God who reveals himself is the source of a comprehensively unified revelation. He is no schizophrenic spirit or vagrant voice in a hierarchy of contending gods."[31] In support of this thesis, Henry cites Wilhelm Schmidt, whose research in comparative religion indicated that the pantheon of many lesser gods alongside a single, dominant deity is a primitive corruption of monotheism.[32] Contrasting with speculative theory and modern theology, orthodox

---

[27]Ibid., 2:61–62.
[28]Ibid., 2:63–64.
[29]Ibid., 2:65.
[30]Ibid., 2:67–68.
[31]Ibid., 2:69.
[32]Ibid., 2:69–71. The Bible is very clear that there is only one God (Deut. 5:23; 6:4; 1 Kings 18:39; Pss. 96:5; 97:7; Isa. 2:8; 37:4; Jer. 10:10; Mal. 2:10; 1 Cor. 8:4). He lives, unlike the idols of the ancient world, and is more powerful than the idols (Psalms 115; 135; Isa. 40:18–20, 26; 41:1–7, 21–24; 43:9–13; 44:6–20; Jer. 2:26–28; 10:1–16).

Christianity has historically insisted on both the continuity and the distinctiveness of general and special revelation. This is an important ground rule for Henry, who once again stakes the claim of the distinctiveness for evangelicalism over its counterparts both within the Christian tradition and in the field of world religions. Moreover, God is the only source of revelation, not human reason or human experience, and his revelation is unified. However, just because his revelation is one, the forms of his revelation need not be so: God reveals himself through creation, in Christ, and at the eschaton.[33]

## Thesis 5

GRA's fifth thesis underscores the sovereignty of God in the composition of theological hermeneutics: "Not only the occurrence of divine revelation, but also its very nature, content, and variety are exclusively God's determination."[34] The Scriptures explain that God could very well have imparted revelation to mankind in only one form or in numerous different kinds. For example, he could have made the angels the recipients of redemption (1 Pet. 1:12). Or, he could have confined salvation to the Hebrews rather than including the Gentiles, or he could have offered it to the Gentiles and not the Hebrews. Jesus could have welcomed rather than refused the intervention of the angelic host when he was apprehended and crucified (Matt. 26:53). God is utterly free to reveal what he wants, in the way he wants, and no human can postulate the nature and form of divine disclosure.

Defying those who caricature Henry as a trenchant modernist, he posits that scientific credibility, historical continuity, and linguistic peculiarities are second-order considerations when one is engaging the texts of Scripture. Contrary to accusations from contemporary evangelical theologians, which will be examined later in this chapter, Henry concedes that these factors are crucial for accurately understanding God's Word, but he is resolute that these methods should not be employed in an a priori or determinative fashion.[35] The greatest challenge facing us is naturalism, which acknowledges no divine

---

[33]Ibid., 2:72–73.
[34]Ibid., 2:77.
[35]Ibid., 2:78.

reality or revelation.[36] The fact that God speaks in manifold ways is the vital theme that must be retained; we must at all costs avoid limiting God to any one conception. To wit, the New Testament writers use numerous terms to characterize God's self-disclosure (e.g., *apokaluptō*, *dēloō*, *phaneroō*, and *deiknymi*). The semantic range of these terms includes the concepts "word," "oracle," "inspiration," and "scripture." John in particular uses "witness" and "testimony" to describe revelation.[37] Henry notes:

> No one has private license to exalt any of these varieties of divine revelation above another, or to dichotomize God's disclosure, or to isolate one strand from the others. No liberty is given to fragment or belittle any of it and thereby to weaken the import of the whole and perhaps even unwittingly nullify it.[38]

The multiplicity of revelational expression decidedly includes the natural order as well. Despite the perception that Henry's doctrine of general revelation is underdeveloped, he states that the way God speaks through the natural order is integral to biblical Christian doctrine. Anyone who denies general revelation opposes not only the Bible, but also historic Christian teaching. Because humans are culpable sinners, denying general revelation destroys the basis of moral and spiritual accountability and obscures humankind's original relationship with God.[39] What sets evangelical theology apart from other alternatives is the affirmation that general revelation does not absolve one from the guilt of sin—only the special revelation found in Jesus can do that. Neither Scripture nor human experience warrants the idea that sinful humanity can translate general revelation into pure, undiluted truth about God.[40]

To receive God's Word, especially in its redemptive form, is to acknowledge our profound debt to the Lord, and to provide the foundations for a doctrine of common grace. God need not have

---

[36] Ibid.
[37] Ibid., 2:80.
[38] Ibid., 2:82.
[39] Ibid., 2:83–85.
[40] Ibid., 2:86.

addressed his soteriological revelation (redemption) to the Hebrews or any subsequent peoples or cultures. For that matter, God is under no obligation to save anyone. But because he willed to make himself known in this way, "he provided a universal revelation in the cosmos and in history, a general anthropological revelation in the mind and conscience of man, and to the Hebrews as a chosen people a particular salvific revelation consummated in Jesus Christ as the promised Messiah and head of the church."[41]

Henry goes even further in his defense of natural revelation. "To proclaim the reality of general divine revelation and yet to abandon the possibility of cosmic revelation [like the neo-Protestants] requires correlating God's universal manifestation with some other arena than nature."[42] Since Descartes, Western thinkers have distinguished nature and history, whereas the authors of the Bible knew of no such distinction. In contrast with the ancient pagan religions, the Bible describes divine activity in nature far more explicitly than the other ancient Near Eastern religions and does not portray man as immersed in nature or as a mystical participant in it.[43] Modern intellectuals tend to view the cosmos through the lens of the physical sciences, a view that by necessity is thoroughly naturalistic. This naturalistic prejudice has been the decisive shaper of post-Enlightenment Western philosophy, and the church must actively commit to reversing this trend. The Christian conception of nature unmasks naturalism for what it truly is, and how it arbitrarily eclipses the supernatural and negates the phenomenal world through its reductive views of human nature and its explication of the cosmos.[44] What is really at stake in the contrast between the biblical and scientistic conceptions of the world is whether the ultimate ontological order is personal or impersonal.[45]

## Natural Revelation

Further demonstrating how biblical theology applies to every aspect of life, Henry explains how a Christian understanding of natural

---

[41]Ibid., 2:87.
[42]Ibid., 2:91.
[43]Ibid., 2:93–94.
[44]Ibid., 2:95–97.
[45]Ibid., 2:97.

revelation can mature into a robust concern for the environment. To affirm that God is exclusively concerned for humankind at the expense of creation is a serious distortion of the whole of scriptural testimony. From creation onward, the Bible correlates the fortunes of the cosmos with those of humans. The burden of creation is the dire consequence of Adam's transgression. Humans, who were once given dominion over nature, must now contend with a terrain cursed by their disobedience. But the radical good news of the biblical narrative is that not only man but nature and the entirety of the cosmos will be redeemed at the eschaton. As ever, Henry remained committed to the proposition that only insights gleaned from divine revelation could be parlayed into true cultural flourishing in general, and with respect to the environment in particular. "Only the theological perspective will overcome also that sentimental reactionary view which speaks of what man can do for nature," he writes, "as if some new burst of human generosity will guarantee fresh concern and tolerance for man's long-neglected minority interest."[46]

Henry's enthusiasm for the revelation within creation, however, does not mean that natural theology can be done with any consistency. According to some philosophers he reviews, the existence of a supreme, supernatural being can be inferred from observational data. The argument has taken on multiple forms: the cosmological argument, the teleological argument, and the moral/anthropological argument. The cosmological argument first appears in Plato's *Phaedrus* and in his later dialogues (especially the *Philebus*, the *Laws*, and the *Timaeus*). It is Aristotle's form of this argument, however, that became most influential, through the theology of Saint Thomas Aquinas. Thomistic naturalism is still, to this day, the unofficial philosophy of the Roman Catholic Church.[47] The most frequent criticism of Thomas's argument is that if everything must have a cause, then so must God. Thomas, of course, does not claim that "everything has a cause" but that "finite/changing/contingent things have a cause."[48]

---

[46]Ibid., 2:102.
[47]Ibid., 2:104–6.
[48]Ibid., 2:108.

Despite this nuance, nearly every significant modern philosopher (e.g., Schopenhauer, Hume, Kant, Bertrand Russell) has leveled critique at Thomas's fivefold argument in some form or fashion.[49] For Henry, Thomism serves the Christian cause least in combining causal and rational concerns into one seamless subject matter. This merger concedes so much to empirical methodology as to render itself incapable of refuting secular, naturalist empiricists.[50]

To the Protestant mind, arguing empirically for God's existence would seem to demote God's agency in revelation, since it dignifies the fallen human mind with the capacity to extrapolate specific revelation from general revelation.[51] As early as the writings of Origen (c. AD 250), Christian theology presupposed that God is given in revelation. But more than anyone, Friedrich Schleiermacher "deliberately disowned the deduction of theological truth from theological revelation."[52] He substituted religious experience for the historic emphasis on revelation.[53] A key insight for understanding Henry's work is how he provocatively connects the logical trajectory of Thomism to modernism. He argues that, just as in Thomism, modernism replaced God as a theological starting point by reversing fields, and thereby has modern theology deified man. Thus, as Harnack states, the "proper object of faith is not God in his revelation, but man himself believing in the divine."[54]

To the last, Henry remained resolute in his thesis that natural theology breeds skepticism. He writes, "A faith in God which tries to establish its case on any proposition derived from general anthropology or philosophy of history or any other basis than the revelation

---

[49]Ibid., 2:108–11. Schopenhauer, for example, argued against the idea of a first cause, dismissing it as logically fallacious. Bertrand Russell argued that the Thomistic system leads to the fallacy of composition: since everything in the universe has a cause, the universe must, too. Hume argued that the explanation of an infinite collection of things is found within the collection, not externally.

[50]Ibid., 2:113.

[51]Ibid., 2:117.

[52]Ibid., 2:119.

[53]Ibid. Cf. Gregory A. Thornbury, "A Revelation of the Inward: Schleiermacher's Theology and the Hermeneutics of Interiority," *Southern Baptist Journal of Theology* 3, no. 1 (1999).

[54]Henry, *God, Revelation and Authority*, 2:120.

of God in his Word is in no sense on the road to monotheism but is already on a one-way street to atheistic humanism."[55]

## The Imago Dei

Henry locates the vast majority of the problems of contemporary philosophy and theology in misapprehensions of human anthropology and the image of God. Although he allows that the Bible does not define the precise content of the *imago Dei*, he does not believe that the doctrine itself is vague. Especially in the Western tradition, the *imago Dei* has been understood as coextensive with humanity's rational and moral faculties. Other options have been the human capacity for self-transcendence, the human exercise of will, immortality, and gender distinction.[56] While the image of God has expressions in all of these, Henry reaffirms the priority of the rational faculty. Once again, though, the reason for this centers on the capacity of human beings to receive divine revelation. Whatever ethical factors are present in the *imago Dei*, without reason, humanity could never intelligibly discern between God and not-God.[57] Henry's doctrine of the *imago Dei*, previously articulated in his *Christian Personal Ethics*, unsurprisingly dissents from other theological proposals. Although he commends Barth for rejecting the modernist divinization of humanity, he believes that the Swiss theologian went too far by asserting that a trace of the post-Eden image in humanity gives aid and comfort to natural theology. But according to Henry, Brunner is likewise mistaken: the image of God is not purely formal and therefore cannot be equated with conscience.[58] Rather, God communicates to us via reason through his spoken Word. The conjoining of these two concepts is crucial in distinguishing Christian theology from its rivals. In fact, it is the Bible itself that considers human reason and conscience to be divinely given instruments that make possible a responsible, human existence in relation to God (John 1:9; Acts 14:17; Rom. 1:20, 28, 32; 2:14–15).[59]

---

[55]Ibid., 2:123.
[56]Ibid.
[57]Ibid., 2:125–26.
[58]Ibid., 2:127–28.
[59]Ibid., 2:129–30.

From here Henry launches his critique against the most trying obstacle through which all modern theology must travel: the epistemology of Immanuel Kant. If the Prussian philosopher is correct that we cannot know a thing-in-itself (*Ding an sich*; noumenal reality) as having independent existence or structure, and that only phenomenal appearances can actually be known, then it stands to reason that there can be neither objective nor conceptual knowledge of God. Simply stated, if sense experience supplies the only content of human knowledge and God is extrasensory, then God cannot be given as content of human knowledge. Henry takes issue with Kant's theory of the transcendental unity of apperception because, at bottom, it is unclear how Kant could even have arrived at any categorical objective knowledge of human epistemology and remained consistent with his theory. His declaration that all knowledge is a joint product of innate forms and sense experience presupposes the existence of a cognitive mechanism that can separate the forms from the sense experience in order that we might know them. Kant avoided theological resources and argued to the contrary that God was not the source of the categories of thought structuring human knowledge. If sensation is separated from an independent and self-existing reality, the entire process of knowledge must be subjective and is therefore reduced to a stream of consciousness. Thus, as Henry points out, all that exists is the ego. But how can the existence of the ego be maintained when not even consciousness is given in sensibility? The ego itself must be only an idea. And if the ego is merely a subjective representation, can we even argue, with Kant, for the necessity and universal validity of human thought? The answer clearly has to be no. Consequently, Kant's view is that we can have no objective knowledge except under the conditions imposed by our minds. While he rejects skepticism, his view nonetheless leads to an overthrow of objective truth.[60]

In the face of the Kantian epistemological drive, only the content of God's intelligible revelation can adequately combine fact and value. Moreover, we should not locate the *imago Dei* only in con-

---

[60]Ibid., 2:130–32.

science or freedom of the will, or even in self-consciousness and self-transcendence; the image of God embraces all psychic elements that elevate humans above the animal world.[61] Only a biblical doctrine of the *imago* can restore the dignity of human beings as Homo sapiens. This is not to say, however, that man's glory was not permanently tarnished by the fall.

> The fall of man was a catastrophic personality shock; it fractured human existence with a devastating fault. Ever since, man's worship and contemplation of the living God have been broken, his devotion to the divine will shattered. Man's revolt against God therefore affects his entire being; he is now motivated by an inordinate will; he no longer loves God or his neighbor; he devotes human reasoning to the cause of spiritual rebellion.[62]

However serious and far-reaching its consequences, the fall of man did not involve the total loss of human knowledge of God, rational competence, or ethical accountability. Though sullied, the *imago* was not completely shattered after the fall.[63] Obliquely referencing the work of Karl Rahner, Henry notes, "Philosophical theists who deny the reality of special revelation sometimes escalate the responses of mankind to general revelation in a way that suggests that even atheists are disguised believers. But only volitional trust in God as a cognitively known reality constitutes genuine personal faith."[64] By staking out this territory, Henry points out the distinctive theological contribution of classic evangelicalism.

## Contra Modern Theology

According to Henry, the most formidable view of revelation in the twentieth century was Karl Barth's threefold form of revelation. In Barth's view, God's Word, the prior form, assimilates Scripture and church proclamation, the second and third forms.[65] It is not clear

---

[61]Ibid., 2:133.
[62]Ibid., 2:134–35.
[63]Ibid., 2:136.
[64]Ibid., 2:137.
[65]Ibid., 2:143.

what Barth meant by the revelation prior to and superior to Scripture. However, what troubles Henry most about this view is that Barthian revelation is noncognitive, and thus it is actually extraneous and dispensable.[66] In addition to his three forms of revelation, Barth also discusses three different kinds of times God speaks: (1) the time of original revelation (God's original utterance), which is the time of Jesus and thus is the time of Abraham (John 8:56) no less than the Gospels; (2) the time of apostolic attestation/the canon; and (3) the time of the church/the derivative proclamation.[67]

Another major player in this field is Jürgen Moltmann, who, insisting that the Bible contains "no unequivocal concept of revelation," still attempts to exhibit one, the character of which is messianic and which implies a history of promise. Along with Barth and Bultmann, Moltmann holds that statements made on the basis of revelation may not be objectified—they give us no valid information about God in himself. As a consequence, Moltmann turns revelation into a predicate of eschatology and thus not correlative with the God who reveals himself intelligibly to humanity.[68]

## Thesis 6

Thesis 6 elegantly states that "God's revelation is uniquely personal both in content and form."[69] God communicates his name to us, and in so doing, reveals to us his divinity (1 Kings 20:13, 28). His divinity is expressed in the audible speaking of his name, and any visual representations made of him serve only to dilute his glory.[70] The theophanies of Scripture hold a special significance in the theology of revelation because they anticipate the coming visual manifestation of Yahweh in Jesus Christ.[71] Understanding God's revelation of himself, that God makes himself known, makes plain the shortcomings of natural theology and its denial that God takes any significant role in

---

[66]Ibid., 2:144.
[67]Ibid.
[68]Ibid., 2:147–48.
[69]Ibid., 2:151.
[70]Ibid., 2:151–52.
[71]Ibid., 2:155.

revelation. God is "the active thinking Subject whose personal initiative is the indispensable presupposition of all knowledge of him."[72]

If the Scripture's own teaching exhibits this level of forthrightness, how did twentieth-century philosophy and theology come to such a strident disavowal of objective knowledge? Having already charted the developments in Kantian epistemology, Henry turns to the impact of German idealism upon Protestant theology. By building on the Hegelian notion that saw the Absolute manifested everywhere immediately, Wilhelm Herrmann (Barth's teacher) emphasized divine self-revelation, the inner, secret experiential correlation of the divine with the human self. The outcome is the nonintellective nature of revelation, the nonobjectifying nature of our knowledge of God, and a dynamic personal actualism that links revelation, action, and special religious knowledge into a single event.[73] Following Herrmann, Barth declared God's supernatural self-revelation to be redemptive communication rather than propositional disclosure, and simultaneously an ongoing sporadic event in which the prophets and apostles hold only chronological priority.[74] Bultmann also shared in Herrmann's perspective, namely, that theological assertions are nonobjectifying, that revelation is cognitively uninformative, and that special revelation is an ongoing event. In so doing, Bultmann unmasked the following weakness in Barth's theology: despite in principle renouncing objectifying metaphysical assertions, Barth had made quasi-objectifying statements about God-in-himself.[75] Bultmann recognized that there is no mechanism by which to do this within the human being's own internal existential controls. Thus, existentialist theology can formulate God's Word and his acts only internally, and in so doing, forfeits God's objective being. Because human experience is an empirical system, it undermines at best or

---

[72]Ibid., 2:157.

[73]Ibid., 2:157–58.

[74]Ibid., 2:159.

[75]Ibid., 2:159–61. For the best single volume on the implications of this view, see Klaus Bockmuehl, *The Unreal God of Modern Theology: Bultmann, Barth, and the Theology of Atheism: A Call to Recovering the Truth of God's Reality* (Colorado Springs: Helmers and Howard, 1988).

disallows at worst God's free action in external nature and history.[76] God's self-revelation is not to be defined or curtailed by special theories that declare him "off limits" to external reality. Henry is clarion that we cannot disbar God from any objective revelation to man.[77]

## Thesis 7

In his seventh tentpole, Henry attempts to show the continuity of divine revelation: "God reveals himself not only universally in the history of the cosmos and of the nations, but also redemptively within this external history in unique saving acts."[78] Twentieth-century higher biblical criticism has questioned not only whether history is a main mode of divine revelation, but also whether the ancient Hebrews even professed to know God as the God of history at all.[79] Humans transcend the biological aspect of reality and engage in social, cultural, and historical activity. But revealed religion repudiates the idea, found both in the ancient pagan religions and in modern Hegelian pantheism, that civilization and culture directly reveal the divine.[80] Current scholarship increasingly affirms the historicity of the narratives in the Old Testament, bolstering the view that Moses did not create Hebrew religion, but appealed to the enslaved Hebrews on the basis of God's earlier revelation.[81] Henry insists on a seamless garment with respect to each stage of God's disclosure. The historical continuity of patriarchal faith is clear: the God of Abraham became the God of Isaac and then of Jacob. As the Bible's narratives unfold, it is clear that true biblical religion has nothing to do with mystic/ecstatic religions, since it embraces history, rather than denying it or being indifferent to it.[82]

In this respect, Henry cites T. F. Torrance, who once remarked that the significance of the Protestant Reformation lies in its reassertion of "the biblical notion of the living God who freely and actively intervenes

---

[76]Henry, *God, Revelation and Authority*, 2:163.
[77]Ibid., 2:166.
[78]Ibid., 2:247.
[79]Ibid.
[80]Ibid., 2:248.
[81]Ibid.
[82]Ibid., 2:249.

in history."[83] Further, the Bible depicts Yahweh as the God who sover-
eignly guides historical events and overthrows nations, protecting Israel
and the remnant. The prophets speak of a final age of salvation and a
day of terror, when Yahweh will overtake wicked humanity, and they
show that his periodic judgments of humanity foreshadow the final
judgment to come. "Salvation is from the Jews" (John 4:22), but the
prophets look forward to a day where salvation will also be shared with
the Gentiles. Thus, in light of all this, the Hebrews saw God as the God
of history—not just Jewish history, but of all nations and generations.[84]

This understanding of the pulse of God's workings throughout
history brings a calm to anyone who accepts its claims. Revealed religion insists that Yahweh intervenes even in events that seem to deny
him, and all historical events are subject to his sovereignty. The *pax
Romana* crumbled, Henry eloquently observes, as did the *pax Britan-
nica*, and as the *pax Americana* now crumbles, but the eschatological
*pax Christi* is biblically assured.[85] For both the Old and New Testa-
ments, faith in the living God cannot be divorced from actual historical
events.[86] Henry confronts the charge head-on that the Jewish writers
of the Old Testament merely borrowed from surrounding Babylonian
and Sumerian cultures. Was the theme of covenant a late invention
redacted back into early Hebrew history? Simply put, no. Although
covenantal pacts were a common feature of the ancient world in the
pre-Mosaic times, the Old Testament covenant texts reflect a stark
departure from the standard fare of suzerainty treaties.[87]

Henry tackles the integration of faith and history as the last
major obstacle in volume 2 of *GRA*. He acknowledges that throughout the history of Judaism, divine revelation came to mean many
different things. Maimonides, for example, would not even comment
on the giving of the law at Sinai and focused mainly on prophetic
intuition. Spinoza dismissed the miracles of the Old Testament
as having originated in prophetic misunderstanding and therefore

---

[83]Ibid., 2:251.
[84]Ibid., 2:251–53.
[85]Ibid., 2:254–55.
[86]Ibid., 2:256.
[87]Ibid., 2:261–62.

bearing no philosophical significance. Today, theologians continually divorce redemptive faith and historical narrative in the Old
Testament.[88] In twentieth-century biblical theology, an array of
suggested models sought a middle way. Gerhard von Rad proposed
reconciliation between history and faith. For him, both religious
and secular approaches are necessary: the theologian accurately
representing Israel's faith perspective and the secular historian
interpreting the past without the hypothesis of God.[89] The school
of Wolfhart Pannenberg insisted that faith and history cannot be
separated from one another. In other words, throughout Scripture,
all of Israel's history has theological relevance.[90] Medieval Jewish
mystics anticipated the move away from external historical revelation; they stressed an immediate revelatory relationship between
humans and God. Twentieth-century kerygmatic theologians—such
as Barth, Käsemann, and Cullmann—internalized revelation, and, as
a result, scholars who were reluctant to let the Bible impinge upon
history sought simply to redefine history.[91] As we learn more about
the pre-Israelite history of Palestine and the ancient Near East,
Julius Wellhausen's skepticism toward Moses increasingly becomes
the critical issue. A decision must be made: if the documents of
the Pentateuch are not firmly rooted in history, then the entirety of
their theological relevance is radically jeopardized. "All too often,"
Henry comments, "it is the critical biblical scholar who is least
able to show how the Bible is spiritually significant for the church
as a corpus of literature."[92] But even unlikely allies such as Martin
Buber indicate that faith and history cannot be divided. Buber argues
against the idea that ethical monotheism arose in Israel only in the
eighth century BC and insists instead that prophetic confidence in
Yahweh extends at least back to Moses's time. Buber's principles
further demonstrate that prophetic confidence in Yahweh extends
all the way back to the patriarchs.[93]

---

[88]Ibid., 2:267.
[89]Ibid.
[90]Ibid., 2:268.
[91]Ibid., 2:271.
[92]Ibid., 2:272.
[93]Ibid., 2:272–74.

In sum, one cannot overestimate the damage wrought by departures from traditional views of revelation upon the fortunes of Christian theism in contemporary culture. The dialectical rupture between the world of transcendence and history, introduced into Protestant thought by Barth, has ironically prompted a string of sociopolitical or liberation theologies in which only the existential experience of a particular group is taken into account.[94] The implications of Barth's theology for the content of the Bible are staggering, namely, that the prophets and the apostles did not convey objective and authoritative truth that have their effects in the present, rather than eschatologically. Likewise, his view has astonishing repercussions for understanding history and nature: the divine being and nature can only interact in terms of negation and protest of the existing order.[95] Seeking to overcome this breach, twentieth-century views that elevate political metaphors to redemptive primacy tend to misinterpret the metaphorical nature of the salvation of God's people into rigid ideological motifs.[96] Henry concludes by tracing the obvious course of this thought: "If God is 'where the (revolutionary) action is' and acts in revolution per se, then no transcendent criterion remains to distinguish one revolution from another as demonic or divine."[97]

Henry further ups the ante for evangelical theology in his contention not only that God reveals himself in history, but also that the very concept of history stems from biblical religion. While no Hebrew etymology can be directly translated by the modern term *history*, the concept is nonetheless appropriate and necessary for expounding Israel's existence.[98] The mystery of how the supernatural intersects with history is a problem for modern-day historians, not a puzzle to be solved by theologians. Unlike C. S. Lewis, whose arguments in defense of miracles provoked a scathing critique from the likes of G. E. M. Anscombe, Henry does not employ apologetics defensively. Whether the historical method can prove the existence of

---

[94]Ibid., 2:275.
[95]Ibid., 2:277–78.
[96]Ibid., 2:279.
[97]Ibid.
[98]Ibid., 2:312.

miracles is not the same question as whether miracles exist. The issue is whether the historian must, in terms of his or her methodology, always explain the past in terms of the nonmiraculous.[99] As with all theoretical thought, Henry asserts that individual presuppositions are the essentially determinative quality for given views of how faith intersects with history.

Illustrations of how interpreters of the past reflect their underlying assumptions through their selection of evidence could continue indefinitely. Plato, for example, in the *Meno*, warned against thinking that historians merely catalog human events, and Aristotle, in the *Poetics*, associated historians with artists and poets rather than with rational philosophers.[100] Without some sort of pattern of importance, events are chaotic. As such, "history requires a meaning-scheme," and this interpretive framework is never an inference from events but a premise of faith.[101] Rather than conceding that the Gospels are demonstrably unreliable, classic evangelicalism challenges and contests the "gratuitous surrender of biblical reliability in historical matters and the ready sacrifice of biblical representations to alien critical theories." Evangelicals also insist that historical investigation and historicist methodology are not sources of faith—the source of faith is God.[102] Henry immediately sets about answering the obvious rejoinder:

> Do we then exercise faith only because we cannot assuredly know that Christ did not rise from the dead? Far from it. If that were the case, our faith would rest not on fact but on superstition. Yet not even "historical probability" can be derived by examining objective data divorced from the "understanding" of "historical truth" that the historian subjectively brings to objective events.[103]

The truth of the matter is that historical method is inherently incapable of coping with supernatural concerns and is unable to demon-

---

[99]Ibid., 2:315.
[100]Ibid., 2:319.
[101]Ibid., 2:320.
[102]Ibid., 2:321.
[103]Ibid., 2:322.

stratively validate any past event.[104] The historian's repudiation of the miraculous is not the evidence of an unbiased observer, but is the evidence of someone covertly committed to practical atheism.[105] In conclusion the biblical understanding of history traces a very careful line between faith and facts. By beginning with a robust understanding of divine revelation, we can combine empirical probability with inner certainty when the meaning of specific events is transcendently vouchsafed by God through his inspired Word.[106]

Just as Henry was establishing evangelical theology on firm foundations, a counterpart in New Haven, Connecticut, was working on developing an alternative proposal for how the Bible could be understood. Missing from this thesis were preoccupations with the philosophical and historical reliability of Scripture, and a call to return to a premodern understanding of God. The work of Hans Frei and his colleagues at Yale promoted a more hermeneutical and narratival understanding of divine revelation. It was a project that would prove seductive to evangelicals, enticing them to move away from the Henry-esque and other classic evangelical understandings of cognitive propositional revelation and toward a more literary way of regarding Scripture.

## Hans Frei, the New Yale School, and the Changing Face of Evangelical Understandings of Divine Revelation
### Biographical Background on Hans Frei

Hans Frei was born in Breslau, Germany, April 29, 1922. His parents, both influential physicians, were Jewish and reared their son in a nominally Lutheran home. At the time of the rise of Nazi government in Germany, the Frei family sent Hans to England to study and to avoid the tumultuous political environment. Not long thereafter, the rest of the family moved to the United States in order to escape the onset of persecution. Owing to his father's failing health, the family was unable to finance a college education for Hans. As a result, he

[104]Ibid., 2:325.
[105]Ibid., 2:328.
[106]Ibid., 2:330.

took the only scholarship he was offered, and in 1942, he graduated with a BS in textile engineering from North Carolina State University.

Having been greatly impressed by a lecture Reinhold Niebuhr gave during a visit to the university, Frei embarked upon a career in theological education. He enrolled at Yale Divinity School, where he could complete his BD. After pastoring a Baptist church in New Hampshire, Frei became an Episcopalian, largely because he appreciated Episcopalian doctrinal inclusivity. He returned to Yale and received a PhD under Niebuhr. His dissertation on the doctrine of revelation in Karl Barth's theology signaled his embrace of neoorthodoxy and simultaneous rejection of traditional theological liberalism. After teaching at Wabash College and the Episcopalian Seminary of the Northwest, Frei returned to Yale for the last time, this time as a member of the religious studies faculty.[107]

Initially, Frei's theological career was largely unrecognized by the academy. Much like his colleague Sydney Ahlstrom, Frei remained in relative academic obscurity until he published the groundbreaking work that would define his career. In 1974, Yale University published *The Eclipse of Biblical Narrative: A Study in Eighteenth and Nineteenth Century Hermeneutics*,[108] and Frei increasingly became recognized as a leader in the field of biblical and theological hermeneutics. This volume and *The Identity of Jesus Christ: The Hermeneutical Bases of Dogmatic Theology*, published in 1985, stood as his primary contributions to theological literature.[109] In 1984, with the publication of George Lindbeck's *Nature of Doctrine: Religion and Theology in a Postliberal Age*, in which Lindbeck cited Frei's work as his inspiration, Frei became regarded as the father of the emerging "postliberal" or "Yale" school of theology. Following a mild stroke, Frei died somewhat unexpectedly in 1988. His students and appro-

---

[107]For additional biographical information on Frei, see William Placher's introduction to Hans W. Frei, *Theology and Narrative*, ed. George Hunsinger and William C. Placher (New York: Oxford University Press, 1993).

[108]Hans W. Frei, *The Eclipse of Biblical Narrative: A Study in Eighteenth and Nineteenth Century Hermeneutics* (New Haven, CT: Yale University Press, 1974).

[109]Hans W. Frei, *The Identity of Jesus Christ: The Hermeneutical Bases of Dogmatic Theology* (Philadelphia: Fortress, 1975).

priators, among the most widely read contributors to contemporary theological method, continue to develop the implications of his work.

## The Eclipse of Biblical Narrative: *A Summary*

Frei's primary thesis in *The Eclipse of Biblical Narrative* maintains that Enlightenment concerns over historical justification undermined the primary quality of Scripture, what he calls "realistic biblical narrative." This development ultimately gave primacy to concerns other than a "literal" reading of the text in biblical interpretation. For nearly seventeen hundred years, Frei argues, the Christian church understood the Bible as the text that shaped and defined the world, and read it literally and figuratively, apart from external metaphysical and historical considerations. To support his contention, Frei turns to the Reformers and Calvin in particular. The emphasis that these "precritical" biblical interpreters placed upon the Bible was its simultaneous literal and figurative nature. It was literal in the sense that the meaning of a text of Scripture is easily accessible to the reader. It was figural in the sense that the narrative internally explains its various parts. Types and shadows prefigure other events, and these occurrences, taken together, constitute the meaning of the text.

Central to Frei's concerns, as we shall see, is that there is no meaning behind the text, and thus no special historical or metaphysical hermeneutical tools are needed for interpretation, just the narrative. As such Frei says that for Calvin, "the only spiritual act is that of comprehension—an act of mimesis, following the way things really are—rather than creation, if it is to be a faithful interpretation." Stated simply, no categories were used to explain the text other than internal references back to the text of Scripture itself. Although he admires much about the Reformers' method, Frei makes very clear that a simple return to a precritical understanding of the Bible is, in fact, impossible since the Reformers actually believed that the explicative interpretation of Scripture was coextensive with historical factuality.[110] For Frei, this kind of assumption is not necessary

---

[110]Frei, *Eclipse of Biblical Narrative*, 40.

to engage in the proper consideration of the text for its realistic biblical character.

Then at the turn of the eighteenth century, Frei explains, a fundamental shift took place as there arose a preoccupation with philosophy and the ability of reason to account for "truth" apart from Scripture itself. The first fissures in the medieval/Reformation synthesis exhibited themselves in the thought of theologians such as Johannes Cocceius, who located the primary meaning of the biblical texts in doctrinal affirmations and in a theological system (federal theology) rather than in the simple literal reading of the past. This was also the age of Locke, who advanced the notion that epistemological certainty is necessary for true knowledge. Followers of Locke, such as Anthony Collins, insisted on rational coherency as a test for justified belief. Frei describes this element as, to some extent, a new emphasis. Consequently, Collins inaugurated a challenge to the orthodox defenders of the Bible that one did not need figural interpretation to understand what the Bible means; one needs only to understand the author's original intention. Any interpretation different from the author's intention is simply mystification and pure imagination.[111] For Frei, this was a precursor for the later historical-critical method, which denied that canonical unity necessarily has to be accounted for in the Bible.

As confidence in empirical investigation grew in both historical and scientific methods, a simultaneous suspicion of supernatural phenomena began to develop, and the Bible became a primary target. Frei summarizes, "First in England and then in Germany the narrative became distinguished from a separable subject matter—whether historical, ideal or both at once—which was now taken to be its true meaning."[112] German interpreters began to shift the terms of the debate as well. The most important German philosopher in this regard was Christian Wolff, who posited that words and narratives themselves refer to external "referents." Because this was true, there must be an "ideal" referent to which statements correlate: "The real-

[111]Ibid., 75–78.
[112]Ibid., 51.

ity to which a concept or a word refers is the ideality of possibility underlying a thing or a general truth."[113]

In light of the changing nature of the debate, theologians began to develop proposals to respond to the new terms of discussion. Both sides to varying degrees became concerned with apologetics and dogmatics: they wanted desperately to prove that the Christian faith would not wither under the advent of the new historical consciousness.

Liberal scholars sought to preserve religious meaning for the Bible in light of the historical criticism of Hermann Samuel Reimarus by arguing that meaning comes from the experiential impact that the text makes upon the reader. Liberal New Testament critics such as D. F. Strauss and Johann Semler and theologians such as Albrecht Ritschl and Friedrich Schleiermacher were all trying to maintain ostensive religious meaning for the Bible, but according to Frei it was a meaning predicated upon a higher truth than the narrative itself.

Likewise, conservative scholars sought to defend the historicity of the Bible against the attacks of the higher critics. The advocates of the "biblical theology" movement sought to establish the unity of the biblical accounts theologically—the thought that the Bible speaks univocally rather than polyphonically. Further, they sought to meet the higher critics on their own battleground: truth was objective and historical, and the Bible could be verified on both counts. Frei's consideration of these eighteenth-century conservative theologians is considerably thinner than his treatment of their liberal counterparts (he treats only Bengel and Cocceius, and consigns their nineteenth-century successors to a brief reference or two). His conclusion is the same: "Hermeneutics stood between the religious apologetics and historical criticism, and these two worked against the narrative option."[114] By the time Schleiermacher and Hegel began theorizing, hermeneutics had become so historicized, and thus so separated from the narrative meaning of the Bible, that the whole interpretive process became historicized.

[113]Ibid., 101.
[114]Ibid., 134.

Frei's critique of both groups of theologians centers on his disavowal of the adequacy (and probably the existence) of propositional truth and revelation. He designates the liberals as "mediating theologians," thinkers who said that revelation has to be mediated in some way, usually through an existential act of faith. (Schleiermacher, Ritschl, Strauss, Brunner, Bultmann, Pannenberg, and Moltmann all receive mention in this regard.) To varying degrees, they sought to separate the "historical Jesus" from the "Christ of faith," thus violating the intention of the realistic narrative depiction. Contrary to the position of these thinkers, Frei thinks that there is no "universal" religious experience on which one can base religious belief.

As for the conservatives, Frei regards with a measured disdain their concern for doctrinal revelation and a particular theory of verbal inspiration. But perhaps more tellingly, Frei maintains that the "supernaturalists" were fighting a losing battle, because they had agreed to the terms of the liberals. For Frei, arguing for the historical reliability of miracles and for a meaning that refers to the author's original intention compromises interpretation. Such an approach, for Frei, is a categorical mistake. Frei considers it unfortunate that the conservatives, in his opinion, replaced biblical narrative with dogmatic propositions that they felt reflected objective reality. He argues that meaning is bound to the narrative sequence itself.[115] He would be extremely uncomfortable with saying that propositional statements or doctrinal affirmations derive their legitimacy in any way from the mind of God.

## The Meaning of "Realistic Biblical Narrative"

As we have mentioned, in *The Eclipse of Biblical Narrative*, Frei's thesis argues that Enlightenment epistemological categories supplanted the central feature of the biblical text: its narrative quality. That is, Frei contends that the Bible maintains a unity because of the story it tells, that of the person of Jesus Christ and his identity. He feels that one can interpret the text internally through the use of what he terms

---

[115]Hans Frei, as quoted by Roger Olson in "Back to the Bible (Almost): Why Yale's Postliberal Theologians Deserve an Evangelical Hearing," *Christianity Today*, May 20, 1996, 32.

"intention-action" schema. Since this story is the central feature of the biblical text, all interpretation of the Bible should flow from narrative alone. As Frei states throughout the corpus of his work, the "biblical narratives mean what they say and say what they mean." In other words, there is no independent "meaning" behind the text of Scripture for Frei. Instead, we are simply to take the words and stories presented to us in Scripture and let them define the way we speak about it. As such, Frei rejects any notion that the interpreter should be concerned with any supposed "objective" truth standing outside the narrative of Scripture. Consequently, Frei avers, we should not be preoccupied with asserting an objective account of reality, or objective truths in particular.

Heavily influenced by the work Eric Auerbach, who held that narratives operate independent of external truth claims, Frei believes that narratives create a "primary world" of their own, a sort of "reality" in which the readers participate. This "primary world" is what is important for the believer in the narrative; exterior concerns about historical facticity are virtually irrelevant since they distract readers from immersing themselves in the categories that the narrative provides for them. For Frei, the biblical narratives are "history-like" while not necessarily claiming to be historical accounts; their history-likeness is all that is necessary for us to claim they are "true."[116] Following his theological predecessor, Karl Barth, Frei advocates an approach to Scripture that isolates its truth claims from any kind of empirical justification.

As Mark I. Wallace summarizes, for Frei:

> The Bible's meaning stems from the internal literary world pictured in its stories, not from the external historical world referred to by these stories. That the Bible is not historical, however, does not entail that it is not history-like; as history-like, the Bible is "literally" though not "historically," true.[117]

Thus truth, for Frei, is internal coherence and dependence on the language of the text rather than some kind of observable phenomena.

---

[116]Frei, *Eclipse of Biblical Narrative*, 10ff.
[117]Mark I. Wallace, "The New Yale Theology," *Christian Scholar's Review* 17, no. 2 (1997): 157.

In Frei's estimation, in order for a text to be "true," the "world of the text's reference" need only "be disclosed as a possibly true world," and so consequently, "it is not clear whether the distinction between 'possible' and 'actual' truth is very sharp in 'meaning as reference.'"[118] Thus, as William Placher, one of Frei's most prolific students, summarizes, for "postliberals" operating out of Frei's understanding of "realistic biblical narrative," the "meaning of a text lies neither in the eternal truths it symbolizes, nor in the way it pictures some independent state of affairs. Rather, the narrative's meaning lies precisely in the story it tells."[119] Ultimately, Frei either obfuscates or disregards the subject of whether the narrative corresponds to some other body of content.

## A Henry-esque Critique of Frei's Approach to Hermeneutical Methodology and the Theological Task

In the following section, we will make a few brief critical observations regarding Frei's thesis as it relates to his ability to engage productively in the theological hermeneutical task. This should not be considered an exhaustive list. More systematic attempts have been made elsewhere.[120]

1. Frei's statement that meaning arises from narrative texts alone equivocates on the critical question of the nature of truth. It certainly seems as though his assertion that meaning arises from texts alone is itself an ontological statement, a category from which he wants to distance himself.[121] Still, Frei would have the theologian continually beg the question of truth outside narrative contexts as an unfortunate "category mistake"—even if he is subconsciously making an epistemological claim through his refuge in ambiguity. There can

---

[118]Hans W. Frei, "Theology and Interpretation of Narrative: Some Hermeneutical Considerations," in Hunsinger and Placher, *Theology and Narrative*, 132.

[119]William Placher, "Scripture as Realistic Narrative: Some Preliminary Questions," *Perspectives in Religious Studies* 5 (Spring 1978): 32–41.

[120]See Carl F. H. Henry, "Narrative Theology: An Evangelical Appraisal," in *Gods of This Age, or God of the Ages?* (Nashville, TN: Broadman & Holman, 1994). See also Nicholas Wolterstorff, "Will Narrativity Work as the Lynchpin?," in *Relativism and Religion* (New York: St. Martin's, 1995).

[121]This is clear, given Frei's negative portrayal of the movement of the epistemological realists in *Eclipse of Biblical Narrative*.

be no doubting that Frei's obfuscation on this point concerning the possibility of objective truth opened the door for Lindbeck's assertion that in Christian doctrine, there need be no such thing as a first-order truth claim. So, for example, when the Nicene Creed refers to Jesus Christ as *homoousios* with the Father, it does not refer to an ontological reality beyond the grammar of the statement. Lindbeck avers, "Thus the theologian most responsible for the final triumph of Nicea thought of it, not as a first order proposition with ontological reference, but as a second order rule of speech."[122]

Frei at several points in his career admitted to his own ambivalence regarding the nature and place of truth as an ontological category. In an article directed to Lindbeck, Frei advised his colleague to cling tenaciously to his presupposition that the "grammar of doctrine" constitutes an "ecumenical reality" of common ground between world religions upon which a rapprochement can be achieved. Deny the call of the propositionalists to pin you down on the nature of truth, Frei warned. "Stick to your guns, treat the truth question also under the auspices of your theme, otherwise you will point us back to the theological past rather than to the future."[123] Frei's agenda, initiated in *The Eclipse of Biblical Narrative*, becomes clear here: subordinate ontological truth claims that you do not like under the ones that you do! This points to the fact that despite Frei's equivocation, he does argue for truth claims on a rational, logical basis much like his putative hermeneutical villains of *Eclipse*. He does so only by hiding behind the obscurity of his concept of realistic biblical narrative.

2. It does not follow that simply because part of the Christian truth claim in Scripture takes place in narrative form, one must disavow propositional theological statements reflecting a state of affairs independent from, but congruent with, the narrative sense. Gabriel Fackre, who considers biblical narrative the central element in positing a Christian theology, contends that, for example, a proper doctrine

---

[122]George Lindbeck, *The Nature of Doctrine: Religion and Theology in a Postliberal Age* (Philadelphia: Westminster Press, 1984), 94.

[123]Hans W. Frei, "Epilogue: George Lindbeck and the Nature of Doctrine," in *Theology and Dialogue: Essays in Conversation with George Lindbeck*, ed. Bruce Marshall (South Bend, IN: University of Notre Dame Press, 1990), 279.

of verbal inspiration helps establish the truth claim of Scripture. He observes: "That inspiration is integral to revelation is crucial to evangelical witness. Evangelicals also agree on why such inspiration is necessary; they contend for its role in making propositional/ affirmational truth claims of a universal nature."[124]

Fackre understands that propositional truth claims undergird the narrative witness: they add to, rather than take away from, the primary missiological thrust of the biblical accounts. Frei did not make the practice of regular biblical exegesis a central part of his defense of realistic biblical narrative as the primary hermeneutical category.[125] Evangelicals do not need to deny that narrative is an important element in interpreting Scripture. Further, it was central to the formulation of the early ecumenical creeds. But contrary to Frei's implication, biblical narrative is not a viciously self-referential language game. Rather, Scripture points to a Trinitarian God who transcends human language, but nonetheless chooses it as a medium to speak to his creatures. As Carl F. H. Henry has posited, "Divine revelation does not completely erase God's transcendent mystery, inasmuch as God the Revealer transcends his own revelation."[126] As such, while on the one hand God transcends his own revelation, on the other (and contrary to Frei's narrative hermeneutic), God is not exhausted by the explanation of him and his work contained in any story or any propositional statement.[127] And yet, he has chosen to accommodate himself in human language in order to speak truthfully to us in meaningful and referential terms. Our knowledge of God and his revelation, though mediated by human language, can be a true knowledge of God without being completely coextensive with the mind of God. Frei's fear of propositional revelation is unwarranted,

---

[124]Gabriel Fackre, *Ecumenical Faith in Evangelical Perspective* (Grand Rapids: Eerdmans, 1993), 101.

[125]More than one reviewer of *Eclipse of Biblical Narrative* has noted the irony that despite the comprehensive nature of his treatment of eighteenth- and nineteenth-century hermeneutics, Frei never undertakes an exegesis of a single biblical text. What is more, Frei rarely does so throughout his scholarly consideration of theological hermeneutics.

[126]Henry, *God, Revelation and Authority*, 2:47.

[127]See also Carl F. H. Henry, *God, Revelation and Authority*, vol. 3, *The God Who Speaks and Shows, Fifteen Theses, Part Two* (Waco, TX: Word, 1979), chaps. 24–28.

given these considerations. His approach is a subtle yet ultimately unsatisfactory attempt to avoid the conclusion that revelation must be mediated in some way.[128] As D. A. Carson notes:

> Because he chooses to communicate with finite mortals in their languages, God cannot possibly communicate all that he is and knows, but I cannot see how that is a barrier to his communicating some true elements of what he is and knows. Of course, we will misunderstand the communication in all sorts of ways, owing to both our finiteness and sinfulness, but the content itself is objectively true.[129]

In short , Frei's concept of "realistic biblical narrative" is not a sufficient hermeneutical concept to help the reader adequately render God's revelatory communication.

3. To separate biblical narrative from a concept of historical revelation is a severe hermeneutical mistake. Since Frei disregards authorial intention as a guide to interpreting biblical passages, he can claim that the text can be read as narrative alone.[130] But while it is not always the case, often the author gives clear indication that his historical concerns are concomitant with his theological and narrative concerns, as with Luke's stated intention in his Gospel and adjoining account of the early church. To ignore this fact is to operate out of a naiveté that places a hermeneutical presupposition before the stated concerns of the text. If Frei's critique of evangelicalism is that it artificially superimposes a theory of inspiration on the text of Scripture, then postliberalism is guilty of the same crime by assuming that every facet of Scripture must be read like a narrative. Amazingly, Frei admits as much.

---

[128]For a critique of narrative theology's doctrine of revelation, see Colin Gunton, *A Brief Theology of Revelation* (Edinburgh: T&T Clark, 1995), chap. 1.

[129]D. A. Carson, *The Gagging of God* (Grand Rapids: Zondervan, 1996), 130.

[130]Frei, in a passage that highlights the inherent ambiguity of his approach, comments regarding his own hermeneutical method, "One *needs*, finally and foremost, to have a text both atemporally distanced from its moorings in a cultural and authorial or existential past and yet also re-entering the temporal dimension at the point of the present, if it is going to have the capacity to inform an understanding that is itself essentially characterized as present." In Hunsinger and Placher, *Theology and Narrative*, 132.

Nevertheless, as Walter Kaiser and Moisés Silva have argued, "It is true, of course, that the historical allusions are usually not the direct point of the narratives. Nevertheless, they do function as corollaries that validate the teaching and claims made in the text."[131] Additionally, as Carl Henry points out in his response to Frei's hermeneutical proposal, "The scriptural narrative is not content to reduce questions of authorship and relationships to universal history to second order questions."[132]

As we have seen, however, postliberal theologians such as Frei and Lindbeck are content to leave the conversation precisely at that point. Frei responds, "So 'reference' again is a difficult thing to get a hold of even though one wants to refer. . . . I think 'reference'—to say nothing of 'truth'—in Christian usage is not a simple, single, or philosophically univocal category."[133] In other words, for Frei, the Christian understanding of truth need not correspond to a reality to which everyone and everything is held accountable. This is the sad legacy of postmodern hermeneutics that can result from a postliberal theological hermeneutic: mutually contradicting metanarratives. Indeed, this is where someone like Lindbeck would like to leave the issue: that our missiological task as Christians is often to help Muslims become better Muslims, Christians better Christians, and so forth.[134] Surely this is indicative of a fundamental disagreement between evangelicals and postliberals concerning the very nature and purpose of the Christian church and Christian Scripture. The debate over external referents is a debate over biblical authority and ultimately whether one must believe in the claim that the Christian gospel is ontologically true. No amount of Wittgensteinian equivocation on the nature of language games can avert this fundamental issue.

4. Finally, as current discussions in theological hermeneutics suggest, Frei's concept of realistic biblical narrative has generated a wide variety of theological claimants. At the heart of much of the

---

[131]Walter Kaiser and Moisés Silva, *An Introduction to Biblical Hermeneutics: The Search for Meaning* (Grand Rapids: Zondervan, 1994), 80.

[132]Henry, "Narrative Theology," 267.

[133]Frei, "Response to Narrative Theology," in Hunsinger and Placher, *Theology and Narrative*, 210.

[134]See Lindbeck, *Nature of Doctrine*, 54.

current debate is the contested nature of the application of realistic biblical narrative for contemporary theological formulation. In the April 1992 edition of *Modern Theology*, on "Hans Frei and the Future of Theology," few of the participants could agree with each other on precisely what Hans Frei felt about such wide-ranging topics as phenomenological hermeneutics, the meaning of realistic narrative as the literal reading of Scripture, and the extent to which postliberal theologians can engage in theological articulation.[135] As Frei's former students and appropriators have shown, an approach to theology predicated upon realistic biblical narrative means a minimalist approach to theological formulation.[136] Charles Wood, citing Frei's concept of realistic biblical narrative as a compromise between the quagmire of traditional liberal hermeneutics and the rigid doctrinal confines of theological conservatism, states that the text of Scripture "in no way oblige[s] the interpreter to accept whatever scriptural texts teach (or disclose, or evoke, or whatever scriptural texts do) as true."[137]

In another chapter of the same volume, entitled "Scriptural Authority and Theological Construction: The Limitations of Narrative Interpretation," Maurice Wiles avers that narrative does not lend itself willingly to either historical verifiability or precise doctrine formulation. As such, narrative theological interpretation is necessarily minimalistic. Consequently, a narrative reading that seeks to show the unity of the biblical witness ultimately remains, in Wiles's estimation, "difficult" and "problematic." In conclusion, theological formulation predicated upon narrative hermeneutics, and the "determination of what can properly be believed, is something that has continually to be discovered in the light of changing experience."[138]

---

[135]See *Modern Theology* 8, no. 2 (1992): iii–214.

[136]This is a recurring theme in *Scriptural Authority in Narrative Interpretation: Essays on the Occasion of the Sixty-Fifth Birthday of Hans Frei*, ed. Garrett Green (Philadelphia, Fortress, 1987).

[137]Charles Wood, "Hermeneutics and the Authority of Scripture," in Green, *Scriptural Authority in Narrative Interpretation*, 18.

[138]Maurice Wiles, "Scriptural Authority and Theological Construction: The Limitations of Narrative Interpretation," in Green, *Scriptural Authority in Narrative Interpretation*, 55.

Like Frei before them, those fascinated by the centrality of real-istic biblical narrative to the theological hermeneutical task find themselves in an endless cycle of pretheological tasks. This is unlikely to change because the method presupposes the relative unimportance of doctrinal propositions in doing theology. There is already emerg-ing evidence of dissatisfaction with Frei's theological hermeneutics. Some of his own appropriators seem to be leapfrogging back in time and reasserting the importance of Barth, rather than Frei, for con-temporary theological method.[139] In the interim, Frei is beginning to suffer the aftereffects of a season of hero worship. Ironically, simul-taneous with this phenomenon is a growing preoccupation among evangelicals with all things postliberal.[140] The appropriation of Frei by certain evangelicals is unlikely, despite their high expectations, to produce any long-term solution to their current identity crisis.

## The Ascendance of Postfoundationalism and the Rejection of Henry

The work of Hans Frei and his colleagues in the New Yale school effectively reset the theological agenda for certain evangelicals from the early 1990s to the present in ways both direct and more diffuse. A skittishness set in when it came to talk of philosophical foundations and apologetics. Polemical theology is out. Ecclesiastical and narra-tive theology is in. From various different sectors, a new conviction seems to have settled that epistemology is irrelevant when it comes to theological method. Although individuals such as Millard Erick-son, Douglas Groothuis, and R. Albert Mohler, among others, have detailed serious concerns about this route, the trajectory of theology has moved, seemingly irrevocably, in a postfoundationalist direction.

The most notable and most scrutinized of these developments comes from a cadre of inheritors and critical appropriators of the Frei-Lindbeck legacy under the moniker of postconservative evangelicals. In tandem with the emphasis of the New Yale school,

---

[139]David E. Demson, *Hans Frei and Karl Barth: Different Ways of Reading Scripture* (Grand Rapids: Eerdmans, 1997). In this volume Demson accuses Frei of a deficient understanding of the presence of Christ for the church.
[140]Timothy R. Phillips and Dennis L. Okholm, *The Nature of Confession: Evangelicals and Postliberals in Conversation* (Downers Grove, IL: InterVarsity, 1996).

postconservatives sought a route that took them around the methodology of classic evangelicalism in general, and Reformed theology in particular. One volume particularly set the agenda for a decade or more of conversation on the basis for theology. The 1996 publication of *The Nature of Confession: Evangelicals and Postliberals in Conversation* was dedicated to the work of Frei and Lindbeck, and looked for ways to galvanize a new movement freed from the concerns of theological propositions that were supposedly holdovers from Enlightenment rationalism. The editors, the late Timothy R. Phillips and Dennis K. Okholm, and the contributors, George Hunsinger, Rodney Clapp, Phillip D. Kenneson, Henry Knight, and Alister McGrath, among others, set an academic conversation that would later find its popular expression in certain emerging and emergent church circles.[141]

For some of these scholars—such as the late Stanley J. Grenz and Roger E. Olsen—the emphasis was to repristinate Anabaptist/Wesleyan/Arminian/Pietist theological traditions in current evangelicalism. The theology of Grenz, a prolific author whose life was tragically cut short in 2005, focused on resetting the methodological agenda for the evangelical movement. Grenz, a one-time student of Gordon Lewis at Denver Seminary, gained a reputation for being one of the most promising thinkers of the second-generation evangelicals with the publication of books like *Reason for Hope: The Systematic Theology of Wolfhart Pannenberg*, and his *20th Century Theology*, cowritten with Olson. The release of *Revisioning Evangelical Theology*, however, signaled a shift in Grenz's theological emphasis. He argued that evangelicalism's distinctiveness lies not in a particular epistemology or its truth claims (as Carnell, Henry, Lewis, Erickson, and others have maintained), but in a shared spirituality that takes place in local, believing communities. He called for a return to Pietism in the face of a postmodern culture that increasingly eschewed rational arguments in favor of personal and social relationships and constructs.

---

[141]Ibid.

Perhaps the most notable change from traditional evangelical epistemologies was Grenz's surprising decision to remove divine revelation from its traditional position as the foundation for religious authority in Protestant theology and consign it to a subcategory of the doctrine of the Holy Spirit in his systematic theology entitled *Theology for the Community of God*. Communal piety and spirituality remained the persistent theme throughout his other works, and Grenz argued that his approach was a matter of "renewing the center" of the evangelical tradition. In response, Mohler parried that, in his estimation, Grenz's project seemed like "a center without a circumference," with no clearly set or evident doctrinal boundaries.

It was Grenz's subsequent work with theologian John Franke, however, that directly brought his work into conflict with classical evangelicalism and the Henry legacy. In *Beyond Foundationalism*, Grenz and Franke sought to set aside the concern for propositional revelation for theological method. Claiming that Henry and others of his generation were held captive by a rationalism alien to the biblical text, Grenz and Franke proposed a course that would place the concerns of the community of faith, led by the Holy Spirit, at the forefront of theological discussion. By adopting key features of the postmodern ethos, they declared, theology could transcend "fundamentalist epistemology" and chart a new course. "Despite the well-meaning, lofty intentions of conservative thinkers to honor the Bible as scripture," the duo wrote, "their approach in effect contributed to the silencing of the text in the church."[142] These serious charges seemed to forecast the response to Henry's theology in years to come, both in postconservative circles and in the assessments of other writers whom it might be best to describe as "denominational theologians."

For example, influenced heavily by the New Yale–school approach, Reformed theologian Michael Horton produced *Covenant and Eschatology*, which operated from Frei's basic premises and sug-

---

[142]Stanley J. Grenz and John R. Franke, *Beyond Foundationalism: Shaping Theology in a Postmodern Context* (Louisville, KY: Westminster John Knox, 2001), 63.

gested that the performative acts of God should be understood as a "divine drama." Here again, traditional epistemic categories come in for critique: "Modern foundationalism has made theology in its image, withholding from theology its own intrasystematic resources. In our approach, we will argue, the covenant and its canon determine theological method, not vice versa."[143] Further, in his proposal Horton seizes upon Henry's critique of theologies of analogy and takes on what he sees as the latter's lack of hermeneutical finesse. In particular, he charges Henry with conflating the concept that biblical affirmations are "literally true" with the notion that they are univocal (i.e., they directly correspond to the mind of God).[144] Here, it seems that Horton is reading Henry in the worst possible light, although Horton is clearly concerned with the matter of univocity. But what I think Henry is trying to say is that in divine revelation, God gets to interpret himself for his creation. The reception of the truth of revelation is not left to human analogical imagination to decipher. If theorists like the later Wittgenstein, Gadamer, Barthes, and Derrida are correct, God (if he exists) is not free to do this. If this is in fact the case, then theology really is nothing more, epistemically speaking, than what Ludwig Wittgenstein dubbed it: "the grammar of faith."

Wittgenstein made this suggestion in his 1953 posthumously published work *Philosophical Investigations*.[145] The comment partially inspired the New Yale school, which views theology primarily as a discussion about the contours of biblical narrative, not propositional content from the mind of God. The work of the New Yale school picked up upon this designation, and thus Paul Holmer entitled his work on the enterprise of theology in precisely the same way.[146] If that is what a new generation of evangelicals claims as the nature of theology, that is their business. But it really should be understood that one cannot easily modify the conclusions

---

[143]Michael S. Horton, *Covenant and Eschatology: The Divine Drama* (Louisville, KY: Westminster John Knox, 2002), 11.

[144]Ibid., 188.

[145]Ludwig Wittgenstein, *Philosophical Investigations*, 3rd ed., trans. G. E. M. Anscombe (Oxford: Blackwell, 2002).

[146]Paul Holmer, *The Grammar of Faith* (San Francisco: Harper & Row, 1978).

of twentieth-century philosophical hermeneutics for the purposes of theology without doing violence to the work of those theorists who advanced these concepts. With a few notable exceptions, they clearly did not believe that Christian doctrines referred themselves to anything like a transcendent metaphysical reality beyond our natural world.[147] For example, as David Vessey argues in his essay on Gadamer and the philosophy of religion:

> Gadamer sought to distinguish his philosophical hermeneutics from theologically driven hermeneutics. Perhaps because of that, even though he has influenced contemporary theological herme-neutics, he has very little to say about theology or religion. What he does say about religion is drawn from a reductive interpretation of religion as myths that posit something transcendent to help us cope with our awareness of our death.[148]

Another example of a conservative theologian who eschews an epistemological orientation to prolegomena is the Baptist thinker Malcolm Yarnell. Although by no means a postfoundationalist in the postliberal sense, he nonetheless has shifted his position on the need for epistemological foundations over the years. For example, in a 2002 conference on the legacy of Henry hosted by Union University, Yarnell praised the work of Henry in his philosophical orientation to method:

> Henry approached the theological enterprise in this manner, apparently for two reasons. First, history demanded it. Protes-tant orthodoxy has long treated revelation as prolegomena to systematic theology proper. In the nineteenth century, liberalism focused attention on epistemology by denying the authority of the premiere conduit of Christian authority, the Bible. In the twentieth century, Neo-Orthodoxy sought to revivify Protestant Christi-anity by reclaiming revelation, but unfortunately, reoriented our

[147]Paul Ricoeur is an exception in this regard.
[148]David Vessey, "Gadamer and the Philosophy of Religion," *Philosophy Compass* 5, no. 8 (2010): 645–55.

knowledge of the divine revelation away from the written text and toward internal encounter.

The second reason Henry approached epistemology first is because although God is ontologically prior to revelation, our knowledge of God must first be established. Answering the epistemological question helps provide the answer to the ontological question.[149]

By the time Yarnell published his *Formation of Christian Doctrine* in 2007, however, his view seemed to have changed. In this volume, he wrote of the need to "liberate" theology from the "captivity of philosophy." While Yarnell rightly points to the reticence of the magisterial Reformers to adopt Aristotelian philosophy and the fact that "philosophy is always fraught with unforeseen difficulties, especially when a culture's worldview changes," one is still left wondering as to the epistemic grounds upon which his confidence in Scripture is established.[150] In other words, one cannot find fault with his desire to orient theology around Scripture. But while he admirably critiques competing views in modern theology that question the full inspiration of the Bible, one still has the uneasy feeling that ideas such as authority and Scripture as the *norma normans non normata* cannot simply be left hanging in midair without a robust prolegomena supporting it. Modern and postmodern interrogations demand this of the contemporary evangelical theologian, and Carl F. H. Henry set forth the correct pattern and approach for the epistemological gravity of divine revelation. Despite his invitation for another generation of evangelical theologians to follow after him, Henry's heirs have spent more time looking over their collective left shoulders.

So if Henry's approach to divine revelation is not good enough, then what is? No more enticing answer to this question is set forth than the one offered by a figure who is arguably current evangelicalism's leading theologian, Kevin Vanhoozer, specifically his adoption

---

[149]Malcolm Yarnell, "Whose Jesus? Whose Revelation?" (paper presented at the "Remaking the Modern Mind" conference, Union University, March 8, 2002).

[150]Malcolm B. Yarnell III, *Formation of Christian Doctrine* (Nashville, TN: B&H, 2007), 66.

of speech-act theory set forth by J. L. Austin and the subsequent work of Austin's chief disciple, John Searle.

## Can Speech-Act Theory Be Deployed in Service to Religious Epistemology?

I am interested in the work of Austin and Searle regarding their respective views on speech-act theory specifically as evangelical theologians have sought to appropriate that methodology in their religious epistemologies. I am particularly curious why theologians such as Vanhoozer and even Erickson believe that speech-act theory is a viable alternative to classic cognitive propositionalist ways of understanding religious authority. Austin's background in analytical philosophy is necessary to understanding whether speech-act theory is intended to bear or even capable of bearing the epistemological weight of divine communication and religious authority. In my estimation, Searle only expands upon Austin's original proposal, but retains continuity with an approach to understanding texts that precludes divine revelation.

For the uninitiated, perhaps a brief explanation of the basic parts of speech-act theory would be helpful at this juncture. For Austin and Searle, the speech act is the basic unit of linguistic measurement. In his landmark work *How to Do Things with Words*,[151] Austin defined a speech utterance as having meaning primarily in its performative capacity. In other words, it is less important to understand that to which a symbol or word refers than to know what it actually *does* in the context of its usage. Stated differently, the truth or falsity of an utterance matters significantly less than the question of whether the utterance "gets the job done." In this sense, then, there is a decidedly Wittgensteinian ring to what Austin was proposing in his William James lectures, later published as *How to Do Things with Words*. Having come up with a basic view of how words work, Austin then laid out a series of ground rules for deciding whether a performative utterance is, to use his own expression, "happy" or "unhappy." Thus, for Austin, the standard for truth becomes not right or wrong,

---

[151] J. L. Austin, J. O. Urmson, and Marina Sbisà, *How to Do Things with Words*, 2nd ed. (Cambridge, MA: Harvard University Press, 1975).

but felicitous or nonfelicitous. At no point in his proposal are grand ontological or metaphysical claims made. He underscored this point repeatedly throughout his career, specifically in his interchange with John Wisdom on knowledge of other minds in a symposium for the Aristotelian Society in Britain. Further, Austin emphasized the emotional background behind speech utterances—the thoughts, feelings, and intent of the author over the abstract or objective truth of the utterance itself. At the conclusion of his proposal, Austin determined that all language is performative in nature and so turns to a broader theory of describing speech acts in general. That job, of course, was left to Searle to do.

In his volume *Speech Acts: An Essay in the Philosophy of Language*,[152] Searle systematizes further the basic contours of Austin's understanding of happy and unhappy performative speech acts. Famously, he separates speech acts into four basic types: the utterance act, the propositional or locutionary act, the illocutionary act, and the perlocutionary act. The utterance act involves the simple pronunciation of words. The locutionary act is intended to add symbols into a coherent statement of fact of a grammatically coherent thought. The illocutionary act calls upon a reader to achieve correct interpretation of an author's wishes, and it is on these grounds precisely that Searle tars Derrida with the accusation that speech acts are always seeking a correct authorial interpretation. As for the perlocutionary act, this comes into play whenever an author makes an appeal for his listener to change behavior or activities. Ultimately, what matters most for Searle is whether any locution holds the notion of both promise and obligation.

This general tack of speech-act theory, then, departs significantly from a cognitive representational account of the truth or falsity of statements of fact. For the propositionalist view, the accuracy and reliability of such declarations is the main concern. What matters is not just the statement's reception from an intended audience, but whether it corresponds to an objective state of affairs independent

---

[152] John R. Searle, *Speech Acts: An Essay in the Philosophy of Language* (London: Cambridge University Press, 1969).

of the author-reader enclosure. Consequently, for anyone wishing to depart from the representational view of symbolic meaning, speech-act theory provides an attractive alternative. But my question is this: Is the Austin-Searle view capable of bearing the epistemological weight of metaphysical statements? Can their thesis be overlaid on traditional notions of divine revelation and biblical authority? A traditional evangelical theologian such as Carl F. H. Henry would argue no. Vanhoozer, however, unreservedly says yes. All of this has direct relevance to the kind of Bible that believers hold in their hands. Both Henry and Vanhoozer want an inspired and truthful Bible. Vanhoozer thinks the Austin-Searle thesis can get him there.

## Henry versus Vanhoozer? Looking Ahead

Perhaps no other figure looms so large over the possible reception of Henry's view of revelation as Kevin Vanhoozer, whose prolific output, scholarly reception, and mastery of current philosophical and theological hermeneutics distinguish him as the leading academic theologian of the evangelical movement today. His theological method differs markedly from that of Henry because he seeks to develop doctrinal categories out of a deep appreciation for the Bible's rich mixture of genres. Doctrine, as such, follows the literary form. With the publication of *Is There a Meaning in This Text?* in 1998, Vanhoozer established himself as the most philosophically informed evangelical theologian since Henry.[153] His command of twentieth-century hermeneutics set him apart from his counterparts in a tradition whose sometimes overly earnest denunciations of postmodern theory sounded very shrill. With many important publications in the interim, Vanhoozer changed the rules of evangelical engagement in the realm of theological prolegomena with the release of *The Drama of Doctrine* in 2007.[154] In *Drama*, he sought to conceive of doctrine differently than did Henry's classic verbal-propositional motif. Instead, he pointed his readers toward thinking about God

---

[153]Kevin J. Vanhoozer, *Is There a Meaning in This Text? The Bible, the Reader, and the Morality of Literary Knowledge* (Grand Rapids: Zondervan, 2009).

[154]Kevin J. Vanhoozer, *The Drama of Doctrine: A Canonical-Linguistic Approach to Christian Theology* (Louisville, KY: Westminster John Knox, 2005).

by way of theo-poetic drama, following the cues of the history of redemption in its canonical linguistic form. This new path was both an arrival and a departure for evangelicalism.

In the past, Vanhoozer has cast doubt upon the helpfulness of Henry's theological methodology. In his 2004 plenary address at the Evangelical Theological Society and its subsequent publication in the *Journal of the Evangelical Theological Society*, Vanhoozer adopted a paternal tone toward Henry's understanding of Scripture as truth. He charged his counterpart with bringing philosophical categories to the text of Scripture, and very directly challenged a core thesis in *God, Revelation and Authority*, which states that all genres in Scripture yield accurate theological propositions and declarations about God. Somewhat severely, Vanhoozer simultaneously lumped Henry's work together with that of Charles Hodge and the early Wittgenstein. This unlikely trio is supposedly guilty of reducing texts to their truth value. Vanhoozer argues:

> The main problem with the picture theory, then, is that it seems singularly inadequate to explain textual meaning.
>
> There are further problems with the picture theory of meaning and truth. First, and most importantly, it fails sufficiently to recognize that we use language to do other things besides referring. And it is far from clear that all reference to the real is best thought of as "picturing." Second, and relatedly, it ignores the role of circumstances, context, and use for determining meaning (e.g. what we are doing with language).[155]

The primary complaint throughout his essay regards authorial intent vis á vis inerrancy, implying that Henry had little appreciation of genre and discourse. Vanhoozer refers to Henry's discussion in volume 4 of *GRA* in which Henry openly worries that a narrow focus on authorial-intent interpretation can tempt commentators to sidestep the matter of the reliability and historicity of texts.[156] As is

---

[155]Kevin J. Vanhoozer, "Lost in Interpretation? Truth, Scripture, and Hermeneutics," *Journal of the Evangelical Theological Society* 48, no. 1 (2005): 96.

[156]Carl F. H. Henry, *God, Revelation and Authority*, vol. 4, *God Who Speaks and Shows: Fifteen Theses, Part Three* (Waco, TX: Word, 1979), 181.

the case with other figures in the critical reception of Henry, Van-hoozer reads Henry in the worst possible light, namely, that Henry claims no more than one way to read a text of Scripture. Vanhoozer's conclusion, aimed at Henry, states: "It is Scripture that reveals God, not a set of detached propositions. Revealed truths are not abstract but canonically concrete. This is our evangelical birthright—truth in all of its canonical radiance, not a diluted mess of propositionalist pottage."[157] If you put the choices like that, who would settle for an allusion to Esau's ill-fated stew?

Although he is certainly right to raise the question of Henry's hermeneutics, Vanhoozer seems disinterested in Henry's fundamental concern in the context of his argument in *GRA*: if one makes the author's intent supreme, and if one says the author's intention was a genre other than historical and scientific accuracy, we have opened up Pandora's box. Once you make this move, Henry warns, you can take any problematic or disputed text in Scripture as a matter of genre confusion. As we will discuss later in this volume, this is precisely the interpretive move behind crucial abandonments of inerrancy in contemporary evangelicalism. So, for example, if you are uncomfortable saying that Genesis 1 literally reveals the way God created the universe, don't worry. Simply say that the author's purpose was literary, poetic, or allegorical, and your problem is solved. This was Carl Henry's fear, and he was right to be concerned—if not with Vanhoozer, then with others who do not possess the better angels of Kevin's theological nature.

All of this resurfaced with the publication of *The Drama of Doctrine*, which represents the mature incorporation of Austin and Searle's speech-act theory into canonical-theological expression. Once again, Vanhoozer expresses his concern over the perceived reductionism of propositional theology, or what he calls "epic classicism."[158] Clearly targeting Lindbeck's typology, Vanhoozer dismisses the notion that God is engaging in "absolute monologue" in the act of divine revelation. He provocatively likens adherence to "Cognitive-Propositional Theology" to a sinful ambition.

---

[157]Vanhoozer, "Lost in Interpretation?," 108.
[158]Vanhoozer, *Drama of Doctrine*, 83.

Propositionalist Theology inevitably succumbs to an "epic" ambition when it aims at producing a set of universal truths. In this respect, one can say of works like Charles Hodge's *Systematic Theology* what Ricoeur has said of Hegel's philosophy: "the greatest attempt and the greatest temptation." What is *tempting* in propositional theology is the idea that one can "master" divinity by learning the system of truths communicated through the literature and language of the Bible.[159]

Although it is possible that Vanhoozer's summary accurately describes Hodge's position, and others' for that matter, one wonders whether his concerns are overwrought or even fair. Does anyone who completes an MDiv truly presume to have "mastered" divinity? Surely Vanhoozer is not speaking of the ability of various theological traditions to fence their doctrinal boundaries, or to say that their confessions of faith and creeds are accurate summaries of what Scripture teaches. Or is he? Such notions question the nature of theology itself.

If indeed theology is a matter of thinking God's thoughts after him in a faithful way, one does not need to propose a view of the univocity of human language with the divine mind in order to state that creeds and confessions can counter heresy with confidence. If this were not the case, then scholars like Bart Ehrman and Elaine Pagels would be correct. There would be no such thing as orthodoxy and heresy—only winners and losers from disparate theological perspectives. Although Vanhoozer wants to move theology away from a "cognitive-propositional" method and toward a genre-informed approach, it is still hard to see how one escapes the inevitable return to the sentences that describe a state of affairs in which some thing or attribute is predicated of a subject, linked by the verbal form "to be." This is, I think, all that Carl Henry was really trying to say, and it is the stock province of classical philosophy: the *Protagoras* of Plato and the *Metaphysics* of Aristotle. This does not mean that the question of how Greek philosophy processes theological questions differently from, say, the Hebrew worldview is not an important

---

[159]Ibid., 87.

consideration when formulating a theological method. But the concern must maintain that there is a very fine line between nuance and confusion. For his part, Henry's governing conviction was that God spoke in intelligent sentences and paragraphs, and this fundamentally set the agenda for how we approach the theological task.

Still, there is no going back to the way theology was done by classic evangelicals like Henry, Schaeffer, and others thirty or forty years ago. As someone whose responsibility it is to teach undergraduates Continental philosophy, I find it irresponsible to regard doctrine as if Wittgenstein, Heidegger, Gadamer, Ricoeur, Lacan, Derrida, and Deleuze never posed their challenges to the conventional notions of the Schleiermachian/Enlightenment proposals regarding hermeneutics, interpretation, and authorial intent.[160] One cannot afford simply to dismiss all things postmodern any more than one can pretend epistemology can be done in the same way after Kant's *Critique of Pure Reason*. And for the record, Henry's work does not interact with Continental philosophy enough to work out the areas of theoretical difference. This work still must be done.

The brilliance in Vanhoozer's more recent work, such as *The Drama of Doctrine* and *Remythologizing Theology,* comes from the erudite, balanced, and informed way he is seeking to move evangelicalism forward. Among the academic community, his "epistemic humility" is appreciated. Although serious work has been done on the nature of theological method from an evangelical perspective by writers as diverse as Richard Muller,[161] John Franke,[162] William Abraham,[163] and Nicholas Wolterstorff,[164] no one project seems so promising about a way forward as Vanhoozer's.

[160]Cf. Richard Kearney and Mara Rainwater, *The Continental Philosophy Reader* (London: Routledge, 1996), various articles.

[161]Richard Muller, *The Study of Theology: From Biblical Interpretation to Contemporary Formulation* (Grand Rapids: Zondervan, 1991).

[162]John R. Franke, *The Character of Theology: An Introduction to Its Nature, Task, and Purpose* (Grand Rapids: Baker Academic, 2005).

[163]William J. Abraham, *Divine Revelation and the Limits of Historical Criticism* (New York: Oxford University Press, 1982).

[164]Nicholas Wolterstorff, *Divine Discourse: Philosophical Reflections on the Claim that God Speaks* (Cambridge: Cambridge University Press, 1995).

That feeling of promise is both Vanhoozer's greatest blessing and his greatest challenge. At the 2011 convention of the Evangelical Theological Society, an impressive trio of scholars was impaneled to respond to *Remythologizing Theology*. All three respondents—Stephen Wellum, John Franke, and Oliver Crisp—praised the monograph. Each one gave suggestions for improvement. For example, Wellum worried that there is little concern in the project for apologetics. Franke queried whether or not Vanhoozer's approach offered enough help for issues confronting the church today (e.g., the debate over the norms of biblical sexuality). Crisp wondered aloud about whether *Remythologizing Theology* contained sufficient epistemological groundwork to rescue Vanhoozer's claim of aspectivalism versus perspectivalism in his attempt to construct a postfoundationalist theology. But the general assessment appeared to be that everyone wanted to claim Vanhoozer as an ally. In his response, Franke playfully noted that Roger Olson had recently claimed Vanhoozer among the postconservative evangelicals and inquired to his colleague as to whether this association made him uncomfortable. In support of Franke's intuitions, it is difficult not to see extensive parallels between his 2005 theological prolegomena *The Character of Theology: A Postconservative Evangelical Approach* and the work in *The Drama of Doctrine* and *Remythologizing Theology*. For his part, Vanhoozer responded to all of these queries with characteristic grace and humility, and agreed that his proposal needed strengthening in the areas indicated by his interlocutors.

Not all reviewers have been as kind. In a series of reviews and reflections on *Remythologizing Theology* on his blog "Helm's Deep," Paul Helm confesses his reservations about Vanhoozer's approach. In his first entry, Helm takes Vanhoozer to task for his distinction between the terms *doctrine* and *theology*:

> What's the difference between doctrine and theology? Something like this, perhaps: a biblical doctrine is a teaching of Scripture. And for Vanhoozer the earlier concern was: how are we to understand such doctrines? Answer: as intrinsic parts of a theodrama, they are what it means to understand God's dramatic work in

Christ, to understand how we ourselves are to be caught up in that drama, participants in it. Doctrine is God in interaction, in dialogue, through the polyphonic character of Scripture, entering the drama himself in the Incarnate Logos. So doctrine is not monologic, nor merely cognitive, or cerebral, teaching, (à la Charles Hodge) but dialogic interaction through the many genres of Scripture, engaging (in one sweep) not only our minds, but our imaginations, affections and wills.

So what is theology, on this view? Theology is a second-order activity, taking the theodrama, and its various elements as just described, and reflecting upon it. What does such theodrama imply about God? To answer this is to be engaged in the remythologizing of theology. The term is potentially confusing, and it seems a pity to have to spend a couple of dozen pages offering an apologia for the use of a word on the title page. But this nevertheless gives the author opportunity to say that remythologizing has nothing to do with Bultmann, but with understanding the Bible not as myth in the sense of a set of ancient fables, but as mythos, a dramatic plot, a plot of this-worldly events, of ordinary as well as heroic stories. That's theodrama again, of course. And remythologized theology is theology which does not proceed from the bottom up, from a merely human set of ideas, such as Hegel or Anselm offer, or the "five speculative 'ways' of Aquinas," but in terms of Scripture's own theodrama, God's ways.[165]

Helm's summary is spot-on, but this does not mean he finds Vanhoozer's approach compelling or helpful. He concludes:

Attempting to make the form of systematic theology more "participatory" by stressing its "dramatic" character, and by talking about speech-acts as its jazzy units, will not ensure participation in the Gospel, nor will it help to ensure it. Its likely outcome is something that will make participation in the Gospel more difficult. For it will fuzzy the distinctive cognitive character of God's

---

[165]Paul Helm, "Vanhoozer's Remythologizing Theology," Helm's Deep, entry posted May 1, 2010, http://paulhelmsdeep.blogspot.com/search?q=Remythologizing+Theology.

revelation, its good news, and make our thinking about divine things less exact, and less exacting.[166]

I am inclined to agree with Helm's assessment, and there is no doubt in my mind that Henry would as well. A reason for my own reticence is that I am suspicious of conscripting the work of an ordinary-language philosopher such J. L. Austin into the service of biblical theology. I do not think it works for a number of reasons. Chief among them is that Austin's work on speech-act theory simply underdetermines its own promise as a device for talking about theological truth. This feature is further complicated in that, although he was perhaps the most distinguished theorist on linguistics of his time, Austin did not publish enough for us to extrapolate grandly from his theory. Further, unless I am misreading his signature contribution, *How to Do Things with Words* is a work of great reserve about what we can expect from locutionary, illocutionary, and perlocutionary acts.[167] His caution, time after time, is that we cannot have grandiose expectations of language when establishing the truth or falsity of a given utterance. Guy Longworth, a leading interpreter of Austin, underscores this point:

> Austin viewed language as a sort of abstraction from the entire history of actions that involve speaking. That is, linguistic expressions and their properties are aspects of repeatable patterns in some of the activities of speakers. In abstracting, we treat bits of language—including both words and the structures through which they combine into sentences—as repeatable types. We thereby allow that the same expressions can be used on a variety of different occasions—in and with respect to different circumstances and for various intents and purposes. On at least some of those occasions, we may use a bit of language to state something that is true or false. And a question then arises as to the role of the repeatable bit of language we use in facilitating our stating truth or falsehood: do the bits of language that we use bear properties

---

[166] Paul Helm, "Propositions and Speech Acts," Helm's Deep, entry posted May 1, 2007, http://paulhelmsdeep.blogspot.com/search?q=Propositions+and+Speech+Acts.

[167] Austin, Urmson, and Sbisà, *How to Do Things with Words*.

that can determine which statement we make on an occasion of speaking and (so) determine, in conjunction with the facts, whether or not what we state is true? Austin gives a negative answer to this question.[168]

In summary, Austin's work does not invite metaphysical conclusions inasmuch as his work is epistemologically modest in the extreme. As such, it is doubtful he would recognize his theory of speech acts as a promising method for theological investigation—especially if doctrine is, on Vanhoozer's account, not intended to be consigned to mythology in the Bultmannian sense of the term, but rather, in its historic context, is the story of the acts of the divine in human affairs. Certainly, this makes sense given Austin's own context and those who followed him. The philosophy of atheist Gilbert Ryle, Austin's close colleague at Oxford, dovetailed with Austin's, as the former teased out the skeptical implications of ordinary-language philosophy. Paul Grice, perhaps Austin's most celebrated student, together with P. F. Strawson, argued that in ordinary-language philosophy, metaphysics merely refers to a descriptive analysis that clarifies the way conceptual frameworks function.[169] Likewise, Searle expounded upon speech-act theory without even mentioning its promise for metaphysical or theological consideration. On the contrary, Searle remains assiduously committed to biological naturalism and the view that we live in a universe "that consists entirely of mindless, meaningless, unfree, nonrational, brute physical particles."[170] In sum, speech-act theory in its genetic form does not seem like very promising territory for the discussion of "God-talk" at all if we intend to remain true to the intent of the original authors.

As commentator Barry Smith points out, Searle's theory of intentionality is "entirely naturalistic," and his ontological thinking is framed by this pretheoretical commitment. So in the *Rediscovery*

[168]Guy Longworth, "J. L. Austin, 1991–1960," accessed, http://www2.warwick.ac.uk/fac/soc/philosophy/people/faculty/longworth/austin_keythinkers.pdf.
[169]Paul Grice, *The Conception of Value* (New York: Oxford University Press, 2001); Robert J. Stainton, "Grice, Herbert Paul," available at http://publish.uwo.ca/~rstainto/papers/Grice.pdf.
[170]John Searle, *Freedom and Neurobiology* (New York: Columbia University Press, 2006), 4–5.

*of the Mind*,[171] for example, Searle avers that "consciousness is a causally emergent property of systems. It is an emergent feature of certain systems of neurons in the same way that solidity and liquidity are emergent features of systems of molecules." Further, in *The Construction of Social Reality*, he says:

> I start with what we know about the world: the world consists of entities described by physics and chemistry. I start with the fact that we're products of evolutionary biology, we're biological beasts. Then I ask, how is it possible in a world consisting of entirely brute facts, of physical particles and fields of force, how is it possible to have consciousness, intentionality, money, property, marriage and so on?[172]

I could go further here, but I think it is fair to inquire, on the basis of authorial intent—which is the central thesis of Vanhoozer's *Is There a Meaning in This Text?*—whether Searle would be horrified to learn that his iteration of speech-act theory was being put into service theorizing about divine revelation? Is such an enterprise legitimate? If it is not based on reception history, what is its basis?

Perhaps I am wrong about these suspicions. Perhaps the notion of theodrama bests Henry's version of God's speaking in intelligible sentences and paragraphs that yield logically sound and yet biblically faithful confessions of belief. Vanhoozer makes a good point that Henry was so focused on maintaining evangelical affirmations that he downplayed the richness of language and its setting in canonical linguistic form. Vanhoozer is also correct that language does more theologically than Henry allows. But after revisiting the first seven theses set forth in volume 2 of *God, Revelation and Authority*, I am not sure that it does less. Henry reminds us that the content of any theological system flows directly from divine prerogatives. The material, expression, and agenda of doctrine either conform to this pattern or set sail into uncertain anthropological and sociological waters.

---

[171]Michael J. Degnan, review of *Rediscovery of the Mind*, by John R. Searle, *Zygon* 31, no. 4 (1996): 735.
[172]John R. Searle, *The Construction of Social Reality* (New York: Free Press, 1995), 273.

One of the most enduring fears of Henry's theological method is that, as was the charge against his forebear Gordon Clark, the result is cold and calculated. This is a real concern. Vanhoozer's brilliant work reminds the evangelical community of the crucial insight of writer Annie Dillard that "we wake, if we ever wake at all, to mystery, rumors of death, beauty, violence."[173] What is more, as J. R. R. Tolkien reminds us in his great essay on Beowulf, there is a danger that attends rational and scientific description: "a plain pure fairy story dragon" can be ruined at the hands of a logical analysis. The interpreter, "unless he is careful, and speaks in parables, will kill what he is studying by vivisection, and he will be left with a formal or mechanical allegory, and, what is more, probably with one that will not work. For myth is alive at once and all its parts, and dies before it can be dissected."[174] Mindful of the fact that Tolkien refers to the Gospel narrative as the übermyth, no one wants to be guilty of killing belief in divine and holy things via vivisection. But God is not a fairy tale dragon, and after many years of reading Carl Henry's approach to theology, I do not think that this is what he was doing. He was a theologian, and theology matters—you cannot be an evangelical without being passionate or serious about it.

---

[173] Annie Dillard, *Pilgrim at Tinker Creek* (1974; repr., New York: Harper-Perennial, 1988), 4.
[174] J. R. R. Tolkien and Christopher Tolkien, "Beowulf," in *The Monsters and the Critics, and Other Essays* (Boston: Houghton Mifflin, 1984), 63–64.

# CHAPTER 4

# Inerrancy Matters

## Biblical Reliability and High Stakes

For Carl F. H. Henry, Easter was not just a Christian holiday; it was *the* Christian holiday. For many years, with the author's permission, Henry would take out a full page ad in his local newspaper and republish the full text of John Updike's poem "Seven Stanzas at Easter." Arguing for a bodily resurrection of Christ in which molecules were reknit and amino acids rekindled, Updike says in stanzas 4 and 7:

> Let us not mock God with metaphor,
> analogy, sidestepping, transcendence;
> making of the event a parable. . . .
>
> Let us not seek to make it less monstrous,
> for our own convenience, our own sense of beauty,
> lest . . . we are
> embarrassed by the miracle.[1]

What Henry loved about Updike's poem was its emphasis on the correspondence between divine truth claims and reality. Christianity, in other words, forces upon us an either–or opposition. Either you believe in a maximalist account of theism as presented in Holy Scripture, or you must abandon the Great Tradition in favor of a completely different proposal. Subtle, middle-of-the-road theological proposals ultimately satisfy neither the skeptics nor the faithful. Updike's "Seven Stanzas" underscores these themes, skewering contemporary proposals that seek to modify the core Christian truth claim "for our own convenience, our own sense of beauty." Henry

---

[1]John Updike, *Collected Poems, 1953–1993* (New York: Knopf, 1993).

taught his entire career that the text that we have in the Bible is not only trustworthy, but capable. It is capable of telling us what has happened in the past, what is happening in contemporary culture, and what will happen, if we listen to its message. It is this conviction that prompted Henry to offer his magisterial treatment of the doctrine of inerrancy in volume 4 of *GRA*. There was a confidence in inscripturated divine utterances that could withstand all analysis and any scrutiny.

This conviction, at the end of the day, was central to Henry's thought. He did not prefer the tone or methodology of his successor at *Christianity Today*, Harold Lindsell, who thought that subscription to the doctrine of inerrancy was some sort of criterion for redemption, or, as Lindsell used to put it, the way you tell the difference between the sheep and the goats.[2] Henry eschewed this notion and invited theologians (e.g., G. C. Berkouwer) who did not precisely share his understanding of biblical authority to write for *Christianity Today* in its early days and years. He was willing to collaborate with anyone who was deeply committed to the Great Tradition of the church more broadly, as his place on the original editorial board of *First Things* indicated. More specifically, he could partner with anyone who could sign on to the following definition of "evangelical" (i.e., being consistent with the "evangel"): "The good news is the scripturally anticipated-and-fulfilled promise that God's sinless Messiah died in the place of otherwise doomed sinners, and moreover, that the crucified Redeemer arose bodily from the dead to resurrection life as the helmsman of the eternal moral and spiritual world."[3]

Though a nonpartisan spirit characterized Henry's deportment toward other like-minded individuals, his work on the centrality of the doctrine of biblical inerrancy to the evangelical future remains perhaps the most defining aspect of his distinguished literary output. He saw, as did many of his colleagues, that inerrancy is the logical entailment of the doctrine of inspiration. Henry thought of iner-

---

[2] Henry reported this to me in a personal conversation in 1997.
[3] Kenneth Kantzer and Carl F. H. Henry, eds. *Evangelical Affirmations* (Grand Rapids: Zondervan, 1990), 76.

rancy as a matter of authenticity and identity—the consequence of believing that we can trust the utterances of God. Despite Scripture's patina of being an ancient text, inerrancy assures us that no aspect of human thought—whether historical, scientific, linguistic, or philosophical—can claim a higher epistemological ground than the Bible alone. Moreover, in the veracity of Scripture, everything is at stake. This is precisely why the apostle Paul

> declares the evangel to be "according to the Scriptures." The good news is scripturally-identified, scripturally-based, scripturally-validated; inspired Scripture is its verifying principle. Without authoritatively true Scripture the good news might be garbled a hundred different ways, as indeed it now often inexcusably is by those who stray from scriptural revelation.[4]

On this point, Henry was crystal clear throughout his career. In *Evangelical Affirmations* he follows up by stating:

> It is unjustifiable therefore to broaden the definition of evangelical identity in a way that excludes a specific view of Scripture. The reduction of evangelical authenticity to the affirmation of a "minimal gospel" (salvation solely on the ground of Christ's substitutionary work appropriated by faith) therefore obscures the inviolable truth of Scripture, which the Apostle Paul affirms. Evangelicals as a body of believers have stood traditionally not for a truncated definition of the good news, but provide an overwhelming precedent for the view that a consistent and complete statement of the Gospel embraces also the truthfulness of Scripture.[5]

## Evangelical Bad Faith

Evangelicals still widely consider themselves to be adherents to the full authority of the Scriptures, but the devil is in the details. To be certain, the annual meeting of the Evangelical Theological Society is larger and more academically robust than it has ever been. All of its members sign off on a pledge that they avow the doctrine of

---

[4]Ibid., 77.
[5]Ibid., 78.

biblical inerrancy. But if ever there was a doctrine that died a slow death by benign neglect, it is inerrancy. In the generation of classic evangelicalism, scholars such as Gleason Archer, Norman Geisler, Walt Kaiser, Millard Erickson, and others offered by theoretical definitions and actual material biblical defenses of the idea that the original autographs, the Old and New Testament Scriptures, perfectly corresponded to the highest levels of truth seeking. Although an array of perspectives were offered and the definition of inerrancy was not always airtight, the Chicago Statement on Biblical Inerrancy of 1978 set a baseline for the evangelical community that was written and endorsed by the leading pastors and scholars of the age: James Montgomery Boice, Kenneth Kantzer, Francis Schaeffer, J. I. Packer, R. C. Sproul, and, of course, Carl F. H. Henry. Whatever one wanted to say about evangelical agreements and disagreements over issues such as soteriology, pneumatology, ecclesiology, and eschatology, American evangelicals by and large stood on the same ground when it came to their position on the Bible as the inerrant word of God.

The ground began shifting in the 1980s, weakened further in the 1990s, and by the 2000s widened into something more like a chasm than a crack in the landscape. As with every generation, it is the theologians who set the agenda that others will follow. Within American Protestantism, on the matter of inerrancy, the first salvo to really set the tone was the Rogers-McKim thesis that while the Bible is infallible in its ability to reconcile us to God, it is not inerrant since it contains so called "technical mistakes."[6] Although the Rogers-McKim proposal made waves that prompted John D. Woodbridge's definitive rebuttal,[7] there was the sense that their critique came from the outside, from mainline Presbyterian theologians.

But that picture began to change with defections from within evangelicalism itself. Two examples highlight the trajectory. Although his early writings affirmed a robust notion of biblical inerrancy in vol-

---

[6]Jack Rogers and Donald McKim, *The Authority and Interpretation of the Bible: An Historical Approach* (San Francisco: Harper & Row, 1979).

[7]John Woodbridge, *Biblical Authority: A Critique of the Rogers/McKim Proposal* (Grand Rapids: Zondervan, 1982).

umes such as *A Defense of Biblical Infallibility*[8] and *Biblical Revelation: The Foundation of Christian Theology*,[9] Clark Pinnock shifted considerably on the matter later in his career.[10] In 1984, he published *The Scripture Principle*,[11] in which he repeatedly revised his former understanding of inerrancy beyond the point of recognition. Favoring a dynamic view of inspiration over verbal-plenary inspiration, Pinnock disavowed classic definitions of inerrancy, including those of B. B. Warfield and the Chicago Statement on Biblical Inerrancy. Further, he allowed that legends, myths, and factual errors exist in the biblical text, stating: "The Bible does not attempt to give the impression that it is flawless in historical or scientific ways. God uses writers with weaknesses and still teaches the truth of revelation through them."[12]

Other influential theologians followed the same path. Donald Bloesch underwent a significant transition on his treatment of Scripture from his earlier work in *Essentials of Evangelical Theology*[13] to his appropriation of Karl Barth's distinction between the Word of God and Scripture, as manifested in Bloesch's multivolume series that included *A Theology of Word and Spirit: Authority and Method in Theology*.[14] In this connection, he states:

> The biblical writings are a powerful testimony not only of people's faith but also of God's truth. They reflect not only the belief of the authors but also the very mind of God. They not only serve to inspire faith in God but also are inspired by God so that our faith can be informed by divine revelation. My sentiments concur

---

[8]Clark H. Pinnock, *A Defense of Biblical Infallibility* (Philadelphia: Presbyterian and Reformed, 1967).

[9]Clark H. Pinnock, *Biblical Revelation: The Foundation of Christian Theology* (Chicago: Moody Press, 1971).

[10]In fact, Pinnock's early teaching on Scripture at New Orleans Baptist Theological Seminary was instrumental in settling the convictions of seminarians such as Paige Patterson, who went on to lead the so-called conservative resurgence in the Southern Baptist Convention.

[11]Clark H. Pinnock, *The Scripture Principle* (San Francisco: Harper & Row, 1984).

[12]Ibid., 99. For a complete list of Pinnock's concessions on inerrancy, see Norman Geisler's compilation at http://www.trinityfoundation.org/horror_show.php?id=7.

[13]Donald Bloesch, *Essentials of Evangelical Theology* (San Francisco: Harper, 1982).

[14]Donald Bloesch, *A Theology of Word and Spirit: Authority and Method in Theology* (Downers Grove, IL: InterVarsity, 1982).

with Barth's: "We know what we say when we call the Bible the Word of God only when we recognize its human imperfection in face of its divine perfection and its divine perfection in spite of its human imperfection."

The object of our faith is not the church or the Scriptures, not even our experience of Jesus Christ. It is Jesus Christ himself, but Christ testified to in Scripture and proclaimed by the Church. He is one whom we meet concretely in the historical witness to his saving deeds. We commit ourselves not to the Jesus of history nor simply to the Christ of faith but to the Jesus Christ of eternity who entered into a particular history and is apprehended only in faith.[15]

One of the stock concerns oft repeated by those who question inerrancy is whether or not the term has any precise definition. Alister McGrath has argued that inerrancy is an American phenomenon introduced into the evangelical bloodstream via B. B. Warfield.[16] In *A Passion for Truth*, McGrath continues along these lines and warns against building a view of Scripture upon "rationalistic foundations."[17] Citing Bloesch as an exemplar, McGrath states that evangelicals have always resisted the temptation to equate Scripture with revelation.[18]

The problem with these assertions is that they are simply not true. Neither the concept of inerrancy nor the conviction that the Bible is actually God's word written are idiosyncratically American or rationalistic. On the contrary, classic evangelicals have always held this view, chief among them being two British leading lights: J. I. Packer and the late John R. W. Stott. As a matter of fact, Stott linked revelation with authority as the basis upon which evangelical unity could be upheld and maintained.[19] For his part, Packer

[15]Donald Bloesch, *Holy Scripture: Revelation, Inspiration and Interpretation* (Downers Grove, IL: InterVarsity, 1994), 37, 39.

[16]Alister McGrath, "Let's Keep Asking Questions: Discussion on the Question of Biblical Inerrancy," *Evangelicals Now*, April 1997, available at http://www.e-n.org.uk/433-Let's-keep-asking-questions.htm.

[17]Alister McGrath, *A Passion for Truth: The Intellectual Coherence of Evangelicalism* (Downers Grove, IL: InterVarsity, 1996), 58.

[18]Ibid., 52ff.

[19]John Stott, *Evangelical Truth: A Personal Plea for Unity, Integrity, and Faithfulness* (Downers Grove, IL: InterVarsity, 1999), 65.

contends that it is actually modern critical scholarship that is based upon rationalistic foundations, and that evangelicals really need to use the term *inerrancy* as a matter of historical continuity and self-definition.[20]

On all fronts, the doctrine of inerrancy is being debated, requestioned, and doubted as never before. The number of incidents have escalated to the point where G. K. Beale dedicated an entire volume to the problem in *The Erosion of Inerrancy in Evangelicalism*.[21] Indeed, everywhere one turns there is an interrogation about the nature and interpretation of the word *inerrancy* and its application to contemporary evangelical scholarship. For several years now, Bruce McCormack of Princeton Seminary has been arguing that evangelicals can come to terms with Barth's view of Scripture, and that the latter's understanding—which is largely McCormack's also—falls under the broad heading "dynamic infallibilism." McCormack parts company with evangelicals like Henry who see Barth's view of Scripture as the message that only "becomes the Word of God" in the moment of encounter between the hearer and the Word. Instead, McCormack argues that Barth's thought is actually circular—that the Bible becomes the Word of God because it is self-authenticating as such.[22] Most significantly, the controversies surrounding the dismissals of Peter Enns,[23] John Schneider, Daniel Harlow, and Mike Licona from their respective posts over charges of violations of inerrancy in their teaching and writing show the high stakes that are involved in the exchange.

To be certain, the concerns about abandoning historic doctrines as a result of modifying one's view of the reliability of Scripture

---

[20]J. I. Packer, *Truth and Power: The Place of Scripture in the Christian Life* (Wheaton, IL: Shaw, 1996), 48–51.

[21]G. K. Beale, *The Erosion of Inerrancy in Evangelicalism: Responding to New Challenges to Biblical Authority* (Wheaton, IL: Crossway, 2008).

[22]Bruce McCormack, "The Being of Holy Scripture Is in Becoming: Karl Barth in Conversation with American Evangelical Criticism," in *Evangelicals and Scripture: Tradition, Authority, and Hermeneutics*, ed. V. Bacote et al. (Downers Grove, IL: InterVarsity, 2004), 55–75. See also William B. Evans's very helpful summary of these matters: http://www.reformation21.org/articles /comments-on-karl-barth-bruce-mccormack-and-the-neobarthian-view-of-scripture.php.

[23]Peter Enns, *Inspiration and Incarnation: Evangelicals and the Problem of the Old Testament* (Grand Rapids: Baker Academic, 2005).

are certainly warranted from those whose charge is to hold their institutions in trust with classic evangelical priorities. The Enns scenario is perhaps most instructive in this regard, since it involves abandoning the notion of Adam and Eve as historical persons—a conclusion that has massive ramifications for soteriology and the entire system of theology. Enns should be commended for his candor regarding the situation, because he clearly advocates for what Stephen Jay Gould once referred to as "non-overlapping magisteria"—the realm of faith and the realm of science. For as Enns writes in *The Evolution of Adam: What the Bible Does and Doesn't Say about Human Origins*:

> Searching for ways to align modern scientific and ancient-biblical models of creation—no matter how minimal—runs the risk of obscuring the biblical texts in question. The creation stories are ancient and should be understood on that level. Rather than merge the two creation stories—the scientific and the biblical—we should respect that they each speak a different language. The fact that Paul considered Adam to be the progenitor of the human race does not mean that we need to find some way to maintain his view within an evolutionary scheme. Rather, we should gladly acknowledge his ancient view of cosmic and human origins and see in that very scenario the face of a God who seems far less reluctant to accommodate to ancient points of view than we are sometimes comfortable with.[24]

Responding to Enns, James K. A. Smith—in the spirit of Continental philosophy—argues that it is a mistake to assume that only the view of the original authors of the text should be the governing assumption of hermeneutics. He helpfully raises the question as to whether God himself has anything to say through the ancient text of the Bible. To be certain, Smith clearly understands what is at stake: "If we don't have an account of the origin of sin we will end up making God the author of evil—a thesis that has been persistently and

---

[24]Peter Enns, *The Evolution of Adam: What the Bible Does and Doesn't Say about Human Origins* (Grand Rapids: Brazos, 2012), 139.

strenuously rejected by the orthodox Christian tradition."[25] Smith is certainly not alone in his reservations about the implications of an evangelicalism that has "gotten over" traditional concerns such as the historicity of Scripture and the logical interconnectedness of doctrine. His thoughtful response to Enns is, however, a good call to step back and ask the question of what might be lost in a program designed to keep evangelicalism alive through a series of rescue attempts via the governing *Zeitgeist*.

Indeed, with the historicity of Adam in question, almost nothing else is sacred. Christology appears to be the next commonplace of the system to go. For instance, in a recent evangelical commentary series, Charles Talbert contends that we need not see the virgin birth as an actual supernatural intervention of the divine into history. Arguing along lines very similar to that of Enns, Talbert says that the virgin birth story is more likely a device that Matthew and Luke use to combat a semi-gnostic heresy that one must achieve moral purity before receiving God's seal of approval. The Gospel of Mark, which contains no miraculous infancy narrative but yet predates the other Synoptics, "was susceptible to this interpretation: a meritorious Jesus who is rewarded by God."[26] To head off this proto-Pelagian notion at the pass, Matthew and Luke incorporated ancient Greco-Roman mythologies about gods being miraculously born as a sign of a much broader metaphysical proof or seal of divine favor and grace apart from good works. Although Talbert may not aver himself an evangelical per se, his work appears in a commentary series whose target audience is this demographic. The nonchalant attitude toward the dismissal of the virgin birth in a series such as this one is but one additional example that evangelicals have lost interest in perpetuating the doctrine of inerrancy as a key evangelical distinctive.

Meanwhile, the coming generation of evangelicals is getting the message. Some within the community are openly questioning whether

---

[25]James K. A. Smith, "Whose Bible? Which Adam?," review of *The Evolution of Adam: What the Bible Does and Doesn't Say about Human Origins,* by Peter Enns, *The Colossian Forum,* April 24, 2012, accessed, http://www.colossianforum.org/2012/04/24/book-review -the-evolution-of-adam-what-the-bible-does-and-doesnt-say-about-human-origins/#_ftn5.
[26]Charles Talbert, *Matthew* (Grand Rapids: Baker Academic, 2010), 47–48.

the term *inerrancy* has any shape at all and should thus be abandoned.[27] In his recent work *Rehabilitating Inerrancy in a Culture of Fear*, Carlos Bovell seeks to address the matter of how this bedrock principle of classic evangelicalism can survive after the advent of the hermeneutics of suspicion.[28] As Bovell himself states: "The inerrantist paradigm is being called into question because the paradigm does not have explanatory power and new ones are needed."[29] Perhaps this is in fact the case, but I, for one, am skeptical. In the spirit of G. K. Chesterton's comment that "Christianity has not been tried and found wanting, but has been found difficult and left untried," I would like to suggest a return to the most magisterial and arguably definitive understanding of inerrancy ever mounted: volume 4 of Henry's *God, Revelation and Authority*.

## Thesis 11

Thesis 11 of *GRA* sets forth what is arguably the hinge point of Henry's work in the entire series: "The Bible is the reservoir and conduit of divine truth, the authoritative written record and exposition of God's nature and will."

### The Modern Revolt against Authority

Early in the largest and most significant of *GRA*'s volumes, Henry indicates how the modern era is characterized by a rejection of authority of any kind other than the autonomous, subjective will of man. To illustrate this point, he turns to the prophetic insight of one of his predecessors:

> Today's authority crisis runs far deeper, however, than simply questioning the propriety or legitimacy of particular authorities. Dietrich Bonhoeffer, writing in *Letters and Papers from Prison*, points to modern man's relegation of God to irrelevance; God is "increasingly edged out of the world." Now that moderns have

---

[27]See http://evanevodialogue.blogspot.com/2008/08/inerrancy-ignore-it-redefine-it-or.html.
[28]Carlos R. Bovell, *Rehabilitating Inerrancy in a Culture of Fear* (Eugene, OR: Wipf and Stock, 2012).
[29]Accessed, http://www.patheos.com/blogs/peterenns/2012/03/inerrancy-and-younger-evangelicals.

presumably "come of age," both "knowledge and life is thought to be perfectly possible without him."[30]

Henry comments that whereas in a previous generation skeptics rejected Christianity on the grounds that it was factually false, now it is denied on the grounds that we are not able to determine the truth at all. Setting the discussion within the debate about human origins, he writes:

> The modern loss of the God of the Bible has at the same time therefore involved a vanishing sense of human dependence on anything outside man himself; man sees himself as living on a planet devoid of any intrinsic plan and purpose, and supposedly born of a cosmic accident. He himself must originate and fashion whatever values there are. The current existential emphasis on man's freedom and will to become himself, particularly on freedom and responsibility as the very essence of human life, regards external authority as a repressive threat. . . . If God does not truly exist and is not Creator; if evolutionary process and development replace the majesty and authority of the sovereign Lord of heaven and earth; if all truth-claims and ethical precepts are relative, then self-determination and personal taste will supplant divine revelation and will become the "rule" of life. The one reality that individual creativity is powerless to fashion, however, is a valid moral norm.[31]

Clearly the antimony between freedom and authority is the fundamental divide that places modern (and postmodern) thought in opposition to the central axioms of the Christian truth claim. If the territory lost to secular culture is ever going to be recovered in our time, Henry avers, the question of authority must be reestablished as coming from divine revelation itself, and a case must be made.

---

[30]Carl F. H. Henry, *God, Revelation and Authority*, vol. 4, *God Who Speaks and Shows: Fifteen Theses, Part Three* (Waco, TX: Word, 1979), 9.
[31]Ibid., 4:11.

## Divine Authority and the Prophetic-Apostolic Word

Henry outlines a biblical-historical argument for a foundational understanding of God as the supreme authority and the subsistence of biblical revelation within the transcendent authority of God. He argues that the authority of historical accounts of the Hebrew Scriptures is maintained by God through the prophetic proclamation of his Word, from the records of Moses, through the words of the prophets, and into the New Testament through the incarnation and apostolic writings. He notes the apostles' emphasis on the word *exousia*—which links the notion that authority and power cannot flourish without each other. Likening the biblical understanding to ancient royalty, he states that "without power, authority becomes hobbled; without authority, power becomes illegitimate."[32]

The move that Henry takes next is logically essential to any Christian worldview, but is very often passed over in debates over inerrancy. He explains:

> The first claim to be made for Scripture is not its inerrancy nor even its inspiration, but its authority. Standing in the forefront of prophetic-apostolic proclamation is the divine authority of Scripture as the Word of God. The main emphasis of the apostolic kerygma in its use of Scripture is that it is divinely authoritative. As in proclaiming the incarnate Word, so in regard to the epistemic Word, the fact of a divine reality holds center stage; related details of birth and growth and underlying psychology have lesser prominence.[33]

Here, Henry directs us away from arguments about interpretations of biblical texts or divergences over doctrine, and he points to the central conviction of evangelicalism that there is a triune personal God behind all biblical affirmations and attestations. Through this God-centered focus, Henry makes debates over the reliability of the Bible a matter of God's ability to speak to his people, the trustworthiness of divine utterances, and so forth. Stated more simply, when it

---

[32]Ibid., 4:24.
[33]Ibid., 4:27.

comes to the matter of divine authority, to use a popular expression, "This time it's personal."

## Modern Reductions of Biblical Authority

Henry recognizes that the modern regard for biblical authority is clearly juxtaposed against his governing thesis—namely, that in the modern consciousness, not only is there no regard for foundational biblical authority, but there is no regard for authority at all. Further, this disregard for an objective standard of authority comes not merely from secular and pagan sectors, but also from within many supposed theological institutions of higher education. Consequently, Henry reiterates the dominant thesis of his whole work, that is, reasserting the centrality and necessity of affirming the ultimate authority of God over all revelation. And in affirming this revelation, we cannot give in to the temptation to subject God's chosen method of communication to the same sorts of proofs we demand of other pieces of evidence. He writes:

> Since its teaching centers in supraempirical realities, much of what the Bible teaches cannot be empirically demonstrated. To replace scriptural authority with some rival authority-principal abridges historic Christian commitments in respect to Scripture as the supreme rule of faith and practice and in other respects also.[34]

The temptation of every age is the same: to place our own controls over God's Word so that we might feign mastery over it. Henry once again turns to Bonhoeffer for assistance in establishing this thesis:

> In the modern demand that Scripture be made culturally "understandable" to contemporary man, Dietrich Bonhoeffer discerns an attempt to escape divine moral obedience and to combine the outward profession of Christianity with an inward autonomy. He detects the same pattern—whether in the eighteenth, nineteenth, or twentieth centuries—of presumably finding an Archimedean

---

[34]Ibid., 4:43.

point in culture or in human reason while the biblical teaching is declared "movable, questionable, uncertain."[35]

Sounding much like John Milbank in a previous era, Henry critiques the age of theory that is based purely on sociological and secular theoretical speculation. Obversely, there are "liberal Protestant churchman" and "Neo-Protestant theologians" who appeal to the authority of Scripture for their pet agendas and causes "in a partisan and restricted way in order to clothe their prejudices with the aura of biblical legitimacy."[36] As such, Henry's line of thought is both simple and brilliant: that all modern theological (and thus philosophical) discourse concerning biblical hermeneutics, linguistic theory, textual criticism, and the myriad theories of historical, anthropological, and sociological theology and philosophy are essentially arguments of authority, specifically the authority of biblical revelation. The question of biblical authority consequently determines intrinsically all subsequent doctrinal affirmations—christology, ecclesiology, soteriology, and so on. Christianity, in Henry's view, must root itself firmly in the assertion that the definitive and final revelatory word for all Christian belief and action is wholly contained in the authority of Scripture. This is the essential disjunction of Henry's entire argument and what he perceives as the fundamental question of modern theology: either the Bible is the transcendentally objective, divinely inspired, God-ordained authority and final word for all standards of truth and value, or the Bible is not and all of life is thus relative and culturally conditioned and thus incoherent.

> The Bible thus remains formally the watershed of present theological debate, even though this fact is not acknowledged. Modern theologians still make special claims for the Bible, and appeal to it to support what they adduce. Yet on their premises they can give no consistent reason for not appealing to the segments that they exclude. The differences between contemporary theologians,

---

[35]Ibid.
[36]Ibid., 4:65.

therefore, turn largely on which facets of the Bible each one elects or rejects.[37]

As Henry sees it, the modern liberal tendency is to redefine inspiration in "non-conceptual" or "existential" categories, a tendency that rises out of modern biblical criticism, whose disciples "disown the revelatory truth-content of Scripture."[38] Regarding this tendency, Henry notes two points: (1) "Most non-evangelical scholars now seem to agree that biblical criticism precludes viewing the Scriptures as a trustworthy literary deposit that conveys divinely revealed truths."[39] (2) This rather casual, semi-arrogant presupposition is demonstrably not the case. Further, any functionalist/empiricist critical theory of biblical inspiration ultimately fails to account adequately for a holistic affirmation of the central tenets of Christianity in their entirety, an affirmation that evangelicalism intentionally holds to as fundamental to true Christian life and practice.

## Is the Bible Literally True?

Henry moves on to tackle the central query of modern philosophical hermeneutics: can theological language convey literal truth about God? He considers numerous attending claims that ensue if one presupposes that it cannot. "Human language is anthropomorphic, it is said, and hence incapable of providing information about God as he is in himself."[40] Since "pictorial" and anthropomorphic language is used of God throughout the Bible, it is assumed that something less than direct assertions about God's being and his ways are intended. If this is the case, Henry warns, "God no longer survives as the living, active, speaking personal deity of the Bible."[41]

In a related matter, Henry takes up the challenge that all language and knowledge are culturally conditioned and therefore relative. He offers a savvy reply to those who say that the biblical authors were

---

[37]Ibid., 4:66.
[38]Ibid., 4:75–76.
[39]Ibid.
[40]Ibid., 4:110.
[41]Ibid., 4:111–12.

so culturally conditioned by their language and setting that they could not deliver timeless truth: "The doctrines which the biblical writers ascribe to Yahweh were not derived from the limited cultural perspectives of their day, but rather from transcendent divine revelation that stands in frequent judgment upon all prevailing cultures."[42] But what of the claim that finite language is too limited to depict the infinite? Knowledge of God, it is said, cannot be compressed into human words because of the finitude of man's thought and language. Henry ripostes with christology: "Christianity counters these claims by insisting upon incarnational theology. It teaches that the Word of God not only became flesh but is also conceptually given, verbally expressible, and verbally expressed."[43]

Further, the debate to maintain a literal truth coming from the Bible is not helped materially by theologians of analogy, Thomas Aquinas being chief among them.[44] This interpretive device, if prioritized as a foundation to metaphysical system, is problematic.

> Analogy is of course a phenomenon of Scripture, and both Jesus and the biblical writers at times refer to likenesses and dissimilarities between the material world and spiritual worlds. That the human person bears the image of God and that the visible world mirrors certain of the Creator's invisible attributes are frequent emphases of Scripture. Yet the Bible does not develop a doctrine of analogical proof of God. . . . Scripture, moreover, does not present the epistemological theory that the nature of human knowledge is such that even on the basis of divine revelation man cannot possess literal truth concerning God.[45]

In other words, the Bible itself nowhere gives us warrant to believe that its teachings are merely metaphorical guesses at the nature of reality, or at the heart of a divine being completely incomprehensible to us, save on the basis of mental pictures. Yes, it is true that

---

[42]Ibid., 4:115.
[43]Ibid.
[44]Ibid.
[45]Ibid., 4:117.

religious language is by nature metaphorical or figurative.[46] But this fact does not give the theologian warrant to sidestep what Henry calls "the ontological question." "Without a literally true ingredient," he observes, "allegorical language cannot insist on a rationally identifiable objective referent. Otherwise symbols would collapse into emotive referents, and this would raise the specter of illusion. If none of our statements about God is literally true, is God truly known at all?"[47] It is Henry's hope that this question settles into a growing discomfort for all who claim to think theologically and who wish to posit the truthfulness of God's Word in the midst of an incredulous age. There really is no other way out. We cannot hide in the shadows of genre and narrative.

> The alternatives to the historic evangelical insistence that Christianity conveys literal truth about God are hardly convincing and lead invariably toward skepticism. There is only one kind of truth. Religious truth is as much truth as any other truth. Instead of being devised for tasks other than to express literal truths about God, human language has from the beginning had this very purpose in view, namely, enabling man to enjoy and to communicate the unchanging truth about his Maker and Lord.[48]

But how is this possible? How can we truly know that God speaks? Those who think they know Henry might be surprised to learn his theory. The answer lies in how much you really believe in the power of the Holy Spirit.

## Thesis 12

As we saw in a previous chapter, one of the oft-cited criticisms of Henry by postfoundationalist thinkers is that he does not emphasize the role of the Holy Spirit in advancing his theory of propositional revelation. After many years of reading and studying Henry, I can say that I honestly have no idea how someone who has actually read

---

[46]Ibid., 4:119.
[47]Ibid., 4:121.
[48]Ibid.

*God, Revelation and Authority* can say that. After all, thesis 12 clearly states: "The Holy Spirit superintends the communication of divine revelation, first, by inspiring the prophetic-apostolic writings, and second, by illuminating and interpreting the scripturally given Word of God." Stated differently, the Holy Spirit is our guarantee that what we read in the Word of God actually results positively in the knowledge of God. The fact that the third person of the Trinity lives and operates in the lives of the apostles and the people of God in the church yields great confidence in the results of biblical inspiration.

## The Meaning of Inspiration

Henry defines inspiration very carefully as follows:

> Inspiration is a supernatural influence upon divinely chosen proph-
> ets and apostles whereby the Spirit of God assures the truth and
> trustworthiness of their oral and written proclamation. Historic
> evangelical Christianity considers the Bible as the essential textbook
> because, in view of this quality, it inscripturates divinely revealed
> truth in verbal form.[49]

This is no theory, but a straightforward reception of the attestations of key texts in the New Testament itself. For instance, in 2 Timothy 3:16–17 we see the character of Scripture: it is *theopneustos*, God-breathed, inspired by God. Henry sees Paul's characterization of the text as an *inclusio* of Genesis 2:7 in which human beings owe their own life existence to the very breath of God. Because God is a person, and because he is eternal, the Scriptures therefore have a "permanent validity." They are not merely assertions of authority based upon prejudices and agendas of the apostles. They are written down so that *through* the apostles, we might understand how God lives and thinks.[50]

Continuing on this theme, he references 2 Peter 1:19–21, which demonstrates that

---

[49]Ibid., 4:129.
[50]Ibid., 4:131.

revealed truth is exalted as something more than just the word of eyewitnesses. What attests its supernatural origin and permanent validity is its nature as the "prophetic word" (1:19, RSV), that is, as scriptural prophecy (1:20). . . . The prophetic word was not brought into being "by the will of man" but was produced, rather, by the Spirit. . . . The reason the prophetic word is sure—surer even than that of eyewitnesses—is that God is its source and that specially chosen men spoke by the Spirit's agency.[51]

Next, perhaps the supreme description on the nature of Scripture comes from the words of Jesus himself in John 10:34–36. "Not only does Jesus adduce what is written in Scripture as law," Henry points out, "but [he] also explicitly adds: 'and the scripture cannot be broken' (10:35, KJV). He attaches divine authority to Scripture as an inviolable whole." What is clear from the Lord's statements is that the biblical text is meant to be taken as a comprehensive authoritative unity—a declaration that promises that theological affirmations can have a definite arc and a systematic shape. Despite the divine origin and Spirit delivery of the biblical writings, Henry is quick to clear up what evangelicals deny with respect to inspiration. First, he deems the dictation theory "untrue to the Scriptures, unrepresentative of evangelical doctrine, and prejudicial to theological understanding."[52] Conversely, the evangelical perspective also eschews the notion that inspiration means merely the heightening of "psychic powers or creative energies"—which has the important implication of saying that the worldview maintained by the prophets and apostles was something far more than an artistic reappropriation of extant ancient Near Eastern sociocultural themes.[53]

Over against the aforementioned denials, the evangelical doctrine of the divine inspiration of the Scriptures makes the following affirmations:

---

[51]Ibid., 4:132–33.
[52]Ibid., 4:138.
[53]Ibid., 4:142.

1. "That the text of Scripture is divinely inspired as an objective deposit of language. The attack on verbal inspiration in the orthodox sense is always an assault on the Bible as a linguistic revelatory deposit."[54]

2. "The evangelical view affirms, further, that inspiration does not violate but is wholly consistent with the humanity of the prophets and apostles. The Spirit of God made full use of the human capacities of the chosen writers so that their writings reflect psychological, biographical and even socio-historical differences."[55]

3. "It affirms also that inspiration did not put an end to the human fallibility of prophets and apostles."[56]

4. "The evangelical view also holds that divine inspiration is limited to a small company of messengers who were divinely chosen to authoritatively communicate the Word of God to mankind. This inspiration is no universal phenomenon, nor is it necessarily or actually shared by all or most spiritually devout and obedient men of God."[57]

5. "The evangelical view believes that God revealed information beyond the reach of the natural resources of human beings, including prophets and apostles. Biblical doctrine has an authoritative basis only because of communication of specially revealed truths to chosen messengers."[58]

6. "Evangelicals insist, further, that God is the ultimate author of Scripture. The Holy Spirit is the communicator of the prophetic-apostolic writings. In view of its divine inspiration, the scriptural message is therefore identified as a content conveyed by 'the Spirit of the Lord,' 'the mouth of the Lord,' and as that which 'the Holy Ghost by the mouth of (his chosen prophet) spoke.' The truth of what the prophets and apostles wrote is guaranteed by the Holy Spirit."[59]

7. "The evangelical view affirms that all Scripture is divinely inspired— Scripture as a whole and in all its parts. . . . To stress verbal-plenary inspiration simply brings out what this view necessarily implies: since it is written Scripture that is in view, inspiration extends to

---

[54]Ibid., 4:144.
[55]Ibid., 4:148.
[56]Ibid., 4:151.
[57]Ibid., 4:152.
[58]Ibid., 4:155.
[59]Ibid., 4:159.

the very words as authoritative (John 10:34–35; Gal. 3:16). The whole content, historical no less than theological and moral, is both trustworthy and profitable (Rom. 4:23; 9:17; 15:4; 1 Cor. 9:10; 10:11; Gal. 3:8, 22; 4:30; 1 Pet. 2:6)."[60]

8. "This view that all Scripture is inspired is the historic doctrine of all denominations. All major bodies have explicitly affirmed the divine inspiration and authority of the Bible. Only in the twentieth century have major Protestant denominations such as the United Presbyterian Church in the United States compromised their traditional commitments in deference to modern critical theories."[61]

Although it may seem pedantic to rehearse Henry's ordering in this way, the precise order and logic of his explanation is clear and, more importantly, explanatory of the classic evangelical position. Moreover, without establishing the foundation of biblical authority and a precise understanding of inspiration first, one cannot proceed to a correct understanding of the doctrine of biblical inerrancy. In other words, inerrancy is mere cant and empty doctrinal sloganeering if it is not settled upon an axiomatic logic of how God "speaks and shows."

## The Inerrancy of Scripture

Henry begins his discussion of inerrancy by stating what the goal of the doctrine is and always must be: faithful biblical exegesis. Although the position is sometimes associated with a culturally isolated fundamentalism, nothing could be further from the truth. Rather, evangelicalism does not reject outright those projects that seek to harmonize scriptural accounts with developments of the modern sciences (historical anthropology, linguistic theory, archaeology, cosmology, etc.). Rather, "evangelical Christianity insists that scriptural revelation is intelligible and propositional, and it therefore cannot dispense with an interest in harmonizing precepts and phenomena. Whatever is logically contradictory and incapable of

---

[60]Ibid., 4:160.
[61]Ibid., 4:160–61.

reconciliation simply cannot be accepted as truth."[62] These words alone, if truly accepted and believed by evangelicals today, might radically revolutionize the integration of faith and disciplines. The evangelical view promises a world in which truth is accessible and can be embraced, but in which also, at the end of the day, wherever truth is found, God's Word will be proved in the right. Much is at stake here, and the reverse proposition is indeed ominous: "If inspired Scripture is inherently errant, then more is compromised than simply the content transmitted by a careless copyist or inexact translator; the very message of the prophets and apostles is shadowed as well, for the inspired biblical writers then are not per se true witnesses."[63]

This confidence in the accuracy of the Bible, however, is not intended to imply that some process of empirical verification must be devised in order to vindicate the legitimacy of the text before a skeptical world of cynics. Henry explains: "The noteworthy factor here is the inability of empirical observation to supply a complete induction. . . . The value of the scientific method lies not in its establishment of final truth but in its establishment of evidentially false hypotheses."[64] What must be exposed is the pretense that one can either validate or invalidate the Scripture merely by scientific or historical research. On the contrary, Henry's main point is twofold. First, one cannot affirm biblical inspiration and authority without the logical entailment of inerrancy following. The Bible cannot be authoritative as a whole when the validity of its contents is in doubt. Second, and related to the first, it is never empirical discovery that throws people's commitment to Scripture in question, but rather prior "philosophical preconceptions to which they alternatively adjust the evidence" in order to devise a God amenable to modern sensibilities. The result is "a conception of God different in many respects from the God of the Bible who himself is the truth and who cannot lie."[65]

Explaining it differently, we might say that empirical or rational considerations can be fine servants to the cause of truth, but ter-

---

[62]Ibid., 4:174.
[63]Ibid., 4:181.
[64]Ibid.
[65]Ibid., 4:192–93.

rible masters. But even if we did allow them sway, we would still be held captive to the prejudices of our hearts. The biography of Bart Ehrman is a good case in point. Ehrman often cites his background as an evangelical and his time at Wheaton—before his going off to Princeton Seminary, where he was exposed to the rigors of higher criticism—as the beginning of his loss of faith in the inspiration and inerrancy of Scripture. But when you actually start reading about the problems he had with "inerrancy," what he really was struggling with was fundamentalist interpretations of the Bible in general, and dispensationalist readings in particular. I think everyone would agree that a disagreement with Hal Lindsay's rendering of the apocalypse is not exactly the same thing as an argument against the notion of inerrancy.[66] It is precisely for reasons such as these that Carl F. H. Henry sought to set forth very clearly what inerrancy does and does not mean.

## The Meaning of Inerrancy

Negatively, scriptural inerrancy does not imply that we can come to some sort of forced peace accord with modern methods of investigation. Ergo, "we have no right to impose upon the biblical writers methods of classifying information that are specifically oriented to the scientific interests of our time."[67] Further, giving full weight to Scripture's multiple genres, Henry makes clear that Scripture need not speak in nonmetaphorical ways in order to get across essential truth about God's being, purposes, and ways. "All language," he admits,

> is in fact symbolic. But anyone who, on this account, argues that language cannot convey literal truth, disadvantages biblical teaching no more seriously than any other communication. If such a theory were consistently applied, it would involve a skeptical view of all statements, and would erase the literal truth even of the critic's assertions.[68]

---

[66] Bart Ehrman, *Misquoting Jesus* (San Francisco: HarperCollins, 2005), 12ff.
[67] Henry, *God, Revelation and Authority*, 4:201.
[68] Ibid., 4:202.

This crucial consideration must be given due weight, since what Henry is saying applies not only to the Scripture's teaching, but also to any commentator, analyst, or critic of any genre. If, for instance, one wanted to write a monograph of analysis of the works of Theodore Roethke or of Shakespearean sonnets, one would certainly not want to hear that such scholarship could not convey genuine understanding of the author's message in these texts simply because they were in the genre of poetry. So what Henry is quite brilliantly stating is this: we should expect no lesser results from the interpretation of the multigenre nature of Scripture than we would of a scholar explaining the meaning of these same types of texts for a receptive audience.

Among other things that inerrancy does not mean, Henry includes the following: that citations of the Old Testament in the New cannot be paraphrastic or christological; that inerrancy requires some sort of bibliolatry in place of christology; and finally, that acceptance of inerrancy necessarily results in orthodox theological formulation. It would certainly be nice if it did, but unfortunately this is not always the case.[69]

Positively, inerrancy does imply the following: First, biblical teaching extends not only to the theological and moral teaching of the text, but also to the historical and scientific matters implied by the text. Second, he contends, inspiration is verbal-plenary, whereby the very words, sentences, and paragraphs of the Scriptures are inspired, not just the ideas of the biblical writers. This is because thought never reaches its highest expression without words. Third, the affirmation of an errorless text extends only to the original autographs first and foremost, "and only indirectly to the copies. The sacred writers were guided by the Spirit of God in writing the original manuscripts in a way that resulted in their errorless transmission of the message that God desired them to communicate to mankind."[70] Finally, "verbal inerrancy of the autographs implies that evangelicals must not attach finality to contemporary versions or translations, least of all to mere paraphrases, but must earnestly pursue and honor the best text."[71]

---

[69]Ibid., 4:202–4.
[70]Ibid., 4:207.
[71]Ibid., 4:209–10.

Thus, a case is ultimately made for the best skills in the original languages.

One might in fact wonder why the distinction between the autographs and the copies is so important to Henry. The answer is that in pursuing the best translation and best manuscript evidence, we bear witness to the fact that our polestar is faithfulness to the initial charges given to the apostles. The one cannot be separated from the other.[72] In other words, our pursuit of the best translation is compelled by the perfection of the original revelation. In the final analysis, the copies of the Scriptures that we possess are an extremely reliable witness that clearly conveys God's will and agenda for his people.[73]

## The Spirit and the Scriptures

Having discussed the reliability of the copies of Scripture we now possess, Henry turns to a much thornier issue in twentieth-century theology: the role of the Spirit in divine revelation. This discussion brought Henry into direct conflict with the governing theological hermeneutic of Karl Barth.

On the positive side, Henry admits the helpful way in which Barth reasserted the role of the Spirit in the life of the church—a teaching that had been suppressed during the high tides of Protestant liberalism, which had removed the attribute of personhood from the third person of the Trinity.[74] Although Henry admired Barth for his emphasis on the Spirit, he remained dubious about how Barth's proposed mechanism for the reception of revelation affected the status of Scripture itself. He explains:

---

[72]"The fact that churches have for nineteen centuries possessed only errant copies and not inerrant autographs, and that these copies have been adequate for effective evangelical engagement around the globe, does not prove that the authority and reliability of the Bible could have been adequately achieved from the outset without errorless apostolic proclamation or autographs. Infallible copies combine the features of divine authority and trustworthiness, but the logical necessity for inerrant autographs still remains. The infallibility of the copies presupposes not only the ongoing special providence of God, and the continuing dependence of copies and translations on the best available texts, but also the inerrancy of the original writings" (ibid., 4:241).

[73]Ibid., 4:250–52.

[74]Ibid., 4:256.

> For Barth, divine authority does not channel into biblical inspira-
> tion; rather, inspiration, subsumed under authority, focuses on God
> as the originator of his Word and is broader than Scripture. . . .
> Inspiration, authority, and interpretation must be understood "spir-
> itually"—that is, in the context of a dynamic, trusting response.[75]

By way of contrast, he asserts that, in keeping with the tradition of
Christian orthodoxy, evangelicalism insists that "at no point is the
Word of God to be considered a merely human phenomenon. . . .
The authority of the Bible is not some authority other than divine
authority."[76] Further, subjective apprehension of biblical revelation
in the life of the believer is crucial to the evangelical doctrine of
Scripture, but this view in no way conditions authority/inspiration
to human volition. According to Henry, Barth aims at protecting
against "bibliolatry" by detaching revelation/inspiration from the
specific activity of the church. Essentially Barth opens the canon
of revelation/inspiration, unique to the prophetic-apostolic written
word of Scripture as objectively inspired and maintained by God, and
subordinates inspiration to the penitence and faith of the believer.
Henry takes pains to explain the difference between this view and the
classic evangelical position, which "insist[s] rather that the authority and sense of Scripture objectively precede the reader's faith; the
Bible's meaning and authority are not definitively conditioned or
dependent upon present-day belief-ful response."[77] Henry worries
that in Barth's view the fixed scriptural canon is dissolved—the Word
of God is only objectively authoritative in its direct imposition upon
the penitent believer's subjective state. As a result of this,

> the Barthian rejection of the fixed written verbalization of revela-
> tion would imply a basically docetic view that involves sporadic
> incarnations. If the restrictions Barth imposes on Scripture were
> applied also to his own view of Jesus Christ then . . . the Word of

[75]Ibid., 4:257.
[76]Ibid.
[77]Ibid., 4:259.

God could in neither case be conceived as an abiding or continuing divine deposit in history.[78]

Henry's reading of Barth, once the standard evangelical position, has been received poorly by recent interpreters. Theologians such as Bruce McCormack, Trevor Hart, and John Webster have presided over a reinterpretation of Barth and have argued that his epistemology and view of Scripture are safe for evangelical consumption. As Webster told *The Christian Century* in an interview:

> From the beginning, it's been common for many readers of Barth to worry about the apparent one-sidedness of his descriptions of the sheer plenitude of God. Perhaps Barth thinks that God's glory has to be maintained at a cost to creatures. Nowadays this worry is often expressed by speaking of Barth's supposed "extrinsicism," that is, his presentation of the Christian faith in terms of an encounter (or collision) of divine and human wills in which creatures are kept separate from God's being. I've tried to suggest that this isn't really the case. From the beginning Barth was deeply interested in the reality of creatures and their acts, and he conceived of Christianity as concerned with the active fellowship between God and creatures.[79]

The debate over how closely Henry read Barth can and should be a matter of ongoing discussion among scholars, although the burden of proof is upon critics to show that the documentary evidence contra Henry's view is convincing.[80] What is very clear is that Barth viewed the canon of Scripture as prone to error on virtually every conceivable matter. He writes in *Church Dogmatics*, "But the vulnerability of the Bible, i.e., its capacity for error, also extends to its religious or theological content."[81] His support for this statement

---

[78]Ibid., 4:262.
[79]Accessed, http://www.religion-online.org/showarticle.asp?title=3553.
[80]In defense of Henry's reading, see Jonathan Gibson, "A Critical Evaluation of Karl Barth's Suggestion that Biblical Inerrancy Is Theologically Indefensible," available at http://www.monergism.com/directory/link_details/29325/A-Critical-Evaluation-of-Karl-Barth039s-Suggestion-That-Biblical-Inerrancy-is-Theologically-Indefensible-pdf/c-56/.
[81]Karl Barth, *Church Dogmatics*, 1.2.509.

makes it apparent that he considers the authors of Scripture bound to the rules, culture, and perspective of their times, but that God is able to use the Bible in the life of the church despite these admittedly embarrassing and severe limitations.

In light of this, one wonders what would attract evangelicals to look to Barth as opposed to, say, Henry. If, as John Webster says, the thing one must admire about Barth is his view on the active relationship between God and his creatures, the same is true, if not in greater measure, about the Henry corpus, particularly Henry's view on the Spirit's work in the life of the believer to illuminate the meaning of Scripture. After all, as he rightly concludes, the lack of "full delineation of the Holy Spirit's work—inspiration, illumination, regeneration, indwelling, sanctification, guidance—nurtures a confused and disabled church. The proliferating modern sects may, in fact, be one of the penalties for the lack of a comprehensive, systematic doctrine of the Spirit."[82] Persistently in his explanation of inerrancy, Henry draws attention to the Spirit as an active and personal stimulant toward understanding, discernment, and regeneration. With great conviction he avers,

> The Spirit of God—not any private interpreter (2 Pet. 1:20), evangelical or nonevangelical—is the authoritative illuminator of the scripturally given Word. . . . It is fully possible that evangelicals, like the Pharisees of Jesus' time, will be chastised for deferring uncritically to certain of their own traditions more than to the Word of God. The baggage of evangelical tradition is no divine criterion with which the Scripture must accord. The Spirit of God alone searches and knows all things, the self-same Spirit from whom the apostles received the inspired Word (1 Cor. 2:11–13), the Spirit who, in illumining the biblical revelation, "judges all things, [while] he himself is judged of no man" (1 Cor. 2:15, KJV).[83]

Powerful observations such as these characterize the prose of *GRA* and, once read, render ridiculous the notion that Carl F. H.

---

[82]Henry, *God, Revelation and Authority*, 4:272.
[83]Ibid., 4:289.

Henry embraced some sort of cold, rationalistic view of God, the Spirit, and revelation.

## Are We Doomed to Hermeneutical Relativism?

Henry turns from the role of the Spirit in illumination to the most ominous of all concerns: that the true meaning of texts, Scripture being chief among them, may be forever beyond our grasp. The modern problem of hermeneutical criticism has created a landscape of theological/philosophical inquiry preoccupied by interpretation and the quest for a satisfactory hermeneutic by which to translate Scripture. Accordingly, Henry points to the "hermeneutical problem" that rises from several historical phenomena:

1. Christian tradition has always been chiefly concerned with understanding and exegesis of Scripture; thus since the New Testament, hermeneutics has been vital for the Christian tradition.
2. The rise of classical philology in the eighteenth century and the refined techniques developed in its pursuit renewed an interest in the interpretation of texts from antiquity, specifically the Bible. "Champions of the historical-critical method in theology and of the grammatical-historical method in interpretation emphasized that the verbal sense of the Bible must be ascertained in the same way as any other book."[84]
3. The rationalistic tendencies of the Enlightenment and scientific prejudices brought an unprecedented skepticism to bear on religious texts, especially the Bible.
4. The rise of Protestant liberalism from the influence of Schleiermacher and those who followed in his train "sponsored an approach to hermeneutics that centered in a new personal attitude or in a special way of understanding and faith response"[85] focused on the moral/ethical character of a desupernaturalized Jesus.

It is the liberal influence of Schleiermacher and his followers (e.g., Harnack) against whom Barth rises with his doctrine of radical transcendence. Barth is right in criticizing the optimism of scientistic

---

[84]Ibid., 4:296.
[85]Ibid., 4:297.

and rationalistic modern criticism by asserting that there is no possibility of a neutral hermeneutic. The contemporary "hermeneutical problem" that concerns Henry arises in large part from Continental philosophy's positioning of language as intrinsic to epistemology and ontology. Twentieth-century Continental philosophy became primarily concerned with hermeneutics and language, which profoundly impacted biblical and theological hermeneutics. Henry clearly realized the stake involved, as indicated in *Truth and Method*:

> Hans-Georg Gadamer has traced the development from Schleiermacher (through Dilthey) to Martin Heidegger, whose existential philosophy expounded "understanding" and "interpretation" as fundamental modes of man's being, thus correlating hermeneutics with ontology and identifying hermeneutics with the phenomenology of Dasein.[86]

What Henry saw nearly thirty years ago was that Protestant liberalism and so-called neoorthodoxy were the least of evangelicalism's worries as it headed into the future. He understood that Continental philosophy held the potential of completely unhinging the metaphysical and ontological claims upon which the Great Tradition of the church had come to rest. He saw that Heidegger's project was perhaps even more radical than those of liberal Protestantism or modern scientism.

> For both Schleiermacher and Dilthey, interpretation involved an underlying body of methodological principles. But whereas modernism retained the attempt to pare theology to scientific respectability alongside an insistence on the inner integrative power of Jesus' moral example, Heidegger considers hermeneutics a philosophical exploration of the character and preconditions of all understanding. The speculative theory of the historicity of understanding shaped by Heidegger exaggerates the obvious fact of basic differences between past and present cultures into a denial of any identity and continuity of meaning. Gadamer extends the Heideggerian approach by asserting the linguistic nature of human

---

[86]Ibid., 4:299.

reality: "Being that can understand is language." (*Wahrheit und Methode* [*Truth and Method*]).[87]

Henry rejects both the Heideggerian and Gadamerian systems because they regard the interpreter as the source of meaning itself, rather than merely an agent of interpretation and translation. The stakes are very high, since ultimately "this theory repudiates, as a by-product of fallacious subject-object thinking and as the correlate of a futile quest for objective meaning, the traditional view of language as an instrument or system of symbols for communicating 'meaning.'"[88] Henry is likely overreading the position of Gadamer, who is largely concerned about the difficulty interpreters have in actually hearing the author in any text and the art of listening well to the other's horizon. In fact, this theme is actually quite compatible with Henry's overall emphasis on the fallibility of interpretation when juxtaposed with the inerrant horizon of the authors of the text of Scripture. Additional affinities between Gadamer and Henry relate to what the latter refers to as "the inescapability of presuppositional interpretation"—a feature that was Gadamer's primary criticism of what he saw as Schleiermacher's naive view that we could easily rehabit the mind of the original author of a text. Still, Henry remained resolute (and for good reason) that there is a notable exception to the rule in all of this: the Scriptures themselves. The Bible does not attribute prejudice in interpretation to an ontological necessity, nor to any lack of objectively given textual meaning. While Scripture assigns an important role to the moral will of the reader and to the Spirit of God's enabling in the efficacious personal appropriation of the truth of the text, Protestant orthodoxy insists upon the perspicacity of the inspired texts.[89] For Henry, revelation is a communication of truth claims that God intends for human beings to know for all times and everywhere. The loss of determinacy when it comes to the teaching of Scripture grew in Henry's mind to a blind alley for the church. It

---

[87]Ibid.
[88]Ibid., 4:300.
[89]Ibid., 4:307.

is either a clear biblical text yielding reliable theological affirmations or nothing at all. And in this, he was most assuredly correct.

Yet, whenever Henry takes a stand, he does so with great humility in the face of truth and the realities of experience. Immediately after his discussion on the specter of hermeneutical nihilism, he offers a lengthy admission concerning the "fallibility of the exegete," followed by candid recognition of "problem passages" in the Scriptures.[90] In so doing, Henry implores his evangelical colleagues to take seriously questions of historical and literary investigation that come from secular critics. At the same time, he reminds us:

> All too apparent, however, is the fact that no exegesis is wholly free of presuppositions. . . . Moreover, their [evangelicals'] disagreement with nonevangelicals is not at all wholly reducible to contrary presuppositions, for the question of which presuppositions most consistently explain the so-called data remains indispensably important. There are, to be sure, no independently existing neutral "data," since the very assertion requires intellectual interpretation.[91]

### The Historic Church, Inerrancy, and the Issue of Canon

Like any responsible theologian, Henry wishes to connect his governing theses with the history of the great intellectual tradition of the church. While he is quick to admit that the word *inerrant* itself is novel, he nonetheless contends that the notion that the Bible is without error is the majoritarian understanding of the postapostolic tradition, the Fathers, the medieval period, and the Renaissance and Reformation. Any departure from this conviction, he maintains, is irreducibly modern in orientation. While skepticism and repudiation of church doctrine have always plagued Christianity from external detractors, it is only in the last century and a half that the doctrine

---

[90]Ibid., 4:316–65.
[91]Ibid., 4:335, 337.

of inerrancy has come under wide-ranging scrutiny and skepticism from within the church itself.[92]

Henry argues that despite the nature of the contemporary debate in contrast to the historic affirmations of the church, progress is being made by evangelicals, mainly in light of the continual failure of twentieth-century rationalistic criticism to adequately understand and address inerrancy. Modern historical criticism misunderstands the issue by "repeatedly confusing inerrancy with mechanical dictation."[93] Without inerrancy and its logically antecedent concepts of authority and inspiration, the entire enterprise of historic Christianity begins to crumble. It is a lacuna that cannot be surmounted. Responding to James Barr's opposition to the concept of a fully trustworthy Bible, Henry poses this challenge:

> One cannot persuasively deny that a thoroughly evangelical theology offers the only consistent course for selecting and retaining authoritative fragments of Scripture. . . . What he [and by extension modern liberalism] seems determined to overlook and avoid is precisely what Christian churches throughout the centuries have kept in the forefront, namely, open acknowledgement that only a sure and intelligible Word of God is the *raison d'être* of revealed religion, and that the Bible is God's authoritative, inspired and inerrant Word.[94]

The rise of historical criticism and doubt that the Bible has a uniquely divine character has made "the problem of canon . . . a central issue in theology," and for good reason.[95] In an extensive handling of the questions about extrabiblical writings such as the Apocrypha and the Pseudepigrapha, Henry moves on to the most serious casualty resulting from wrong-headed thinking on both of these matters: the unity of the Bible. "Time after time," Henry observes,

---

[92]Ibid., 4:374.
[93]Ibid., 4:381.
[94]Ibid., 4:384.
[95]Ibid., 4:405.

critical scholars have failed to elaborate a cohesive pattern of theological unity, so that their endless reformulations now imperil even an assured christology, the very lifeline of New Testament concern. On this chaotic outcome of brilliant critical theorizing Gerhard Maier gives the verdict that modern historical criticism has come to the end of its tether (*Das Ende der historisch-kristischen Methode*).[96]

Such a severe judgment corresponds to the high stakes involved. Simply put, no true biblical theology can neglect to presuppose that the Bible is actually the Word of God. This much is clear: "Without literal meaning and literal truth (which Barr disowns) no proper idea remains of what the biblical writers affirm about God, creation, salvation or last things; the very possibility of an intellectually cohesive theology is shattered."[97] Without the biblical story as metanarrative—the story to interpret all stories—culture faces a major crisis of meaning. "The lost unity of the Bible," Henry soberly concludes,

has resulted for modern man in a miserable disintegration of his spirit. A society that refers origins to evolution, conscience to culture, nature and history to happenstance, morality and religion to personal preference, is not only on its way to civilizational end time, but is also, in fact, already at the gates; it is, moreover, totally unprepared for the End of all ends.[98]

In addressing matters this way, Henry takes his place as the pioneering canonical theologian of the evangelical movement with his work in *GRA*.

## The Spirit and Church Proclamation

Although Henry opened himself for critique by not focusing much on ecclesiology through his career, it is important to remember that he ends his consideration of inerrancy in volume 4 of *GRA* with a

---

[96] Ibid., 4:450.
[97] Ibid., 4:463.
[98] Ibid., 4:468.

discussion of the implications of inerrancy for preaching and teaching in the church today. He defines preaching thus:

> Authentic proclamation is simply the declaration of the original Christian message of redemption and its immediate relevance to man and society. The hermeneutical problem of proceeding from the biblical words and sentences to their exposition in contemporary life must proceed in all confidence that in the scriptural revelation God has already proceeded once-for-all from his enduring truth to appropriate and proper words.[99]

Throughout his distinguished career as a writer, Carl Henry sought, sometimes desperately, to reawaken pastors and church leaders to their responsibility to bring biblical exegesis to bear on contemporary problems and social ills. For him, kerygmatic preaching necessarily includes application to the crises of the hour. The gospel does not address individuals only—although it always must address them—but also communities, cities, nations, governments, and the principalities and powers of the age. With confidence Henry lays down the following challenge and encouragement to preachers of the Word of God:

> The Christian faces the world armed with a truly creative word, a word that is intelligible, authoritative, and enduring. What originally gave and still gives power to the Word of God is not tradition somehow brought to life by it, or architecture and ritual that some trust to impart potency to proclamation. Nor is sincerity by the one who proclaims the Word the key to its power; many humans after all have been sincerely wrong. What lends power to the Word is rather that God himself is pledged to be its invisible and invincible herald: he tolerates no fruitless proclamation of his Word; he has ordained fulfillment of its mandated mission.[100]

Never naive, Henry realizes that none of these emphases will take root or have effect apart from what he outlines in his thirteenth

[99]Ibid., 4:490.
[100]Ibid., 4:493.

thesis: "Bestower of spiritual life, the Holy Spirit enables individuals to appropriate God's truth savingly, and attests its power in their personal experience."[101] Perhaps most beautifully, Henry maintains the power of the preached Word—not just through inscripturated revelation or systematic theology—but also through the testimony of all those who exhibit solidarity with the risen Christ. Reversing the force of the second commandment into its obverse expression of love, he speaks of "God's graven image: Redeemed Mankind." The greatest witness to the truth of an inspired and inerrant Bible will be a loving, gospel-motivated church engaged with the concerns, ails, joys, and sorrows of the planet around them. Thus, "God will finally publish his holy will not simply in inspired books, but also in the lives of all the redeemed, even as he already has done in the person of the incarnate Jesus."[102] But this emphasis of the new birth can only be sustained, promoted, and protected if a commitment to inerrancy is maintained, for the message of conversion only holds if the Bible is true. The same holds for the mandate that the church look like the kingdom of God; the "community of the faithful ignores distinctions of color and country and class, and summons each and all to yield talent, possessions and time to God's service."[103] "Underlying much of the contemporary disinterest in the biblical image of the new man, and in Christ as the ideal image of man, is the secular modern notion of 'the good life'—a slogan in which the term good may encompass even the selfish and prurient preferences of the morally profligate."[104]

The proclamation of the good news via the power of the Spirit through the gift of Christ's heralds builds toward the lovely description of the church in Henry's thesis 14: "The church approximates God's kingdom in miniature, mirroring to each generation the power and joy of the appropriated realities of divine revelation."[105] Providing perhaps the most poetic description of ecclesial grandeur ever written, Henry turns finally in his great defense of biblical inspiration,

---

[101]Ibid., 4:494.
[102]Ibid.
[103]Ibid., 4:496.
[104]Ibid., 4:498.
[105]Ibid., 4:496.

authority, and inerrancy to the terminus of all of these theoretical and doctrinal affirmations: the fact that this is all "good news for the oppressed." Thus, critically,

> the Gospel resounds with good news for the needy and oppressed. It conveys assurance that injustice, repression, exploitation, discrimination and poverty are dated and doomed, that no one is forced to accept the crush of evil powers as finally determinative for his or her existence. Into the morass of sinful human history and experience the gospel heralds a new order of life shaped by God's redemptive intervention.[106]

As we will see in the next chapter, Henry envisions a seamless garment linking biblical verities to social responsibilities, and the evangelical community must not shirk its responsibilities in this regard. The gospel implies global solutions that have real-world application, or it becomes something less than good news—a Gnostic gospel. He pleads with his readers as an entailment of the doctrine of inerrancy:

> Not only evangelical rescue operations but also remedial programs belong to the social concern implicit in redemptive religion. The evangelical community is indeed to establish love-missions or pilot projects of social concern. . . . Social justice is not, moreover, simply an appendage to the evangelical message; it is an intrinsic part of the whole, without which the preaching of the gospel itself is truncated. Theology devoid of social justice is a deforming weakness of much present-day evangelical witness.[107]

Even more pointedly, he says:

> Christians must speak not as outside of or peripheral to the movement of human transformation, but as central participants and agents in it. The Christian should know himself by spiritual birthright to be in the fallen world as a member of the already existing

---

[106]Ibid., 4:542.
[107]Ibid., 4:551.

"new community" which is not only called "out of the world" but also dispersed through it as "salt" and "light."[108]

## Inerrancy or the Alternative

Many critiques of the concept of biblical infallibility have been offered through the centuries, from David Friedrich Strauss through Adolf von Harnack, to Rudolf Bultmann, to modern-day figures like Elaine Pagels, Bart Ehrman, Marcus J. Borg, John Dominic Crossan, and John Shelby Spong. Most of these attempts are designed to convince Bible believers that, based on historical, archeological, and scientific evidence, their faith is no longer tenable and must be replaced with something else.

In response, an array of evangelical worthies have sallied forth to say to the skeptics, "Not so fast." The combined armaments protecting the historical validity of the faith have, in many important respects, never been stronger. When one considers the collective scholarly corpus of figures such as D. A. Carson, Walter Kaiser, N. T. Wright, Ben Witherington III, Peter Williams, Darrell Bock, Craig Blomberg, and so many others, the boundaries of Zion and the credibility of the Bible have never been so well protected. There is much promise in the recovery of biblical credibility today and so much good news as arguments are being composed from the right perspective. For example, in his recent work *Scripture and the Authority of God*, Tom Wright presents the matter of authority from the doctrine of creation first and foremost. He writes, "The real point, which is also a signpost to many other issues when people ask 'Why should Christian morality be good for non-Christians?' is the Christian claim that in Jesus of Nazareth the creator of the world—the whole world, not just a Christian subset of the word!—is being renewed."[109] This is so helpful. And what evangelical would not give thanks for the massive contribution that D. A. Carson has made to the field of New Testament studies and biblical theology—an inspiration for generations of aspiring Christian scholars to come. As his *Collected Writings on*

---

[108]Ibid., 4:553.
[109]N. T. Wright, *Scripture and the Authority of God* (San Francisco: HarperCollins, 2011), 192.

*Scripture* demonstrate, Carson has surveyed the field of challenges to the classic evangelical doctrine of inspiration with extraordinary ability, wisdom, and verve.

The argument of this volume, however, is that Carl F. H. Henry was tuned into another frequency—that of theory and epistemology. Although he was keen to defend the specifics of inerrancy on material grounds, his project in *GRA* was much greater. In essence, *GRA* sought to demonstrate that metaphysics is still philosophically and theologically viable. Ultimately, that is where the real debate lies. Henry sought to repair the great Copernican divide initiated by Kant and perpetuated by virtually every significant theologian of the twentieth century. In this sense, "foundationalism" was his chief and primary concern.

For reasons I have highlighted in previous chapters, much of the leading thought in evangelicalism has sought to find a way around the impasse, through sometimes all-too-nifty appropriations of contemporary postmodern theory and hermeneutics. I am not convinced this will work. That is not because I do not think it important to learn from the giants of Continental philosophy and their concern about objective interpretations of texts, figures such as Wittgenstein, Husserl, Heidegger, Gadamer, Derrida, Lacan, Ricoeur, and others—I do. I am simply not convinced a *via media* exists between Continental thought and historic Christianity—a path to the "second naïveté" and a premodern view of the Bible that ignores the perils of contemporary philosophy. So many evangelicals are seeking to forge a compound between these two phenomena, but the compound is unstable.

A good illustration that a middle position is not tenable is the contemporary debate over the existence of God. Specifically, I am less interested in the exchange between traditional theists and the so-called new atheists—which mostly are pedantic restatements of eighteenth- and nineteenth-century positions—and more intrigued by the conversation between, say, Slavoj Žižek and the British radical theologian John Milbank. In that debate, the world comes alive, and the weight of the twenty-first century lies in the balance. On the one side, Žižek seeks to maintain all of the key features of the biblical witness, but interprets them through the lens of radical leftist politics.

The Bible is the textbook for the coming social revolution—even if we conceive of the cross as the ultimate statement that everything is *not* going to be all right, and the resurrection as being Christ's bodily departure from earth to heaven and leaving us with just the Holy Ghost within a community of profound solidarity. Žižek seems to be saying that Christianity's true message is: "Kids, you're on your own now." For his part, Milbank finds it very strange that a materialist like Žižek would fail to appreciate the richness of the double materiality of Augustine: one in the city of man, and one in the city of God. The resurrected Christ inhabits the one and plans to return to those being made in his image in the other.

Both men are concerned with, to use Francis Schaeffer's phrase, "the God who is there." Says Žižek, referencing Chesterton, believers ironically

> "are frightened of four words: He was made Man," [but] what frightens them is that they will lose the transcendent God guaranteeing the meaning of the universe, God as the hidden Master pulling the strings—instead of this, we get a God who abandons this transcendent position and throws himself into his own creation, fully engaging himself in it up to dying, so that we, humans, are left with no higher Power watching over us, just with the terrible burden of freedom and responsibility for the fate of divine creation, and thus of God himself. Are we not still too frightened today to assume all these consequences of the four words?[110]

Milbank does not buy Žižek's deconstruction as authentic. Rather, he posits:

> My case is that there is a different, latent Žižek: a Žižek who does not see Chesterton as sub-Hegel, but Hegel as sub-Chesterton. A Žižek therefore who has remained with paradox, or rather moved back into paradox from dialectic. And this remaining would be suf-

---

[110]Slavoj Žižek and John Milbank, *The Monstrosity of Christ: Paradox or Dialectic?* (Cambridge, MA: MIT Press, 2009), Kindle edition, 387/5120.

ficient to engender a Catholic Žižek, a Žižek able fully to endorse a transcendent God, in whom creatures analogically participate.[111]

Whether or not one follows the Žižek-Milbank exchange blow for blow, what makes their conversation significant is the grounds upon which the debate is happening. Both thinkers are Hegelians of different varieties.[112] Both have abandoned traditional approaches to metaphysics with its appeals to some sort of publicly available reason. Both appear to assume that such appeals are no longer possible. For Milbank, Hegelianism frees us from the Kantian divide between transcendent categories and the human mind—the transcendental unity of apperception. For Žižek, Hegel levels the playing field and reduces all distinctions to the even turf of a materialist account of history. But what they hold in common is their belief that there is no way to go back to a world in which human beings can stir their minds to metaphysical heights through the resources of natural law, or that God can reach down to them on a bridge constructed of logically meaningful sentences and paragraphs via special revelation—divine writings that can be marshaled into dogma. There is no going back.

As I see it, Carl F. H. Henry would have been the ideal third party to the Žižek-Milbank debate. Like Žižek, he was intimately concerned with the plight of the globe and suffering peoples. Like Milbank, he resolutely defended the right of theologians to maintain divine prerogatives in theological expression. But unlike the contemporary pair, he was no idealist or mystic—he was a realist and sought for biblical authority to be defended on proper grounds. Henry would not have condoned either a conceptual or actual collapsing of theological verities into a Hegelian scheme. In *Introducing Radical Orthodoxy*, James K. A. Smith likened Milbank's work to that of the twentieth-century Dutch philosopher Herman Dooyeweerd, a comparison to which Milbank has responded favorably.[113] Henry, appreciative of Dooyeweerd's relentless quest to reorient all of knowledge as modes

---

[111]Ibid., 1817/5120.

[112]See Marcus Pound, http://www.zizekstudies.org/index.php/ijzs/article/viewFile/269/344.

[113]James K. A. Smith, *Introducing Radical Orthodoxy: Mapping a Post-Secular Theology* (Grand Rapids: Baker Academic, 2004), 13–14 and elsewhere.

or aspects of reality consistent with a revelation of the biblical type, expressed reservations about the latter's denial that "the cosmos has a logical structure."[114]

Indeed, the question of whether or not theology is rational and can be squared with the traditional Western insistence upon metaphysics stands at ground zero of all current and future theological debate. This was the governing question behind Carl Raschke's pathbreaking book *The End of Theology*, first published in 1979. Following Derrida, he argues that metaphysics is the "pursuit of the signified," a search that is "unreservedly quixotic; it is like searching for the bottom of a bottomless well." Raschke goes on:

> "Nothing" is before language in the logical sense. Yet the signs still seduce us. What then is the source of our enthrallment? . . . The sign, Derrida declares, is simply a "trace." A trace is a hint, a seeming sedimentation, of something that cannot in itself be discovered. The trace suggests a "presence," but it is a presence which, from the immediate point of view, is always absence. The trace is significant, but we can never be sure what it signifies.[115]

What is the actual text of the Bible, Raschke would say, but a series of these traces? To uncover their meaning, he maintains, is to "overcome metaphysics" and "theo-logic" altogether.[116] The goal is not to do biblical exegesis in order to recover real "presences" in an ancient text, or to hope for the breaking in of the Word of God into history from outside space and time: "Assuredly we cannot think of it as some voice which irrupts from 'on high,' an entirely 'new' manifestation of the 'Word of God' which falls within the province of historical 'revelation.'"[117] Theology as such has come to an end, yielding to "dialogue" in the face of

---

[114]Carl F. H. Henry, *God, Revelation and Authority*, vol. 5, *God Who Stands and Stays, Part One* (Waco, TX: Word, 1982), 346.

[115]Carl Raschke, *The End of Theology* (Scholars Press, 1979; repr., Aurora, CO: Davies, 2000), 42.

[116]Ibid., 124.

[117]Ibid., 128.

the threshold for the unobtrusive advent of shining divinity. The glimmerings of transcendence in language itself, wrested and given play through the hermeneutical self disclosure of the unsaid, signal the dawn of *parousia*. The *parousia* is not "advent" from outside the tradition but the manifestation of the tradition's hidden capacity for signification.[118]

Raschke concludes his thesis by stating that "the Word of God, cherished, embellished, and illumined for untold generations, must be released from its tutelage to the written letter. Dialogue does not take place between words, but between living persons."[119]

The mediating positions of recent internecine evangelical theology with respect to theological method, inspiration, authority, inerrancy, and doctrinal formulation do not seem robust enough and appear to lack verve when compared to the bracing positions of the likes of Raschke, Milbank, and even an atheist such as Žižek. Could it be that a recovery of confidence in propositional revelation and an inerrant Bible is, despite now decades of neglect and/or disdain, the last stand between the evangelical community and a new era of radical hermeneutics? These may well be the only honest alternatives left to those who take theory and their own convictions seriously.

---

[118]Ibid., 129.
[119]Ibid., 139.

# CHAPTER 5

# Culture Matters

In 1527, the bubonic plague swept throughout Germany, decimating the population, and eventually found its way to the tiny town of Wittenberg. Martin Luther was forced to confront the threat while tormented with various digestive-tract ailments of his own—so much so that he reached the point of despair. "I felt," Luther wrote to his closest friend, Philipp Melanchthon, "completely abandoned by Christ." Melanchthon himself had already fled the plague.[1] Despite these convulsions, both personal and national, Luther intervened on behalf of the masses who were being stricken by the plague. The elector had begged him to leave, but the Reformer instead disseminated an essay entitled "Whether One May Flee from a Deadly Plague," and urged political leaders and church leaders to stay behind and set up homes for the sick. True to his word, Luther soldiered on in Wittenberg, lecturing to empty classrooms and returning home each night to his Katie and a house filled with those afflicted by the plague. In fact, their home remained under quarantine until after the plague had lifted.

It was during these days that Luther penned the words to "A Mighty Fortress Is Our God." Everyone has his or her own favorite lines or phrases from *Ein feste Burg*, but the final verse is perhaps most especially apt to what one of Luther's inheritors, Carl F. H. Henry, saw as his vision for an evangelical view of culture:

> That Word above all earthly powers,
> No thanks to them, abideth;
> The Spirit and the gifts are ours
> Through him who with us sideth;

---

[1]See James M. Kittelson, *Luther: The Reformer* (Minneapolis: Augsburg, 1986), 211.

Let goods and kindred go,
This mortal life also;
The body they may kill:
God's truth abideth still;
His kingdom is for ever.

Although "A Mighty Fortress" is often viewed as upholding the gospel against attacks by the Roman curia and the papacy, in context, it seems to have been more about what to do when there is no political solution to the threats that society faces. The hymn reminds us about gospel prerogatives in the face of human helplessness. When the plague strikes, what can save a nation? Americans, are, of course, divided as to whether or not a societal plague is upon us. They are also deeply at variance over whether Christianity, or specifically a conservative evangelical version of it, holds the promise of moving us beyond the current lack of social cohesion, morality, and economic verve. Some still answer that question with an enthusiastic yes. Others, weary of the promises of religion, at best say no. At worst, they mock the notion that religion can really solve anything.

In spite of this, evangelicals continue their passion for sociopolitical engagement. The numbers of books on this subject alone in the past couple of years is eye-watering. It is a situation that brings to mind Jacques Ellul's observation in *New Demons*:

Everything is political. Politics is the only serious activity. The fate of humanity depends upon politics, and classical philosophical or religious truth takes on meaning only as it is incarnated in political action. Christians are typical in this connection. They rush to the defense of political religion, and assert that Christianity is meaningful only in terms of political commitment. In truth, it is their religious mentality which plays this trick on them. As Christianity collapses as a religion, they look about them in bewilderment, unconsciously of course, hoping to recover where the religious is to be incarnated in their time. Since they are religious, they are drawn automatically into the political sphere like iron filings to a magnet.[2]

---

[2]Jacques Ellul, *The New Demons*, trans. C. Edward Hopkin (New York: Seabury, 1975), 199.

Evangelicals have been fascinated by political involvement in part because they believe that it is a way of bringing all things in subjection to the lordship of Christ. They want to change the world. Isn't that the boilerplate mission statement of every evangelical college or university? But is that possible? Can evangelicals change the world? Two of America's most prominent sociologists have taken up this question in recent days. James Davison Hunter's *To Change the World* aims to put an end once and for all to the whole "Christian worldview" racket, revisit the bipolar nature of evangelical fundamentalism, both on the left and on the right, and even take a whack at good-old-fashioned Anabaptist/Pietist/Wesleyan approaches to cultural engagement just for auld lang syne. Because the monograph came from an author whose background is evangelical, the primary genre of discourse is, of course, self-critical. Hunter's analysis is penetrating and convicting, and to his credit he takes theology very seriously. Unlike so many evangelical theologians who seem really to want to be sociologists when they grow up, Hunter is a sociologist who wants to be a theologian when he grows up. Perhaps for this very reason, then, contra the language of "culture change," he proposes the category of "faithful presence." But what this means proves to be somewhat trickier. He explains in two lessons, as follows:

> The first is that *incarnation is the only adequate reply to the challenges of dissolution; the erosion of trust between word and world and the problems that attend it.* From this follows the second: *it is the way the Word became incarnate in Jesus Christ and the purposes to which the incarnation was directed that are the only adequate reply to challenge of difference.* For the Christian, if there is a possibility for human flourishing in a world such as ours, it begins when God's word of love becomes flesh in us, is embodied in us, is enacted through us and in doing so, a trust is forged between the word spoken and the reality to which it speaks; to the words we speak and the realities to which we, the church, point. In all, presence and place matter decisively.[3]

---

[3]James Davison Hunter, *To Change the World* (New York: Oxford University Press, 2010), 241, his emphasis.

In the end, Hunter seems to be talking along the same lines as C. S. Lewis—about Christians doing their work with their Christianity latent in their approaches to art, economics, and medicine.[4] It is hard to find much fault in this, but I have to admit that "faithful presence" as a category by itself—without a macro goal of broader cultural ambition (e.g., Wilberforce and the Clapham Sect)—might be interpreted by people of my generation and the next to mean a quasi-quietism. And, as we shall see, it falls short of the original vision of classic evangelicalism set forth by Carl Henry.

By way of contrast, the volume *American Grace,* by Robert Putnam (Harvard) and David Campbell (Notre Dame), is much more sunny about the whole state of Christian engagement of culture, partly, I think, because they *don't* take theology all that seriously. What Putnam likes about believers, specifically the evangelicals, is that we're already doing what Hunter is proposing in *To Change the World.* We *are* a faithful presence in our neighborhoods and communities. Putnam shows that church attendance is actually the best indicator predictive of civic involvement and engagement. He and Campbell also add that according to their research the single best indicator of neighborliness and generosity is regular attendance at religious services. As it turns out from their survey, even if one does not actually affirm the faith tradition, attendance at religious services enhances health, concern for others, involvement in the community, and the like.[5]

---

[4]Lewis states: "I believe that any Christian who is qualified to write a good popular book on any science may do much more by that than by any direct apologetic work. . . . We can make people often attend to the Christian point of view for half an hour or so; but the moment they have gone away from our lecture or laid down our article, they are plunged back into a world where the opposite position is taken for granted. . . . What we want is not more little books about Christianity, but more little books by Christians on other subjects—with their Christianity latent. You can see this most easily if you look at it the other way around. Our faith is not very likely to be shaken by any book on Hinduism. But if whenever we read an elementary book on Geology, Botany, Politics, or Astronomy, we found that its implications were Hindu, that would shake us. It is not the books written in direct defense of Materialism that make the modern man a materialist; it is the materialistic assumptions in all the other books. In the same way, it is not books on Christianity that will really trouble him. But he would be troubled if, whenever he wanted a cheap popular introduction to some science, the best work on the market was always by a Christian." C. S. Lewis, *God in the Dock* (Grand Rapids: Eerdmans, 1994), 93.

[5]Robert Putnam and David Campbell, *American Grace* (New York: Simon and Schuster, 2010).

So as evangelicals, maybe we ought to just congratulate ourselves and stop beating ourselves up so much. Maybe we *are* a faithful presence as a default feature of our DNA. Though we might think that, Putnam is convinced that our good deeds and our general "who are our neighbors?" mien has nothing to do with whether what we believe is actually true in a critically real sense, for even if it is, it does not matter. Speaking at the Southern Festival of Books in Nashville in the fall of 2010, Putnam remarked that British prime minister David Cameron recently summoned him to 10 Downing Street to talk about whether and how Britain might revive community as a largely secular culture. The prime minister wanted to exploit that intangible something that religious people have without endorsing religiosity or confessing any one given theological tradition.

The Hunter-Putnam dichotomy only serves to underscore the deep, abiding nature of the problems evangelicals face when it comes to mounting a public theology. What is the basis or point of social justice? Everybody knows it's going to be tougher sledding from here on out. Evangelicals are on the skids in terms of their political influence in Washington, and books like Jonathan Merritt's *A Faith of Our Own* report that younger evangelicals feel burned by what's happened to theology in the public square.[6] We are entering a season of real need for leadership. Sociologist Jacob Taubes observes, "As there is no theology without political implications, there is no political theory without theological presuppositions."[7] We cannot avoid the political dimension, but if we "go there," we wonder whether we're going to be cheapening the gospel or creating more problems than we can solve.

What is ostensibly the case is that evangelicals lack a coherent definition of the common good and a common platform for sociopolitical engagement. There are pronounced differences among the camps. In one arena, you have Darryl Hart versus the Kuyperians.

---

[6]Jonathan Merritt, *A Faith of Our Own* (New York: FaithWords, 2012). See also Matt Anderson's excellent response to the title at http://www.christianitytoday.com/ct/2012/mayweb-only/faith-of-our-own-review.html?start=3.

[7]Jacob Taubes, "Theology and Political Theory," in *From Cult to Culture: Fragments toward a Critique of Historical Reason*, ed. Charlotte Elisheva Fonrobert and Amir Engel (Stanford, CA: Stanford University Press, 2010), 215.

In another, Kevin DeYoung versus David Platt having a very edifying debate on the matter of the church's responsibility to the poor and to culture. Elsewhere, you have John MacArthur versus the signatories to the Manhattan Declaration. Much helpful conversation has taken place to clarify matters related to these discussions, especially, for example, Kevin DeYoung and Greg Gilbert's recent offering, *What Is the Mission of the Church? Making Sense of Social Justice, Shalom, and the Great Commission*. Still, as a student of evangelicalism, one cannot help but feel a sense of loss that conservative evangelicals are so divided on how to engage the public square, whether theoretically or practically.

We have come full circle to where Carl Henry began with evangelicals after World War II in *The Uneasy Conscience of Modern Fundamentalism* (1947). Evangelicals have no consistent program to speak to the sociopolitical climate of our time, and I think that within the confines of our current environment, we need to ask ourselves whether that's even possible anymore. But before we give up hope, I want to plead *ad fontes* for my fellow evangelicals to revisit the manifesto that, at least culturally speaking, started it all. We need to return to the central claims of Carl Henry's landmark book.

*Uneasy Conscience* exhibited confidence that even in the worst imaginable period in world history, a globe confused and battered emerging from the Second World War could look to the good news of the Lord Jesus Christ and be transformed—not just as individuals, but as a society. Because Henry held confidence in the epistemological gravitas of an inerrant and infinitely applicable Scripture, he believed that the church had the greatest potential to help meet the needs of an ailing planet. It was this ambitious, optimistic, and robust vision that stood at the genesis of the evangelical movement. By addressing the political, social, economic, and intellectual questions of the age, God's people have an opportunity to share the gospel that not only makes us right with God, but also makes human flourishing possible. This was the vision of classic evangelicalism.

## The Uneasy Conscience of Modern Fundamentalism

Henry's central aim in *Uneasy Conscience* is to challenge the pre-dominant cultural prejudices held against biblical Christianity and to assert a right understanding of the core tenets and mission of Chris-tian evangelicalism. This project is simultaneously a polemic against modern liberalism and against the myriad strains of Christianity that denominate themselves as "evangelical," "fundamentalist," or both, but have misapprehended the purpose and calling of authentic evangelicalism. Henry confronts critics on all sides by arguing that evangelicalism is intrinsically linked to the redemptive energy of the Christian evangel in the active and practical opposition of social and spiritual evils. This mission, he claims, is the only means by which substantive, meaningful, and sustainable change can be effected upon cultural and social ills.

## The Evaporation of Fundamentalist Humanitarianism

Henry's opening salvo addresses the modernist critique against evan-gelicalism's lack of social conscience. He distinguishes between two categories—the nonevangelical and the evangelical—to indicate the differences in prevailing cultural paradigms. He does so out of a very immediate awareness that modern liberalism, in all its forms, is "foredoomed to failure." His critique is hot on the heels of two disastrous world wars and the world climate these crises have inaugu-rated. Henry diagnoses the malady of social apathy within Protestant fundamentalism and likewise reevaluates a right understanding of what constitutes true biblical Christianity.

> Against Protestant Fundamentalism the non-evangelicals level the charge that it has no social program calling for a practical attack on acknowledged world evils. . . . But what is almost wholly unintel-ligible to the naturalistic and idealistic groups, burdened as they are for a new world order, is the apparent lack of any social passion in Protestant Fundamentalism. On this evaluation, Fundamentalism is the modern priest and Levite, by-passing suffering humanity.[8]

---

[8]Carl F. H. Henry, *The Uneasy Conscience of Modern Fundamentalism*, with foreword by Richard J. Mouw (Grand Rapids: Eerdmans, 2003), 2.

Henry points out that not only has evangelical fundamentalism become indifferent toward social evils and reform; it has adopted an aggressive stance against many institutions whose efforts are exerted toward the alleviation of social evils, both secular and religious, effectively quashing the social voice of fundamentalist evangelicalism almost wholesale.

> The social reform movements dedicated to the elimination of such evils do not have the active, let alone vigorous, cooperation of large segments of evangelical Christianity. In fact, Fundamentalist churches increasingly have repudiated the very movements whose most energetic efforts have gone into an attack on social ills. . . .
>
> Now, such resistance would be far more intelligible to non-evangelicals were it accompanied by an equally forceful assault on social evils in a distinctly supernaturalistic framework. But by and large, the Fundamentalist opposition to societal ills has been more vocal than actual.[9]

Further, the argument in *Uneasy Conscience* seeks above all else to revive the true spirit of Christian fundamentalism away from the degenerate qualities that have come to typify its cultural identity as regarded by "modern prejudice." "Modern prejudice, justly or unjustly, had come to identify Fundamentalism largely in terms of an anti-ecumenical spirit of independent isolationism, an uncritically-held set of theological formulas, an overly-emotional type of revivalism."[10] And can anyone doubt that these problems are still extant in evangelical Christianity today?

Against these imputed qualities, Henry lays out his working definition for authentic and thus exemplary evangelical fundamentalism. It was the ethically alert fundamentalist minority who recognized that such tendencies do not express the inherent genius of the great evangelical tradition. Spokesmen, particularly among orthodox Reformed groups, saw that the title "fundamentalism" was applied initially with doctrinal fidelity, rather than ethical irresponsibility, in mind.

[9] Ibid., 3.
[10] Ibid., 5.

Fundamentalism was a Bible-believing Christianity that regarded the supernatural as essential to the biblical view. The miraculous was not to be viewed, as in liberalism, as an incidental and superfluous accretion. This was, after all, the central argument of J. Gresham Machen's *Christianity and Liberalism*. Henry explains:

> It was from its affirmation of the historic evangelical doctrinal fundamentals that modern orthodoxy received its name, and not from its growing silence on pressing global problems. This was clearly seen by spokesmen for contemporary Fundamentalism like . . . Machen, who vigorously insisted that Christianity has a message relevant to the world crisis, however staggering the issues.[11]

On every page, Henry has a laser-like focus on his central agenda: to undermine the marriage of Protestant evangelicalism to apathy and willful ignorance of social evil. Of all the seemingly incongruous weddings in church history, he finds this one the most striking: "That Christian supernaturalism, which as a matter of historical record furnished the background and in some sense[s] the support for the modern humanisms and idealisms, should be accused of having lost its own devotion to human well-being is indeed a startling accusation."[12] He clarifies:

> This is not to suggest that Fundamentalism had no militant opposition to sin. Of all modern viewpoints, when measured against the black background of human nature disclosed by the generation of two world wars, Fundamentalism provided the most realistic appraisal of the condition of man. . . . But the sin against which Fundamentalism has inveighed, almost exclusively, was individual sin rather than social evil.[13]

This condition of evangelicalism that favors a gospel of individual sin management divorced from any program or principle of ethico-social reform is, as Henry sees it, the root cause of the prob-

---

[11]Ibid., 6.
[12]Ibid.
[13]Ibid., 7.

lem his book seeks to address: "The Evaporation of Fundamentalist Humanitarianism."

> This modern mind-set, insisting that evangelical supernaturalism has inherent within it an ideological fault which precludes any vital social thrust, is one of the most disturbing dividing lines in contemporary thought. In the struggle for a world mind which will make global order and brotherhood a possibility, contemporary speculation has no hearing whatever for a viewpoint which it suspects has no world program.[14]

And so it dismisses fundamentalism by concluding that the concern for human beings as human beings "has evaporated from Christianity."[15]

## The Protest against Foredoomed Failure

Henry inveighs against the assumptions outlined in his opening argument by insisting not only that the core tenets of evangelicalism demand a robust social conscience and rigorous service against social evils, but also that evangelicalism, by its nature, is more adequately equipped to take this stance than any other philosophical system. After all, an evangelical message vitally related to world conditions is not precluded by New Testament doctrine. Indeed, conservative Protestantism insists that only this estimate of human sinfulness and the need of regeneration is sufficiently realistic to afford any securely grounded optimism in world affairs. Any other framework can offer only what Henry memorably calls a "bubble and froth cure."[16]

But from whence comes the "uneasiness" that fundamentalists are supposed to be feeling? It rises from the awareness that Christianity's mission and message have become irrelevant and unnecessary within the larger cultural conversation of correcting the ethical crises of modernity. While modern minds wrestle with global concerns, the Christian conscience is disturbed because its historic message is dismissed as a nonoption for solving the ills of Western culture.

---

[14]Ibid., 11.
[15]Ibid.
[16]Ibid., 13.

Fundamentalists, for their part, respond with a yawn. For them, as long as people are getting "saved" who cares if the world was going to hell?[17]

Contrary to the current attitude, which sees evangelicals constantly second guessing themselves, Henry argues for swagger. Rather than being an outdated, irrelevant philosophy, evangelicalism is instead uniquely positioned to offer radical and poignant critiques of both social conditions and the modern optimism that initiated them. It is the radically divergent ideological position held by evangelicals that makes such a critique possible in the first place. "The evangelical is convinced that the non-evangelicals operate within the wrong ideological framework" to make cultural achievement possible. Secularists nurture "a naive and misplaced confidence in man, growing out of a superficial view of reality." By way of contrast,

> only an anthropology and a soteriology that insists upon man's sinful lostness and the ability of God to restore the responsive sinner is the adequate key to the door of Fundamentalist world betterment. Any other approach is a needless waste of effort and, in effect an attack on the exclusive relevance, . . . of the historic redemptive Gospel.[18]

Henry thus theorizes that any strain of evangelicalism not motivated to transform the world radically through a direct opposition of social evils is not true to the Christian gospel, and ultimately cannot be the message that reaches troubled souls with the good news of Christ the Lord. In sum, Christianity without a passion to turn the world upside down bears no relation to apostolic Christianity.[19]

Essentially, as modern liberalism and its "social gospel" rose to prominence and began its own attack on social evils, evangelicalism focused its efforts on resisting movements hostile to fundamentalist ideology, and thus became preoccupied with philosophical and

---

[17]Ibid., 14.
[18]Ibid., 15.
[19]Ibid., 16–17.

theological self-justification rather than practical, ethical change in the world. Henry comments:

> The recoil of Fundamentalism from such moralism cut loose from Biblical redemption, might have been pursued without a divorce between evangelical doctrinal and evangelical ethical insistence. Historically, Christianity embraced a life view as well as a world view; it was socially as well as philosophically pertinent.[20]

But in doing this, fundamentalists have staged a terrible reversal from tradition. "Whereas once the redemptive gospel was a world-changing message, now it was narrowed to a world-resisting message. . . . In protesting against non-evangelical ideologies, Fundamentalism came to react also against the social programs of the modern reformers."[21]

The original spirit of historic Christianity was a social conscience deeply rooted in an apostolic understanding of the New Testament, a way of thinking that realized that any social effort or program of reform not rooted in the redemptive, world-changing power of the gospel is ultimately unsustainable and inadequate to offer substantive solutions to social evil. The failure of modernity to redress the calamities of the nineteenth and twentieth centuries indicates the timeliness of Henry's call to reclaim the prophetic voice that characterizes the spirit of authentic Christian evangelicalism.

## The Great Evangelical Divorce

Typically, jeremiads are boring and uninspiring, but in *Uneasy Conscience*, the sense of outrage at what has been lost is both terrifying and motivating. Henry states that "for the first protracted period of time in its history, evangelical Christianity stands divorced from the great social reform movements."[22] What makes matters worse, he maintains, is the divorce of modern Protestantism from the social convictions inspired by the Reformation. This cleavage is for Henry the locus of evangelicalism's social irrelevance in the modern era,

---

[20]Ibid., 18.
[21]Ibid., 19.
[22]Ibid., 27.

unlike the entire ethical tradition of Christian history. In its true genius, historic Christianity provided an idealistic atmosphere of prophetic insight regardless of the cultural context—whether embattled or privileged—in which it found itself. Fundamentalism today, however, denies that Christian ethics is in any sense identified with the vision for human flourishing set forth by modern reformers and social-change agents. Consequently, the most vocal, vigorous, and courageous attacks on admitted social ills come from humanists and secularists, while the church remains quarantined in its holy huddle. "As a consequence," says Henry, "Protestant evangelicalism without a world program has largely relegated itself to a secondary, or even more subordinate, role of challenge to the prevailing cultural mood."[23]

In the aftermath, what evangelicalism has sacrificed in its divorce from social concerns is a rootedness in the historic ethical mandates of the Hebrew-Christian tradition, and thus it has essentially severed itself from orthodoxy. By demonstrating the necessity of active social participation inherent to Christian theology, Henry aims to correct the misunderstanding that equates fundamentalism with social apathy. Hebrew-Christian thought has historically stood as a tightly knit world-and-life view. Metaphysics and ethics were seen as biblically inseparable. The great doctrines of the faith implied a divinely given social order with correlative expectations for all humanity.

> The ideal Hebrew or Christian society throbbed with challenge to the predominant culture of its generation, condemning with redemptive might the tolerated social evils, for the redemptive message was to light the world and salt the earth. No insistence on a doctrinal framework alone was sufficient; always this was coupled with the most vigorous assault against evils, so that the globe stood anticipatively at the judgment seat of Christ.[24]

Additionally, the historic identity of the Hebrew-Christian tradition, as Henry argues, was essentially one of challenge to the standards

---

[23]Ibid., 28.
[24]Ibid., 30–31.

of prevailing cultural norms and outright rejection of any and every social evil. Historically, Christianity was, by its very character, positioned as a prophetic reality within and to its given cultural identity. Henry emphatically asserts that any culture, movement, or program that attempts to flourish apart from the ethical standards of biblical revelation is condemned to failure at the outset.

What believers have to offer the world is far more than a mere strategy to avoid hell after one dies. In both Old and New Testament thought there exists but one sure foundation for an enduring civilization, and its cornerstone is a vital knowledge of the redemptive God. This only makes sense since the universe is designed along moral lines. All attempts to build civilization on other foundations, whether before or after Christ's coming into the world, are doomed before they begin. "The ten commandments disclose the only secure foundation for a society without the seeds of dissolution; all cultures, cut loose from these principles, have in them the vitiating leaven of decay."[25]

Not only the biblical authors, but also the forebears of evangelicalism understood this. Henry briefly gives an account of the Christian ethical tradition from the New Testament Gospels and apostolic period, through Augustine and Aquinas, and on to the Reformation (Luther, Zwingli, and Calvin). Henry juxtaposes this historical perspective with the modern fundamentalist position and locates the titular "uneasy conscience of modern fundamentalism" at the moment in which evangelicalism woke up to find itself pitted against its own history.

For Henry, all problems are ultimately rooted in poor theory. As a result, he examines eschatological theology and the philosophy of history to find the offending concepts and rehabilitate them. To do this, he contrasts two ideological frameworks that characterize this problem; the kingdom-*now* systems and the kingdom-*then* systems. Kingdom-now systems, generally characterized by liberal reform movements, assume a paradigm of kingdom utopianism, which places the inauguration of a perfected social order on the agency and will

---

[25]Ibid., 31–32.

of man. Kingdom-then systems relegate the possibility of a perfected social order to a future era, the inauguration of which is essentially unaffected by human agency.

Against these disparate options, Henry asserts that evangelicalism is essentially distinct from any of the now/then philosophies in that it accepts both now and then as proper kingdom orientations, simultaneously present and future. It appears more in accord with the biblical philosophy of history to think of the church age in terms of divine continuity with the inaugurated kingdom of heaven rather than a parenthesis, in terms of the amazing unity of the redemptive plan rather than an amazing interlude.[26]

In sum, contemporary evangelicalism needs (1) to reawaken to the relevance of its redemptive message to the global predicament; (2) to stress the great evangelical agreements in a common world front; (3) to discard as contradictory to the inherent genius of Christianity any elements of its message that cut the nerve of world compassion; and (4) to restudy eschatological convictions for a proper perspective that will not unnecessarily dissipate evangelical strength in controversies over secondary positions in a day when the primary insistences have international significance.[27] Out of this awesome vision for the future, many worthy evangelical institutions, publications, and organizations were either born or sustained. *Uneasy Conscience* gave permission to a new generation of evangelicals to dream. And I submit that if it is read again against the current backdrop of evangelical fracturing and discord, concord can be found once again.

In a final call to hear his passion for engagement, Henry points toward the conclusion of his program by offering an analogy. The two thieves crucified with Christ are exemplary of the two disparate views under consideration throughout the book: humanism and fundamentalism. The thief on the left "felt that Jesus had no momentous contribution to suffering humanity, while the one on the right was convinced of His saviourhood but wanted to be remembered in the

---

[26]Ibid, 47. For an excellent review of these matters and an updating of the Henry program, see Russell D. Moore, *The Kingdom of Christ: The New Evangelical Perspective* (Wheaton, IL: Crossway, 2004).

[27]Henry, *Uneasy Conscience of Modern Fundamentalism*, 53–54.

indefinite future, when Jesus would come into His kingdom."[28] Those who hold a biblical worldview need to meditate on Jesus's reply: "Today you will be with me in Paradise" (Luke 23:43). The message for decadent modern civilization must ring with the present tense. We must confront the world now "with an ethics to make it tremble, and with a dynamic to give it hope."[29] Henry entreats his audience:

> Fundamentalism insists upon a purposive and moral as over against a purely mathematical universe; it insists upon a personal God, as against impersonal ultimates whether of space-time or élan vital variety; it insists upon a divine creation as over against a naturalistic evolution; it insists that man's uniqueness is a divine endowment rather than a human achievement; it insists that man's predicament is not an animal inheritance nor a necessity of his nature but rather a consequence of his voluntary revolt against God; it insists that salvation can be provided only by God, as against the view that man is competent to save himself; it insists that the Scriptures are a revelation lighting the way to the divine incarnation in Jesus Christ as the Redeemer of mankind, as against the view that they stand among many records of religious experience without a difference in kind; it insists that history is bound up with man's acceptance or rejection of the God-man, rather than that history is primarily what happens among nations; it insists that the future is not an open question, but that world events move toward an ultimate consummation in a future judgment of the race.[30]

If historic Christianity is again to compete as a vital world ideology, evangelicalism must project a solution for the most pressing world problems. It must offer a formula for a new world mind with spiritual ends, involving evangelical affirmations in political, economic, sociological, and educational implications for all of life. "A truncated life results from a truncated message," Henry says.[31] But despite his criticism of "conversion only" approaches to cultural engagement, he nonetheless knows that the core tenet for evangeli-

---

[28]Ibid., 55.
[29]Ibid.
[30]Ibid., 58.
[31]Ibid., 65.

calism must be the redemptive message of the gospel. He remains adamant that any nonredemptive solution cannot sustain itself. And as Henry was famous for saying on many different occasions, "The gospel is only good news if it gets there in time." Bringing men and women to repentance and faith in Christ must always be the clear outcome of all efforts to speak to sectors of culture. Evangelicalism will be presumed not to have a mind on great world issues unless it speaks, but there is no justification for evangelical attempts at solutions that do not possess a framework for the salvation of souls. The social gospel alone has been tried and found wanting. From here on out, Henry calls out to his co-laborers in the gospel, let evangelicalism now speak out of the resources of the redeemed mind.[32]

## The Dawn of a New Reformation

The need for vital evangelicalism is proportionate to the world need. The days are as dark as Nero's Rome, and they demand attention as immediate as Luke's Macedonia did. The cries of suffering humanity today are many. No evangelicalism that ignores the totality of man's condition dares respond in the name of Christianity. Though the modern crisis is not basically political, economic, or social—fundamentally it is religious—evangelicalism must be armed to declare the implications of its proposed religious solution for the politico-economic and sociological contexts for modern life.[33] There is no satisfying rest for modern civilization if it is found in a context of spiritual unrest. This is but another way of declaring that the gospel of redemption is the most pertinent message for our modern weariness, and that many of our other so-called solutions are inadequate for the present hour, to say the least.[34] While it is not the individual Christian's task to correct social, moral, and political conditions as his primary effort apart from a redemptive setting, simply because of his opposition to evils he ought to lend his endorsement to remedial

---

[32]Ibid., 73.
[33]Ibid., 83.
[34]Ibid., 85.

efforts in any context not specifically antiredemptive, while at the same time calling for the ultimate, redemptive solution.[35]

In the end, here is Henry's deepest conviction: when the current evangelical community begins to "out-live" its environment as the first-century church outreached its pagan neighbors, the modern mind will stop casting about for other solutions. The great contemporary problems are moral and spiritual. They demand more than a formula, more than political will, more than economics. The evangelicals have a conviction of absoluteness concerning their message, and not to proclaim it, in the assault on social evils, is a dereliction of duty. But the modern mood is far more likely to react first on the level of Christianity as a life view than as a mere message about how to make it to heaven.[36]

## After Henry's Vision: Looking Back to Look Forward in Christian Witness Today

### "Mugged by Reality"

It is remarkable to see how fresh, crisp, and contemporary Henry's proposal is more than six decades removed from its original publication. As Richard J. Mouw remarked in his new foreword to *Uneasy Conscience* in 2003: "The agenda that Henry laid out in this book still deserves sustained attention. It must also be said that his actual suggestions as to what is required in a well-formed biblical orthodoxy continue to ring true for many of us."[37] Moving forward, we must strategize how to connect the Henry vision with the state of affairs on the ground today in the second decade of the twenty-first century.

Speaking to the *New York Times* in December of 1981, Irving Kristol memorably defined a neoconservative as a "liberal who has been mugged by reality."[38] Kristol's pithy description reminds us that the kinds of crises one undergoes often cause him to reevaluate his view of the world. In the mood in which our society hears the

---

[35]Ibid., 87.
[36]Ibid.
[37]Richard J. Mouw, foreword to Henry, *Uneasy Conscience of Modern Fundamentalism*, xiii.
[38]Irving Kristol, as cited in Fred R. Shapiro, *The Yale Book of Quotations* (New Haven, CT: Yale University Press, 2006), 437.

historic Christian message, Christians increasingly find themselves in a position quite like Kristol's archetypal "neoconservative." After years of making historic arguments for belief and morality, we feel "mugged" by reality. Are fewer and fewer people listening, we find ourselves wondering? There seems to be something of a malaise, at least in evangelical circles, with respect to diminishing returns on their witness to the broader culture.

If, as I will argue, people are irrepressibly religious beings, why is secularism advancing so rapidly in Europe and now America? The answer has its origins, of course, in understanding the declining fortunes of Christianity in culture. And if some of what I say sounds like a *mea culpa*, then that is certainly intentional. If the Christian community is indeed interested in reaching an ideologically laden age with the gospel, as did Henry, then perhaps it is appropriate to begin not so much with an apologetic, but with the words, "We're sorry."

Remarkably, few things have really changed since the founding editor of *Christianity Today* first sat down behind his typewriter to compose what then became the bombshell that fell on the fundamentalist playground. What Henry perceived to be true is still the case: the persistent fascination with transcendence in culture, and the reality that secularism fails to offer a better solution for cultural flourishing. In light of these, I want to take into account the prospects for cultural engagement for the two concepts that concerned Carl Henry and his heirs: reason and revelation. And I would like to juxtapose those topics with the following query: Is there hope for rapprochement between natural law (about which Henry expressed reservations) and theologies of revelation (Henry's agenda in *GRA*) when it comes to the common project of reintroducing the Christian witness to the Western world?

In chapter 2, I outlined the reasons why an evangelical theory of epistemology, based on categories in Henry's reappraisal of the tradition of the Reformers, cannot be composed with a Thomistic worldview. Although I have argued that he was completely on target, the crisis that all Christians operating out of the great Christian intellectual tradition are facing is so great, we must find new ways for both evangelical and nonevangelical (Roman Catholic, Orthodox) philosophies to partner their best arguments for cultural renewal while respecting one another's nonoverlapping epistemologies. We can begin with the fact that, despite the best efforts of a secular age to drum it out of us, people long to see the world through a spiritual lens.

## Irrepressibly Religious

In his 1887 notebook entry on "European Nihilism," Friedrich Nietzsche looked forward to his preferred future for the Continent. In his litany of antivirtues, Nietzsche celebrated the idea that there are no "final goals" to existence, repudiated the notion that every human being has "infinite value," and relished the extinction of spiritual consolation. The "strongest" persons, in this dawning era of self-reliance, "are those who have no need of extreme dogmas, those who not only concede but love a good measure of chance and nonsense." "God," Nietzsche alleged, "is much too extreme a hypothesis."[39]

Despite attempts to kill the Deity, the project to end religion in the West has failed rather miserably. Even such a dedicated nihilist as Michel Foucault hears someone whisper in his ear, in the closing sentence of *The Archaeology of Knowledge*, "You may have killed God beneath the weight of all you have said; but don't imagine that, with all you are saying, you will make a man that will live longer than he."[40] Foucault, of course, flattered himself by taking up Nietzsche's mantle to, once again, declare the death of God. Throughout history, human beings have proved to be irrepressibly religious creatures. Culture, after all, reflects the deepest longings and aspirations of the human spirit. We find something to give the status of being ultimate, something having the status of not depending on anything else. And what is the divine if not something of fundamental importance? That really is the best definition of religion: the reverence, worship, and awe of something ultimate.[41]

---

[39]Friedrich Nietzsche, "European Nihilism," in *The Nietzsche Reader*, trans. Keith Ansell Pearson and Duncan Large (Oxford: Blackwell, 2006), 386.
[40]Michel Foucault, *The Archaeology of Knowledge and the Discourse on Language*, trans. A. M. Sheridan Smith (New York: Pantheon, 1972), 211.
[41]See, for example, Roy Clouser, *The Myth of Religious Neutrality*, rev. ed. (South Bend, IN: Notre Dame University Press, 2005), 24.

Even avowed atheists, at the end of the day, still have to come up with some sort of placeholder for the God of Abraham, Isaac, Jacob, and Jesus Christ in order to explain how the universe got here. For instance, what is Richard Dawkins's reverential treatment of Darwinian natural selection if not an attempt to suggest that something other than the God of the Bible—in this case, the laws of biology—is absolutely necessary to explain the origin, diversity, and beauty we find on planet earth and in the cosmos? Throughout the course of human civilization, what has been seen as ultimate has been worshipped. And that which is worshipped always makes demands upon its followers. In that sense then, everyone is religious. Dawkins's god may not be personal, but his worldview bears the marks of religious fervor. He has a list of orthodoxies and is quick to cast out heretics from his midst. Despite earnest attempts to do away with religion in modern times, it cannot and will not go away. Faith shapes culture. It is simply a matter of which belief system a society chooses and how effectively that faith nourishes the animating impulses of a people.

There is, then, a crucially important difference between institutionalized religion and religion itself. Institutionalized religion focuses on organization, church hierarchy, bodies of formalized doctrine, and ecclesiastical structure. We can safely say that this aspect of religion is in grave circumstances—particularly in its Christian expressions—in the secular West. But the religious impulse itself is fundamental to the human condition. For this reason, despite the best efforts of those who would wish to stamp it out, religion will never go away. The question before us then is, which religious expression/identity will capture the minds of this generation? Goethe put it soberingly well: "The destiny of any nation at any given time depends on the opinions of its young men under twenty-five."

## Wars of Religion: Damage to Christian Credibility in the Public Square

To raise the question of the declining fortunes of institutional Christianity is, of course, to invite a much, much larger question: Why was the Christian religion abandoned in the first place by the leading intellectuals and cultural elites on the Continent? Although the process of secularization is a well-worn tale for some, the story bears repeating. Christian apologists describe secularization (i.e., the removal of dominant religious ideas and symbols from the public sphere) as a reaction against traditional religion.[42] While this is certainly a part of the big picture, there is another way to look at things. Simply put, secularism became plausible in light of certain events in seventeenth- and eighteenth-century Europe.

The first event worth mentioning involves Savonarola's attempt at reform in late fifteenth-century Florence. Denouncing the corruption and the worldliness of the church, the Dominican friar called for a political revolution based upon moral and spiritual reform. He condemned the art, culture, and literature that flourished in the time of Lorenzo the Magnificent. In his now infamous "Bonfire of the Vanities," Savonarola sought to purify the church by banning, destroying, and/or burning Renaissance art, secular books, game tables, chess tables, and literary texts related to humanist thought. Upon the death of Lorenzo, Savonarola and the political party he inspired rose to power and repudiated the contemporary Italian culture in a radical attempt at national holiness. Their requirements for morality were harsh, but they justified their actions by claiming that what they were building was a Christian nation. But Savonarola's preaching failed to inspire the nation to repent or rally to his cause. He received a condemnation from Rome for claiming prophetic powers for himself and was eventually burned at the stake by Alexander VI.

Niccolò Machiavelli took special note of Savonarola's inability to reform Italy both morally and politically. For the author of *The Prince*, attempts to change culture by first appealing to holiness and right living paled in comparison to the more persuasive method of a quartered army. "If Moses, Cyrus, Theseus, and Romulus had had no weapons, they could never have imposed their institutions on their peoples for so long." "In our own times," Machiavelli averred, "there is the example of Fra Girolamo Savonarola, who collapsed with all of his new ordinances as soon as the people ceased to believe

---

[42]For an excellent summary of the process of secularization, see Peter Berger, *The Sacred Canopy* (Garden City, NY: Doubleday, 1967), 105–25.

in him; he had no way of keeping the backsliders in line or of converting the doubters."[43] What mattered for the prince, Machiavelli
concluded, was not religious zeal but the power to enforce one's will
on others. As a result, those who follow in Machiavelli's train view
the church as gravitating to one of two extremes: it is either corrupt
or harshly moralistic. In either case, the law of parsimony reveals
what really matters when it comes to governance: the sword. The
church's distinctives, derived from divine revelation, thus do not play
a meaningful role in government. This point of view increasingly
came to be regarded as "realism."

The sixteenth and seventeenth centuries turned out to be an
unmitigated disaster for the reputation of the church's engagement
with culture. The French Wars of Religion (1562–1598), with their
mixture of Protestant and Catholic intrigue, proved that arguments
over theological orthodoxy and attempts to purge heresy make for
dangerous domestic policy. Even at the level of popular culture, the
St. Bartholomew's Day massacre still lives on in infamy. A failed
assassination attempt on Protestant leader Gaspard de Coligny turned
into a mass slaughter against Huguenot (Calvinist) men, women,
and children. In the weeks after August 24, 1572, the city of Paris
devolved into anarchy.

Despite recent Marxist attempts to portray the French Wars of
Religion as little more than socioeconomic class warfare, the evidence
resists interpretations that sweep away the origins of these conflicts
in worldviews. As Mack P. Holt contends in his contribution to the
Cambridge New Approaches to European History, the conflagration
is best understood as having religious roots, with "religion" being
defined not only as mere theological doctrines, but also the complex
sociological entailments and group interests that result from what
people believe.[44] Thus, the question became, who (i.e., which inter-

---

[43]Niccolò Machiavelli, *The Prince*, trans. Robert M. Adams (New York: Norton, 1977), 18.

[44]Accordingly, Holt explains, "In these terms, Protestants and Catholics alike in the sixteenth
century each viewed the other as pollutants of their own particular notion of the body social,
as threats to their own conception of ordered society. When a mob of Catholic winegrowers
set fire to a barn in Beaune where a clandestine group of Protestants had observed the Lord's
Supper in both kinds on Easter Sunday of 1561, for example, their actions went far beyond
an expression of discontent and intolerance of the Calvinist theology of the Eucharist. Those

est group) has the right to define culture? And even with all of the complex sociological data taken into consideration, there can be no denying that people in the sixteenth and seventeenth centuries dealt with such weighty matters through their worldview. Inevitably, worldviews deal with ultimate questions; and ultimate questions inexorably result in religious commitments. And no one can deny that religion precipitated or aggravated much of the violence.

In Germany, in the wake of the Protestant Reformation, Martin Luther himself had some difficulty explaining how one could be free from the dictates of the papacy when it came to matters of faith, but still beholden to the princes when it came to the matter of civil obedience. To resolve the paradox, Luther penned an essay entitled *On Temporal Authority, and the Extent to Which It Should Be Obeyed*. In it, he proposed a "two kingdoms" view. The church, he argued, knows no law but the love of the gospel as the people of God; it is the colony of heaven residing temporarily on earth. The other kingdom, however, belongs to secular rulers. Arguing from Romans 13, the Reformer claimed that earthly government is the purview of sinners. Still, God uses the sword of the state to keep law and order and instill terror in those who do evil. These two kingdoms, however, can never be conflated. They are, in this world at least, separate.[45]

With this "two kingdoms" model, Luther introduced a terrible conundrum into Western thought. Although the Reformation accelerated the dissolution of the medieval synthesis between church and

---

winegrowers were cleansing the body social of the pollutant of Protestantism, and in the process, preventing a dangerous and threatening cancer from spreading. By setting ablaze the barn where that pollution had taken place, they were purifying by fire the social space that those Protestants had desecrated." Mack P. Holt, *The French Wars of Religion, 1562–1629*, 2nd ed., New Approaches to European History (New York: Cambridge University Press, 2005), 2.
[45]Luther wrote: "If anyone attempted to rule the world by the gospel and to abolish all temporal law and sword on the plea that all are baptized and Christian, and that, according to the gospel, there shall be among them no law or sword—or need for either—pray tell me, friend, what would he be doing? He would be loosing the ropes and chains of the savage wild beasts and letting them bite and mangle everyone, meanwhile insisting that they were harmless, tame, and gentle creatures; but I would have the proof in my wounds. Just so would the wicked under the name of Christian abuse evangelical freedom, carry on their rascality, and insist they were Christians subject to neither law nor sword as some are already raving and ranting." "Temporal Authority," in *Martin Luther's Basic Theological Writings*, ed. Timothy Lull (Minneapolis, MN: Fortress, 1989), 665.

state and opened up the possibility for religious freedom, Luther simultaneously (and quite unwittingly) sowed the seeds for the demise of religion's role as a source of cultural authority. Certainly Luther could not have imagined a Germany in which the princes would no longer take stock of their Christian heritage. Despite his theorizing, Luther's contemporaries and successors strived to govern on the basis of theological distinctions. And by doing so, both Protestant and Catholic forces at work inside Germany presided over one of the darkest chapters in European history.

On the heels of the Reformation, the Thirty Years War (1618–1648) further besmirched the reputation of religion's involvement in matters of the state. The war scarred the German landscape. Mercenary armies were set loose on the people, resulting in devastating population losses by the end of the war.[46]

## The Plausibility of Secularism

Clearly, during the wars of religion, Christianity became terribly distorted as compared to the witness of the early church, when Christians gained social capital and credibility in the Roman Empire. But is it any wonder in the wake of this experience why the cultural elite of Europe would want to revisit the centrality of Christianity as the defining worldview for European culture? So, when Voltaire criticized, against this backdrop, what he viewed as the all-too-Pollyannish worldview that "God is working everything out for the greater good," we can better understand the energy behind his dictum *Écrasez l'infâme*— "Crush the infamous!" by which he meant religious superstition.[47] And when Immanuel Kant declared, "*Sapere aude!* 'Have courage to use your own reason!'—that is the motto of Enlightenment," we

---

[46]For a chart showing the population losses in Germany, see Mark Kishlansky, Patrick Geary, and Patricia O'Brien, *Civilization in the West*, 5th ed. (New York: Person Longman), accessed March 30, 2008, http://wps.ablongman.com/wps/media/objects/262/268312/art/figures/KISH312.jpg.

[47]Voltaire wrote *Candide* as a send-up of Gottfried Wilhelm Leibniz's response to the problem of evil. Leibniz attempted to argue, on the basis of modal logic, that the current world is the greatest possible world. Voltaire often closed his correspondence with this as a peroration. Its usage is often applied to the Christian religion or clergy. See Voltaire, *Letters on England*, trans. Leonard Tancock (New York: Penguin, 1980).

184 RECOVERING CLASSIC EVANGELICALISM

can see the impetus behind this declaration of cultural independence from the dictates of the clergy and the theologians.[48]

In the English-speaking world, no philosopher levied a more trenchant critique of theology's role in forming government than Thomas Hobbes (1588–1679). Hobbes's worldview took shape in the light of the English Civil War, which, once again, was largely religious in nature. Hobbes feared Catholicism's unification of church and state because it centralized power. But he just as strongly worried that the Protestant doctrine of the priesthood of believers would lead to anarchy. For this reason, the author of *Leviathan* sought to remove political questions from the arena of theological debates and turned them into a science of common sense and natural justice. And so political "science" as we know it was born. Columbia University professor Mark Lilla sums up Hobbes's contribution:

> Before Hobbes, those who sought to refute political theology kept finding themselves driven deeper into it as they tried to solve the many puzzles of God, man, and world. Hobbes showed the way out by doing something ingenious: he changed the subject.
>
> The aim of *Leviathan* is to attack and destroy the entire tradition of political theology, what Hobbes called the "Kingdom of Darkness." Yet the treatise begins, not with theology or politics, God or kings, but with physiology. Specifically, it begins with an exploration of the human eye and how it perceives the world. On the very first page of his work Hobbes makes an implicit profession of faith: that to understand religion and politics, we need not understand anything about God; we need only understand man as we find him, a body alone in the world.[49]

---

[48]The full context for the quote is as follows: "Enlightenment is man's release from self-incurred tutelage. Tutelage is man's inability to make use of his understanding without direction from another. Self-incurred is the tutelage when its cause lies not in the lack of reason but in the lack of resolution and courage to use it without direction from another. Sapere aude! 'Have courage to use your own reason!'—that is the motto of enlightenment." Immanuel Kant, *Foundations of the Metaphysics of Morals and What Is Enlightenment?*, trans. Lewis White Beck (Indianapolis: Bobbs-Merrill, 1959), 85.

[49]Mark Lilla, *The Stillborn God: Religion, Politics, and the Modern West* (New York: Alfred A. Knopf), 75–76.

## Hell above Ground

Hobbes's dream to relegate the study of politics to the study of the brute realities of man's physical existence known through the vehicle of modern science, however, left the human being vulnerable to any ideology predicated upon appeals to scientism. By the end of the twentieth century, estimates for the number of innocents killed under the auspices of governments run by secular utopian (and often antireligious) ideologies ranged between one hundred million and two hundred million persons. The First and Second World Wars, Mao's Revolution, Stalin's slaughter of innocents, and the killing fields of Cambodia clearly were not conflicts fought upon religious grounds, but resulted in horrors completely out of proportion to the wars of religion in the sixteenth and seventeenth centuries. As George Steiner wrote in his 1970 T. S. Eliot Memorial Lectures, Voltaire predicted that mass brutality from authoritarian rulers or despots would come to an end with the demise of religion's influence in the public square. Voltaire could not have been more wrong, says Steiner. On the contrary, "indifference" on the subject of religious truth breeds "intolerance."[50] Steiner continues, "The epilogue to belief, the passage of religious belief into hollow convention, seems to be a more dangerous process than the philosophes anticipated." In place of a literal hell to punish those who did evil in this life, Steiner observes, modern ideologies relocated hell above ground.[51] The twentieth century bears ample witness to the results of this new barbarism. The problem, then, appears not to be religious ideas about man, but the man himself.

In this light, postmodernism must be seen primarily as a protest against these totalizing metanarratives about reality that ruled the modern world, what Jean-François Lyotard calls "crimes against humanity."[52] The postmodern project attempts to subvert, resist, and undermine ideologies that oppress groups who live on the boundaries

---

[50]George Steiner, *In Bluebeard's Castle: Some Notes toward the Redefinition of Culture* (New Haven, CT; London: Faber, 1971), 47.

[51]Ibid., 56.

[52]See, for example, Jean-François Lyotard, "Defining the Postmodern," accessed October 9, 2012, http://philosophyatalbertus.wordpress.com/assignments/lyotard-defining-the-postmodern/.

of culture on the basis that there is some independent and rationally verifiable means of telling human beings how things must be for everyone at all times in all places. The concept of deconstruction, therefore, offers a method whereby the imperious power structures of a text may be undermined, whether that text is *The Communist Manifesto*, *Mein Kampf*, or even the Bible. As philosopher John Caputo has put it, "Whenever deconstruction finds a nutshell—a secure axiom or a pithy maxim—the very idea is to crack it open and disturb this tranquility."[53]

As such, a feeling of irritation characterizes postmodern life in the West. Certitude is in short supply. Despite this set of conditions, thoroughgoing nihilism, both intuitively and practically, seems to be very difficult to practice. Not even Nietzsche managed to do it!

I remember several years ago when US National Public Radio host Renee Montagne noted with incredulity during an interview that rock performer David Bowie's 2002 album actually had the theme of hope, in contrast to the starkness and bleakness of Bowie's previous recording catalog. The artist responded with a reference to the then fifty-five-year-old's young family: "I think I have to imbue my songs with a certain sense of optimism now, more than I ever did before, because I have a child."[54] Indeed, it is very difficult being a nihilist with a two-year-old running around the house. Optimism, hope, and love: these are categories that are metaphysical in nature. They speak of transcendence and the permanence of things beyond the mere physicality of the world.

But despite such trends, something of substance is most certainly necessary to respond to this interest in transcendence. Toward this end I would like to reflect on the future for both natural law and the church's witness in this period after the crisis of faith in religious institutions. There is great hope at this time, despite feelings of apocalyptic gloom in many quarters. But the hope will not come from trying to make peace with theologies of absence or from concessions

---

[53] John D. Caputo, *Deconstruction in a Nutshell: A Conversation with Jacques Derrida* (Bronx, NY: Fordham University Press, 1996), 32.
[54] Renee Montagne, "Interview with David Bowie," *Morning Edition*, August 28, 2002, accessed January 9, 2008, http://www.npr.org/templates/story/story.php?storyId=1149058.

to cultural relativism. For as Kierkegaard once averred, "He who marries the spirit of the age is likely to be a widower in the next." Interest in the transcendence of human life and a religious instinct by themselves, of course, do not automatically translate into good news for traditional religious structures. New practices in traditional Christian thought and witness are needed.

## Hope for Rapprochement between Natural Law and Theologies of Revelation

Following Carl Henry's aversion to natural law strategies for engagement, which I reference in chapter 2, I confess that I have been of late something of a skeptic when it comes to the persuasive power of natural law in matters related to public square issues.[55] Indeed, Henry's 1989 Rutherford Lectures, later published as *Toward a Recovery of Christian Belief*, sought to defend presuppositionalism contra evidentialism as its main and unswerving emphasis.[56] Still, Henry's presence on the board of *First Things* and his glad acceptance of all manner of data that corroborated the Christian worldview showed that at the level of *reaching culture*, he was willing and energetic to partner with anyone who could adhere to core biblical axioms. Before I go any further, however, let me make a disclaimer. I certainly have no qualms with Robert P. George's definition of natural law in *First Things*:

> Natural law is nothing other than a doctrine of public reasons that . . . "would command a universal consensus under ideal conditions of discourse and meanwhile are available to, and could be accepted by, anyone who is willing and able to give them fair and adequate attention." These reasons, embraced and proclaimed by the Catholic Church, can be, and have been, affirmed by people who know nothing of, or do not accept, Jewish or Christian revelation or the authority of the Church or any other institution. Respect for these reasons as reasons accounts for the honored place of dialectic in the tradition of natural law theory and the emphasis of contemporary natural law theorists on full and fair debate in

[55] Carl F. H. Henry, "Natural Law and a Nihilistic Culture," *First Things*, January 1995, 55–60, accessed February 26, 2002, http://www.firstthings. com/ftissues/ft9501/articles/henry.html.
[56] Carl F. H. Henry, *Toward a Recovery of Christian Belief* (Wheaton, IL: Crossway, 1990).

the forums of democracy on such issues as abortion, euthanasia, embryonic stem-cell research, human cloning, and marriage.[57]

My reservations are more practical than epistemological at this stage. In sum, here are a few:

First, Leo Strauss, perhaps the most notable natural law theorist of the twentieth century, expressed a genuine reticence about the ability of natural law to settle questions about morality without getting into debates over theology and revelation. As Alex Burns reflects in the *Harvard Political Review*, "For Strauss, nature was supposed to be a place of 'pure and whole questioning,' not a 'defense against assaults on convention.'"[58] The followers of Strauss see themselves as taking natural law and applying Occam's razor. What is left on the cutting room floor are the moral issues near and dear to the agendas of most Christians—whether evangelical *or* Roman Catholic. If Straussians doubt the potential of the natural law approach to solve matters like the marriage debate, it raises the question as to whether this is simply an internal dispute in the natural law tradition or a genuine fissure in this method of cultural engagement.

Second, it appears that a growing number of public intellectuals and pundits are wary of the close connection between the leading proponents of natural law and various faith traditions. This phenomenon was nowhere more obvious than in the reception of a massive report by the President's Council on Bioethics, which was stacked with prominent natural law advocates. Writing for *The New Republic*, Steven Pinker, *L'enfant terrible* among secularists, observed regarding President Bush's Council on Bioethics and its magnificent report on human dignity:

> Though [Bioethics Council Chair Leon] Kass has jawboned his version of bioethics into governmental deliberation and policy, it is not just a personal obsession of his but part of a larger move-

---

[57]Robert P. George, "Public Morality, Public Reason," *First Things*, November 2006, accessed September 29, 2008, http://www.firstthings.com/article.php3?id_article=5344.

[58]Alex Burns, "Who Was Leo Strauss?," *HPROnline*, accessed, http://hprsite.squarespace .com/who-was-leo-strauss/; see also Anne Norton, *Leo Strauss and the Politics of American Empire* (New Haven, CT: Yale University Press, 2005).

ment, one that is increasingly associated with Catholic institutions. (In 2005, Kass relinquished the Council chairmanship to Edmund Pellegrino, an 85-year-old medical ethicist and former president of the Catholic University of America.) Everyone knows about the Bush administration's alliance with evangelical Protestantism. But the pervasive Catholic flavoring of the Council, particularly its Dignity report, is at first glance puzzling. In fact, it is part of a powerful but little-known development in American politics, recently documented by Damon Linker in his book *The Theocons*.

Since episodes of divine revelation seem to have decreased in recent millennia, the problem becomes who will formulate and interpret these standards. Most of today's denominations are not up to the task: Evangelical Protestantism is too anti-intellectual, and mainstream Protestantism and Judaism too humanistic. The Catholic Church, with its long tradition of scholarship and its rock-solid moral precepts, became the natural home for this movement, and the journal *First Things*, under the leadership of Father Richard John Neuhaus, its mouthpiece. Catholicism now provides the intellectual muscle behind a movement that embraces socially conservative Jewish and Protestant intellectuals as well. When Neuhaus met with Bush in 1998 as he was planning his run for the presidency, they immediately hit it off.

Three of the original Council members (including Kass) are board members of *First Things*, and Neuhaus himself contributed an essay to the Dignity volume. In addition, five other members have contributed articles to *First Things* over the years. The concept of dignity is natural ground on which to build an obstructionist bioethics. An alleged breach of dignity provides a way for third parties to pass judgment on actions that are knowingly and willingly chosen by the affected individuals. It thus offers a moralistic justification for expanded government regulation of science, medicine, and private life. And the Church's franchise to guide people in the most profound events of their lives—birth, death, and reproduction—is in danger of being undermined when biomedicine scrambles the rules. It's not surprising, then, that "dignity" is a recurring theme in Catholic doctrine: The word appears more than

100 times in the 1997 edition of the Catechism and is a leitmotif in the Vatican's recent pronouncements on biomedicine.[59]

Pinker's assessment is interesting not because it is right—or even insightful (it's not)—but because of its gamesmanship. Try as you might to persuade an audience that your position on human dignity, for example, is derived purely from natural law, as long as you bear the stigmata of being a Christian, whether Roman Catholic or evangelical, or, in Kass's case, Jewish, you might just as well go ahead and cite Scripture passages in support of your position while you're at it. The connection will inevitably be made. It is guilt by association to be certain—and we all know that it's a logical fallacy.

Third, the natural law approach to public policy may, at times, appear to be in danger of denying the phenomenological proof that although truth may be objective, knowledge is always personal. This, of course, was the key insight of the twentieth-century chemist-turned-philosopher Michael Polanyi, who argued that we often embrace truth having originally begun with passions and pretheoretical faith commitments.[60] As my colleague Jimmy Davis has argued, sometimes those presuppositions can act like windows and point us in the direction of truth when it conforms with the preponderance of the evidence. At other points, they may be blinders, narrowing our field of vision so greatly that we cannot accurately see the big picture.[61] Polanyi's doctrine of personal knowledge serves as a much-needed explanatory filter for how public policy is cast and explained. At times, a preexisting belief might consider a natural law argument (e.g., maintaining the definition of marriage as a one-flesh relationship of the reproductive type) and be strengthened because it adds an important set of evidences to the belief. This would suggest that sometimes natural law might function more in a ministerial role to

---

[59]Stephen Pinker, "The Stupidity of Dignity: Conservative Bioethics' Latest, Most Dangerous Ploy," *The New Republic*, May 28, 2008, accessed May 13, 2008, http://www.tnr.com /story_print.html?id=d8731cf4-e87b-4d88-b7e7-f5059cd0bfbd.

[60]Michael Polanyi, *Personal Knowledge: Towards a Post-Critical Philosophy* (Chicago: University of Chicago Press, 1958), 249ff.

[61]Jimmy Davis, "Faith and Learning," in *Shaping a Christian Worldview*, ed. David S. Dockery and Gregory Alan Thornbury (Nashville, TN: B&H, 2008), 136ff.

encourage the faithful that they have not lost their minds, rather than in the magisterial way that it is sometimes envisioned.

These reservations seemingly received further confirmation recently in an exchange between John Wilson and Michael Novak with respect to the latter's central arguments in his book *No One Sees God*. Wilson's review of the volume examined what he considered to be a certain set of "muddles" in Novak's line of thinking. On the one hand, Novak forcefully counters proponents of the new atheism by defending both the rationality and the power of traditional proofs for God's existence. On the other hand, notes Wilson, Novak concedes later in the book that "neither the atheist nor the believer sees God. Both must live in darkness." How can the proofs for God's existence be compelling one second, Wilson queries, while later Novak takes it all back by saying that we all have our walls of doubt, and that the playing field is leveled between the atheist and theist when it comes to epistemic certitude.[62] Had one of the most articulate defenders of natural theology entered a blind alley?

At first, I thought Wilson had caught Novak in a real bind. That is, until I read Novak's rejoinder. The noted Catholic philosopher made no attempt to brush aside Wilson's critique. He responded with something far more powerful: epistemological honesty. Novak did not back off of the explanatory philosophical power of the theistic proofs for a moment. But he simultaneously acknowledged the tacit dimension to our knowledge of God in a manner similar, in fact, to Polanyi. In so doing, he acknowledged—with remarkable candor—that even though we might admit the rational validity of an argument, there is yet a universe left to explore—that of the heart. In the world of the heart, there is a difference between out-and-out doubt and what Novak calls the "dark knowledge of 'the cloud of unknowing.'"[63] He spoke movingly about his own mother, who suffered through an intense wilderness of doubt in her pilgrimage with God. It was a very Pascalian approach to the issue.

---

[62] John Wilson, "Out of Darkness," *National Review*, December 1, 2009, accessed, http://nrd.nationalreview.com/article/?q=ZjZlYjZkOWYzN2MxMzRjODQwMGZhMjk4NGGJmMWE0MmQ=.

[63] Michael Novak, "No One Agrees about God," *National Review*, December 15, 2009, 3–4.

Around the same time, J. Budziszewski published his essay "Natural Law Revealed" in *First Things*. In it, the University of Texas professor spoke eloquently of the ways in which the book of Revelation affirms and narrates the mirror of nature. The typical debates between nominalism and realism were temporarily set aside. And for the first time, I began to be hopeful that Protestants and Catholics really might be able to move beyond their epistemological impasse on the matter of natural theologies versus theologies of revelation. Timothy George, addressing the matter of Calvin and natural law, spoke of a mode of discourse with which all adherents of the Great Tradition can agree:

> . . . the option of an intentional community of faith set over against its environing culture, a company of men and women who bear faithful witness in the name of him whose crown rights can never be assimilated to the kingdoms and societies of this world. . . . I submit that Christians today can best shape the public policy of their society by refusing to reduce the faith to the religion of the *polis*, whether that religion be based on natural or positive law.[64]

Nothing could restore the fortunes of historic Christianity more in postmodern times than a unified thesis of public reasons for traditional morality complemented by an authentic recognition that there is an existential dimension for why people disagree with our views on marriage, abortion, and other related life issues. Untangling that ball of yarn will require all hands on deck engaged in the effort, combined with a singular authenticity in the church's behavior and practice before a watching world that is very cynical of the claims of the church.

## Hope for the Church after the Crisis of Faith in Institutional Religion

Such distrust, however, certainly is not new—at least not for the church in Europe. In America, Christians living in rapidly changing cultural conditions have much to learn from the past. For example, as

---

[64]Timothy George, "A Response to Susan E. Schreiner," in *A Preserving Grace: Protestants, Catholics, and Natural Law*, ed. Michael Cromartie (Grand Rapids: Eerdmans, 1997), 83.

the Protestant church faced the prospects of life in Germany immediately after the Holocaust, it had to face up to the grim reality that its own response in opposing Hitler had been too little, too late. Much of the blame lay at the feet of the Lutheran church, which was easily co-opted into becoming the Reich church. As heroic as the Confessing Church movement had been, the reality was that the movement against Hitler led by church leaders such as Karl Barth and Dietrich Bonhoeffer had been a rear-guard action. With the notable and admirable exception of strong resistance from Roman Catholic territories in Germany, most German Christians welcomed the rise of the führer. They did so because, as the journalist Milton Mayer so powerfully pointed out in his extensive series of postwar interviews with German citizens, "they thought they were free."[65]

This state of affairs was not lost on Bonhoeffer himself. He commented to his friend Eberhard Bethge about the culture now thrust upon the West, "We are now moving to a completely religionless time; people as they are now simply cannot be religious anymore." The traditional structures and hierarchies of the church had failed to stop genocide. Writing from his cell at Tegel Prison in May 1944 to his godson on the occasion of his baptism, Bonhoeffer reflected:

> We have grown up with the experience of our parents and grandparents that a man can and must plan, develop, and shape his own life, and that life has a purpose, about which a man must make up his mind, and which he must then pursue with all of his strength. But we have learnt by experience that we cannot plan even for the coming day, that what we have built up is being destroyed overnight, and that our life, in contrast to that of our parents, has become formless or even fragmentary. In spite of that, I can only say that I have no wish to live in any other time than our own, even though it is so inconsiderate of our outward well-being. We realize more clearly than formerly that the world lies under the wrath and grace of God. We read in Jer. 45: "Thus says the Lord: Behold what I have built I am breaking down, and what I have planted I am plucking up. . . . And do you seek great things for yourself? Seek

---

[65]Milton Mayer, *They Thought They Were Free: The Germans, 1933–45*, 2nd ed. (Chicago: University of Chicago Press, 1966).

them not; for, behold, I am bringing evil upon all flesh; . . . but I will give your life as a prize of war in all places you may go." If we can save our souls unscathed out of the wreckage of our material possessions, let us be satisfied with that. If the Creator destroys his own handiwork, what right have we to lament the destruction of ours? It will be the task of our generation, not to "seek great things," but to save and preserve our souls out of chaos, and to realize that it is the only thing we can carry as a "prize" from the burning building. "Keep your heart with all vigilance; for from it flows the spring of life" (Prov. 4:23).[66]

Bonhoeffer understood that Christians would have to inhabit an entirely different type of existence if the church in the postwar environment was to once again truly be what God wanted it to be. Rather than making its plans on the basis of what would be the best "strategy for engagement" to improve its position with the society that emerged after the Nazis, Bonhoeffer believed that the spiritual power for God's people to be salt and light would have to be given back to them by God himself. This modern martyr saw a new cultural environment ensuing in which the church would have to once again become like its Lord Jesus, who came into the world not to be served, but to serve and give up his life for the many. The church, like Jesus himself, must become the guileless "man for others." As the apostle Peter reminded a persecuted group of first-century Christians, followers of Jesus should "live such good lives among the pagans that, though they accuse you of doing wrong, they may see your good deeds and glorify God on the day he visits us" (1 Peter 2:12, NIV). Bonhoeffer realized that rather than enjoying a position of privilege as elites in a cultural hierarchy, "The church stands, not at the boundaries [of culture] where human powers give out, but in the middle of the village." We must not seek great things for ourselves, Bonhoeffer maintained, but rather seek the welfare of the actual communities in which individual churches find themselves. Put differently, there must be a transparent goodness and way of life practiced by the

---

[66]Dietrich Bonhoeffer, *Letters and Papers from Prison*, enlarged ed., ed. Eberhard Bethge, trans. Reginald Fuller et al. (New York: Touchstone, 1997), 297.

church that can be easily detected by the neighbors of local Christian communities. Somehow, everyone—both those who profess Christ and those who do not—should be able to see that in some very real sense, the church is there for them and their children.

In the Sermon on the Mount, Jesus told his disciples that the meek will inherit the earth. They must not seek great things for their own benefit, but rather seek the good of the communities in which individual churches and faith-based organizations find themselves. After the Holocaust, Christianity could never again afford to run the danger of being regarded as just another ideology or party to the prevailing will to power. Rather, the church, as Tim Keller of Redeemer Church in New York City has put it, must be "in the city, for the city," seeking common ground: the health of our communities, families, and neighborhoods. Regaining the trust of one's neighbors is the first step to building cultural credibility. Christians who invest themselves wholeheartedly in the local contexts where they are planted—and this not for merely utilitarian reasons—see themselves, said Bonhoeffer, as "belonging wholly to the world." In their example, he wrote his friend Bethge, "Christ is no longer [merely] an object of religion, but rather something entirely different: Lord of the universe."[67]

And let us not forget that this was the way a small, ragtag, imperially persecuted group of Jesus's followers effected change in the second, third, and fourth centuries. As sociologist Rodney Stark has demonstrated, the success of the early Christians began with their theological convictions. Here was a group of people who actually believed that the God who created the universe subjected himself to weakness by becoming a human being and opened himself to sharing, and taking upon himself, the sufferings common to humanity. "For God so loved the world" was not an esoteric philosophy of some sort. As the Gospel of John so memorably puts it, "The Word became flesh and dwelt among us" (John 1:14). When earthquakes, famines, race riots, and plagues swept through communities, the early Christians nursed those with no hope back to health. In time, the evident

[67]Ibid., 281.

goodness of Christians in meeting human needs had a cumulative effect on Roman culture. For example, they stayed behind in cities like Antioch to care for the sick and dying who were abandoned by the cultural elites wealthy enough to flee the city to avoid the spread of disease or social calamity. The people left behind began to believe that maybe this message of Jesus really was true. And thus, over time, the world of Caesar became the world of Christ. As Stark concludes: "What Christians gave to their converts was their humanity" in the midst of a brutish pagan culture. "In this sense virtue was its own reward."[68] Stark also describes the effect of Christians on their communities in the midst of social crises:

> [Antioch was] a city filled with misery, danger, fear, despair, and hatred. A city where the average family lived a squalid life in filthy and cramped quarters, where at least half of the children died at birth or during infancy, and where most of the children who lived lost at least one parent before reaching maturity. A city filled with hatred and fear rooted in intense ethnic antagonisms and exacerbated by a constant stream of strangers. A city so lacking in stable networks of attachments that petty incidents could prompt mob violence. A city where crime flourished and the streets were dangerous at night. And, perhaps above all, a city repeatedly smashed by cataclysmic catastrophes: where a resident could literally expect to be homeless from time to time, providing that he or she was among the survivors. . . .
>
> Christianity revitalized life in Greco-Roman cities by providing new norms and new kinds of social relationship able to cope with many urgent urban problems. To cities filled with the homeless and the impoverished, Christianity offered charity as well as hope. To cities filled with newcomers and strangers, Christianity offered an immediate basis for attachments. To cities filled with orphans and widows, Christianity provided a new and expanded sense of family. To cities torn by violent ethnic strife, Christianity offered a new basis for social solidarity. And to cities faced with epidemics, fires, and earthquakes, Christianity offered effective nursing services.[69]

---

[68]Rodney Stark, *The Rise of Christianity* (San Francisco: HarperCollins, 1997), 215.
[69]Ibid., 161.

This sort of doctrine and behavior made Christianity unique among the world religions. In stark relief to the other great mystery religion of the first few centuries AD, Mithraism, Christianity was not a "power religion." In Greco-Roman mythology, Mithras killed the bull Taurus, which gave him the right to rule the stars and control the seasons. Jesus of Nazareth came to die, but conquered death through his resurrection, which made him the Lord of life instead of death.[70]

Engaging our communities in the way described above, however, must not be mistaken as a call for some sort of quietism. Certainly, Bonhoeffer was no shrinking violet. He did, after all, openly oppose the Nazi regime and actively sought to undermine Hitler—to the point of involving himself in a plot to assassinate the führer. Certainly, evil must be stopped when it threatens the lives of the innocent and the defenseless. This stance characterized the Christian position from the early centuries, as believers opposed the brutality of the Roman gladiatorial games, infanticide, and the horrendous treatment of women in the ancient world.[71] But at its best, Christianity has affected the prevailing culture through the solidarity of its community and the social presence of its people. And so, for example, when a nonbeliever walked into a celebration of the Lord's Supper at a Christian gathering in the early centuries, he or she witnessed a remarkable phenomenon taking place. Members of the privileged classes, for example, would be serving the agape meal to members

---

[70]There is a good reason for the starkly different reactions of Islam and Christianity to cultural challenges. There are, after all, two very distinct theological worldviews at work. Islam stresses the power, perfection, glory, and unassailability of its religion. Allah is a solitary and even arbitrary sovereign. His word, the Qur'an, was purportedly delivered perfectly to Muhammad in Arabic and thus is untranslatable in any other language. According to Islam, Muhammad cannot be maligned in even the slightest way without swift justice. For a fundamentalist Muslim, all blasphemers must die. This is not the case with Christianity. God is a Trinity of loving persons, living in community. His followers are encouraged to translate his Word into every tongue known to man. In the person of Jesus of Nazareth, God became flesh, and associated himself with all sorts of unsavory characters—prostitutes, tax collectors, and even a murderer-turned-apostle like Paul. And most importantly, Christ Jesus "did not count equality with God a thing to be grasped, but emptied himself, by taking the form of a servant . . . . he humbled himself" (Phil. 2:6–8). Indeed, he opened himself up to all manner of blasphemy, humiliation, and torture—even to the point of death on a cross. He welcomed all of these in order to save sinners because he loved them.

[71]See, online, the *Kairos Journal* occasional paper, "Legatees of a Great Inheritance: How Judeo-Christian Tradition Shapes the West," PDF.

198 RECOVERING CLASSIC EVANGELICALISM

of the slave class—a very powerful image that repudiated the hierarchical class structure of Roman society.[72]

## Conclusion

The coming years will require renewed efforts that demonstrate the attractiveness of traditional Christian thought and practice in ways that are winsome both intellectually and existentially. Our cultural strategy must equally focus on both the mind and heart. Historic orthodoxy must be seen to be true intellectually and communally at the same time. As we think about a future for making men moral, we will see that the future of Christianity in Europe and America rests not upon the will to power, but the will to do the good and believe the tradition. If Christianity is to be seriously regarded once again in the West, then the church will have to regain the ground that has been lost over the past five centuries. As important as making the rational argument in favor of Christianity is and will continue to be, the church must realize that the objections that modern persons have to traditional religion are not finally rational. They are emotional, deep-seated, and embedded in individual biographies and family histories. So what evidence for Christian belief can be marshaled under such adverse conditions? The church must return to the materials Paul outlined as the basis for social capital: "love, joy, peace, patience, kindness, goodness, faithfulness, gentleness, and self control." "Against such things," wrote the apostle, "there is no law" (Gal. 5:22–23).

If, however, the prevailing *Zeitgeist* of the twenty-first century is "Show, don't tell," Christians will happily engage in their own project of deconstruction against secularism and respond along Henrynian lines: "Show *and* tell." By demonstrating their faith in tangible ways that anyone can understand, and by articulating *why* they believed in the first place, followers of Jesus have the opportunity to prove that the fabric of society can be held together by traditional religious belief once again. The lifeblood of culture and the flow of moral energy

---

[72]See, for example, Robert M. Grant, *Early Christianity and Society* (San Francisco: Harper & Row, 1977), 130–34; Ray Vander Laan, *In the Dust of the Rabbi* (Grand Rapids: Zondervan, 2006), 109ff.

that keeps a society intact, I believe, rests upon such a recovery.[73] More pointedly, it is crucial that this élan penetrates into the hearts of the coming generation of Britons, Europeans, and Americans.

Which brings to mind Goethe's insight with which we began. So, to restate the question: If religion shapes culture, for Europe, Britain, and America, which religion will it be? Which worldview? Which belief system will capture the imagination of the greater part of the coming generation? And second, what do we stand to lose if the answer to that question is not "Judeo-Christian"? The stakes have never been higher. No words in conclusion could be more fitting than the ones Henry himself spoke at the close of his Rutherford Lectures in Edinburgh:

> The Christian belief system, which the Christian knows to be grounded in divine revelation, is relevant to all of life. For unbelieving multitudes in our times, the recent modern defection from God known in His self revelation has turned the whole of life into shambles. Ours is the first society in modern history to have ventured to erect a civilization on godless foundations; it may well be the last.
>
> . . . even the classic ancient Greek philosophers still warn us through their extant writings that no stable society can be built apart from durable truth and good and that any eclipse of these realities robs human survival of meaning and worth. Their writings are not the last word, however. Echoing from Creation to Calvary to Consummation, God's eternal Word invites a parched humanity to the Well that never runs dry, to the Water of Life that alone truly and fully quenches the thirst of stricken pilgrims.[74]

---

[73]I am employing a definition of culture here first outlined by Johann Herder.

[74]Henry, *Toward a Recovery of Christian Belief*, 114.

# CHAPTER 6

# Evangelicalism Matters

In a recent interview with the *Columbia University Journalism Review*, the celebrated filmmaker Errol Morris speaks about the documentarian's task of helping audiences "rediscover reality." He begins with a consideration of what biography and history are, and how authors write texts about these things. In thinking through the trope of writing about the past with a "beginning-middle-end" methodology, Morris notes something "almost insufferable" about thinking that simply giving the appropriate genre a nod is good enough. No, he concludes, it is not good enough. What people long to know is the gritty specifics about a particular moment in time, a realization that something significant both historically and existentially happened at a previous juncture. He discerns:

> Someone comes up to you and they say, "Well, I'm a post-modernist. I really don't care about truth, truth is subjective, or there are all kinds of different versions of truth: your truth, my truth, someone else's truth." And then so you say to them, "Well, then it doesn't matter to you who pulled the trigger? It doesn't matter to you whether someone committed murder or not or someone in jail is innocent or not? That's just a matter of personal opinion?"
>
> Our intuitions, I believe our intuitions strongly are it does matter. It matters a great deal what happened in the world. You know, our vision is incomplete in every respect. We try to find out about the world by collecting evidence, by thinking about things, by looking at things. Nothing that we ever create is complete, but you try to figure out what our relationship is to reality, to the real world, to what happened, to what transpired. You use every means at your disposal. To me, journalism is—it's an attempt, again, to recover reality. You know, I'm very fond of pointing out to people,

people talk about reenactments, why do you use reenactments. I'd like to point out that reality is reenacted inside of our skulls routinely. That's how we know about the world. We walk around in the world. The world isn't walking around in us. You know, we take in evidence, you know, in our senses, and we try to figure out on the basis of what we learn, what we read, what we see, what's out there. And it may sound horribly grandiloquent and pretentious and pompous, but the issue is what is out there, what is true, what is false, what really happened, and the question of what were people thinking, which is a question that really deeply fascinates me. I think photography does it by creating portraits, too. You take a picture of someone's head, you know, their face, and you sort of look at it. Maybe we're programmed to do this. You look at their face, and you think like, "What are they thinking? What is going on here?"[1]

Morris's instincts about journalism have a refreshing self-authenticating quality about them. At the end of the day, this interrogative really does matter: "What is the case?" Carl F. H. Henry began his career as a journalist, and despite an incredibly distinguished career as a philosopher, theologian, editor, and author, he remained a journalist at heart. Like Tintin in the comics, trying to get to the facts of a good story, Henry approached most issues in this manner:

What is really the case about the Bible? Did the events described within it happen or not?

Or:

What is really the case about the great doctrines of the faith? Do they accurately help us understand the mind of God?

Or:

---

[1]Errol Morris, "Recovering Reality: A Conversation with Errol Morris," *Columbia Journalism Review*, accessed, http://www.cjr.org/video/recovering_reality.php; also available at http://www.youtube.com/watch?v=OHNf4No5WtY.

What is really the case about a lost world? Is Christ the only answer?
Does the Bible contain enough resources to answer the challenges
faced by the present hour? If so, what do we do?

If this way of approaching the matter of evangelical identity
sounds too straight or old-fashioned, well, Carl Henry stands guilty
as charged. After all, we began this book with an invitation to recover
the "lost world" of classic evangelicalism through the thought of the
founder of *Christianity Today* and the leading evangelical theologian of the twentieth century. In that lost world, evangelicals once
believed that evangelicalism held distinct beliefs theoretically and
practically. There was an élan to the movement that prompted a
progressive culture of literary, artistic, and theological ambition
that gave boundless energy to new projects, and sustained existing
institutions. All of this work, however, never lost sight of the goal
that the central task of evangelicalism was, in fact, reality testing
in service of seeing people "born again." It was the age of notable
conversions, with figures such as the late Chuck Colson, convicted
and sent to prison in the Watergate scandal, coming through on the
other side with a life of awe-inspiring service because he knew he was
redeemed. When I was growing up in the 1970s, it seemed as though
every Christian household in America had a copy of Colson's *Born
Again*. It was a poignant reminder to the nation that although the
White House might fail you, the gospel never will.

Carl Henry believed that evangelicalism represented biblical
Christianity in a way that distinguished it from rival secular philosophical systems of thought head-on, Roman Catholicism behind,
Protestant liberalism or neoorthodoxy to the left, and fundamentalism to the right. He committed himself to the task of showing
the strength of evangelicalism at the level of epistemology—in its
presuppositions, claims, and understanding of divine revelation. This
more philosophical bent proved to be what some might call a bad
career move for Henry because his books lacked the popular appeal
of those by figures such as Francis Schaeffer. Henry sometimes wrote
in difficult (although often poetic) prose, further distancing himself
from a generation of legatees to follow him. Although once heralded

as the leading theologian of the evangelical movement, Henry drew considerable antipathy from a younger generation of scholars who sought to move evangelicalism in a different direction than that of propositional revelation.

Despite the slings and arrows of outraged scholarly reception, I have sought in this volume to keep the emphasis where Henry himself placed it. Evangelicalism will never rise above the strength of its epistemological outlook, its confidence in an inerrant Bible and in the promise that through the life and work of Jesus of Nazareth one can "rediscover reality." If it is the case that the Scriptures take us beyond the confines of human experience and usher us into a real world of transcendence—a world of Word and Spirit—then we can have faith that the gospel of that divine Word breaking into the stream of human history and culture can bring hope to the nations and world community. We can put the principalities and powers of this age on notice that God's people will not accept alternatives—whether philosophical, political, economic, or naturalistic—to confidence in the power of (as Pascal so memorably put it) "God, not of the philosophers, but of Abraham, Isaac, Jacob, and Jesus Christ."

In a consultation on the life and work of Carl F. H. Henry at the 2009 annual meeting of the Evangelical Theological Society in New Orleans, a common theme of the impaneled guests—Russell D. Moore, Richard J. Mouw, Craig Mitchell, and Peter Heltzel—was that Henry died a disappointed man. This assessment is almost certainly accurate. If one surveys some of his later volumes—titles like *Twilight of a Great Civilization, Has Democracy Had Its Day?*, and *Christian Countermoves in a Decadent Culture*—the themes are darker, and the prose more severe. In sum, two main worries colored Henry's final phase: (1) evangelical theology was abandoning its key epistemological distinctives; and (2) evangelical institutions and organizations had failed to live up to their potential, choosing instead to protect their own interests rather than contributing to the common evangelical weal.

Speaking at a symposium in his honor at The Southern Baptist Theological Seminary in 1997, Henry addressed both areas of concern in separate lectures: "The Instability of 20th Century Theology" and "A Troubled Conscience Fifty Years Later." Having been in the room at the time, I can affirm that his tone was one of both grace and gentle regret. In fact, these were the last major statements Henry made before succumbing to a terrible spinal stenosis that kept him in agony until his death in 2003. In the former paper, Henry restated his worry that "mediating evangelicals" were exchanging their heritage for a mess of postmodern pottage, and here it is worth quoting him at length.

> Mediating evangelicals are currently seeking linkage with narrative theory. This approach foregoes emphasis on a divinely inspired inerrant Bible; it weakens the insistence on propositional revelation, and it clouds the need to insist on the historically factual character of defining elements of Scripture. At the same time postliberals insist on Christianity's distinctiveness and on Scripture as the "supreme source" of Christian ideas and values. They affirm the centrality of the figure of Jesus in the thought and life of the church. They emphasize the faith response of the Christian community in contrast to 20th century cultural norms.

> For all that, evangelicals would be imprudent to shift interest from Christian orthodoxy to narrative theology. Postliberalism rightly insists that historical criticism cannot with certainty either confirm or disconfirm the factuality of biblical events. But it seems to imply that this situation abandons us to skepticism except for the faith of the Christian community. Evangelical Christianity insists also that Christians have another access to biblical history than historical method offers. That access is what divinely authoritative, inspired, and wholly trustworthy Scripture teaches. It is not enough to emphasize the believing faith of the Christian community. If Christ be not risen, Christian faith is in vain. The Bible tells us not merely a story in which the history-like resurrection of Jesus is an essential ingredient; it tells us in propositionally revealed truth what events are both historically factual and decisively important for human destiny. In the absence of this revelation Postliberalism cannot be identified by a shared set of doctrines. It is merely the latest fashion in a century of constantly changing theological

frontiers. By the turn of the century some of its champions will
likely be marching to a very different drummer.[2]

Henry refused to be sanguine about the theological choices of
younger evangelicals, and wondered aloud which "drummer" might
be leading the parade next. He expressed some incredulity and perhaps a bit of hurt to see the epistemological, metaphysical, and ontological program that he and so many of his colleagues had outlined
so carefully in scores of monographs, courses, and confessions of
faith left in favor of less weighty hermeneutical options. "What is
wrong with classic evangelicalism?" we can almost hear him say.

In "A Troubled Conscience Fifty Years Later," Henry revisited
his thesis in *Uneasy Conscience*. Although he celebrated the growth
and influence of evangelicals in the public square, he expressed some
dismay in that believers had increasingly been co-opted into political
and cultural agendas that ultimately caricatured the evangelicals as
right-wing fanatics, on the one hand, or accommodationists to the
spirit of the age, on the other. Reacting to what he viewed as unfortunate detours in the evangelical project, he claimed:

> *Uneasy Conscience* had in view not a confrontational assault on a
> cultural arena already largely dominated by modernist and emerg-
> ing humanist motifs, but rather a measured program of education
> and of political participation and penetration. It did not anticipate
> that through their own writing and unwitting concessions to the
> culture evangelicals might themselves be placed on the defensive.
> It did not call for political protest movements or the development
> of huge mailing lists through which eager mediators other than
> elected officials would exploit the anxieties and fears of the citi-
> zenry, negotiate evangelical fortunes, and become supposedly able
> to deliver an evangelical bloc vote.
>
> It hoped rather for education with a view toward political
> penetration of the corridors of power in a culture in which evan-
> gelical colleges and universities would define the cultural dilemma,
> identify the Christian mind, and formulate a compatible world-life

[2]Carl F. H. Henry, "The Instability of 20th Century Theology," unpublished manuscript, 1997.

view. . . . A political movement lacking a canopy philosophy could offer no stable alternative to the reigning cultural dilemma.

But the hoped for educational thrust would prove to be disappointing. Proposals in the 1950's for a Christian university in the New York area crumbled. The Coalition of Christian Colleges and Universities soon reflected weakening epistemic controls as many presidents of member institutions excelled at fund raising more than at the formulation of theological essentials. Even sound bellwether evangelical colleges could hardly restrain faculty assaults on biblical inerrancy.[3]

Looking like he was cast in some sort of cruel allegory, Henry was describing what he always wanted but never had: an urbane evangelicalism bristling with ideas coming from the best minds and faithful institutions carrying them forward into a reluctant, but hopefully winnable society. In sum, he longed for the creation of a real evangelical milieu—a nurturing perspective with like-minded compatriots—like the one Roman Catholics have created and sustained. If he were alive today, Henry would likely survey the steady stream of formerly Protestant thinkers and writers converting to Roman Catholicism, and while disagreeing with their theological reasons for leaving, would probably sigh and quietly say to the evangelical community who had lost them, "I saw all of this coming. You can't say I didn't tell you so." The converts are leaving for a milieu with a robust epistemology, a church convinced of its own doctrinal heritage, and a community not accustomed to so much self-criticism or so many second glances about things like truth, marriage, and what ultimately is the basis for human flourishing. Henry envisioned but never saw the realization of his dream for such a robust community. Although he would have celebrated current movements to defend and preach the gospel, and while he would have supported passion for renewed focus on local churches, he would have wondered whether all the good will was just one strategic set of skeptical philosophical questions away from a relapse into fundamentalism at best, or outright heterodoxy at worst. In the balance of confusion lies the soul

---

[3]Carl F. H. Henry, "A Troubled Conscience Fifty Years Later," unpublished manuscript.

of a world that does not know Christ and awaits the reclamation of evangelical confidence in the good news.

Throughout this volume, I have focused largely on Carl F. H. Henry's contribution to the field of theological method and his vision for evangelical engagement with the broader world. As I stated from the outset, he is deserving of a definitive biographical study that would survey the important roles he played in the areas of world evangelism, publishing, and the life of key institutions that still define the evangelical movement. Specifically, I have focused on certain key works in Henry's written corpus with the conviction that, if they were paraphrased and given a new hearing, the verve and pluck within them might somehow revive interest in the foundations of the faith. Although I have sought to indicate throughout this book that there are many other important voices who exhibited solidarity with Henry's main emphases, I see him in particular as a lens through which to understand the current scene and make an honest judgment as to whether there is still any purchase left in what I have called "classic evangelicalism."

On some days, I feel like the Henry of the *Uneasy Conscience* and *God, Revelation and Authority* years, bursting with confidence that the future is bright if the matter of epistemological origins can be reset. On others, my mood darkens, and I fear that evangelicalism was a brilliant "almost," and all we are left with now are "brands" of ecclesial difference and emphasis that rise and fall with the men (and women) who represent this or that organization for a limited time only. What I am convinced of is this: if the philosophical foundations are not taken seriously once again, if our explanations of the gospel are not rooted in reality, we lose. We lose big. We come up short because we live in an age of ideology that *does* take these matters seriously. The disciples of Nietzsche, Hegel, Marx, and Lacan stand at the door and knock. They wait for our university students to invite them in, for they would be more than happy to sit down and explain how everything works at the level of theory behind all that we see, say, and support.

Also at the beginning of my argument, I indicated that I was intentionally playing on a key concept in the title of this book: recovery. I mean this both in the sense of reclamation and in the sense of therapy. We must reclaim the essentials of our Protestant heritage in the spirit of the seminar Kenneth Kantzer and Carl Henry used to convene at Trinity Evangelical Divinity School, called "Know Your Roots." But we must also get over our addiction to novelty and the misperceived pursuit of freedom from tradition, which leave us lifeless to the legacy of those who went before us. For as Paul reminded the church in Corinth: "Though you have countless guides in Christ, you do not have many fathers" (1 Cor. 4:15). If we cannot reconcile our theology with the sturdy basis for biblical Christianity that framed evangelicalism and once made it great, we will find ourselves and our children cut loose from our tradition. While some might celebrate this severing of ties with the past, the loss of one's heritage is always filled with regret.

# Selected Bibliography of Works by Carl F. H. Henry

A fuller bibliography of writings by Dr. Henry, compiled by William H. Bates, is available at http://www.henrycenter.org/about/carl-f-h-henry/published-works/.

## Books

Henry, Carl F. H. *Answer for the Now Generation*. Chicago: Moody Press, 1949.

————. *Aspects of Christian Social Ethics*. Grand Rapids: Eerdmans, 1964.

————, ed. *Basic Christian Doctrines*. Grand Rapids: Baker, 1962.

————. *The Biblical Expositor: The Living Theme of the Great Book, with General and Introductory Essays and Exposition for Each Book of the Bible*. Grand Rapids: Baker, 1994.

————. *Carl Henry: At His Best*. Portland, OR: Multnomah, 1989.

————. *Christian Counter Moves in a Decadent Culture*. Portland, OR: Multnomah, 1986.

————, ed. *Christian Faith and Modern Theology*. Grand Rapids: Baker, 1971.

————. *The Christian Mindset in a Secular Society*. Portland, OR: Multnomah, 1984.

————. *Christian Personal Ethics*. Grand Rapids: Eerdmans, 1964.

————. *The Christian Vision: Man in Society*. Hillsdale, MI: Hillsdale College Press, 1984.

————. *Confessions of a Theologian*. Waco, TX: Word, 1986.

————, ed. *Contemporary Evangelical Thought*. New York: Channel, 1957.

————. *Conversations with Carl Henry: Christianity for Today*. Lewiston, NY: Mellen, 1986.

————. *The Drift of Western Thought*. Grand Rapids: Eerdmans, 1951.

————. *Evangelicals at the Brink of Crisis*. Waco, TX: Word, 1967.

————. *Evangelical Responsibility in Contemporary Theology.* Grand Rapids: Eerdmans, 1957.

————. *Evangelicals in Search of Identity.* Waco, TX: Word, 1976.

————. *Fifty Years of Protestant Theology.* Boston: Wilde, 1950.

————. *Frontiers in Modern Theology.* Chicago: Moody Press, 1964.

————, ed. *Fundamentals of the Faith.* Grand Rapids: Baker, 1969.

————. *God, Revelation and Authority.* 6 vols. Waco, TX: Word, 1976–1983. Reprint, Wheaton, IL: Crossway, 1999.

————. *The God Who Shows Himself.* Waco, TX: Word, 1966.

————, ed. *Horizons of Science.* San Francisco: Harper & Row, 1978.

————. *The Identity of Jesus of Nazareth.* Nashville, TN: Broadman, 1992.

————. *The Ministry of Development in Evangelical Perspective.* Pasadena, CA: William Carey Library, 1979.

————. *New Strides of Faith.* Chicago: Moody Press, 1972.

————. *Notes on the Doctrine of God.* Boston: Wilde, 1948.

————. *Personal Idealism and Strong's Theology.* Wheaton, IL: Van Kamper, 1951.

————. *A Plea for Evangelical Demonstration.* Grand Rapids: Baker, 1971.

————. *The Protestant Dilemma.* Grand Rapids: Eerdmans, 1948.

————. *Remaking the Modern Mind,* 2nd ed. Grand Rapids: Eerdmans, 1948.

————, ed. *Revelation and the Bible.* Grand Rapids: Baker, 1958.

————. *Toward a Recovery of Christian Belief.* Wheaton, IL: Crossway, 1990.

————. *The Twilight of a Great Civilization: The Drift toward Neo-Paganism.* Westchester, IL: Crossway, 1988.

————. *The Uneasy Conscience of Modern Fundamentalism.* With foreword by Richard J. Mouw. Grand Rapids: Eerdmans, 2003.

————, ed. *Wycliffe Dictionary of Christian Ethics.* Peabody, MA: Hendrickson, 1973.

Henry, Carl F. H., et al. *Quest for Reality: Christianity and the Counter Culture.* Downers Grove: InterVarsity, 1973.

Henry, Carl F. H., Everett F. Harrison, and Geoffrey W. Bromiley, eds. *Baker's Dictionary of Theology*. Grand Rapids: Baker, 1960.

Henry, Carl F. H., and Kenneth Kantzer, eds. *Evangelical Affirmations*. Grand Rapids: Zondervan, 1990.

## Articles and Book Chapters

Henry, Carl F. H. "Agenda for Evangelical Advance." *Christianity Today*, November 5, 1976, 38.

———. "American Evangelicals and Theological Dialogue." *Christianity Today*, January 15, 1965, 27–29.

———. "The Authority of the Bible." In F. F. Bruce, J. I. Packer, Philip Comfort, and Carl F. H. Henry. *Origin of the Bible*, 13–27. Wheaton, IL: Tyndale, 1992.

———. "Barth's Turnabout from the Biblical Norm." *Christianity Today*, January 4, 1963, 28.

———. "The Bible and the Conscience of Our Age." *Journal of the Evangelical Theological Society* 25, no. 4 (1982): 403–7.

———. "Biblical Authority and the Social Crisis." In *Authority and Interpretation: A Baptist Perspective*, edited by Duane A. Garrett and Richard Melick Jr., 203–20. Grand Rapids: Baker, 1987.

———. "Canonical Theology: An Evangelical Appraisal." *Scottish Bulletin of Evangelical Theology* 8 (Autumn 1990): 76–108.

———. "Carl Henry on Hierarchy." *Theological Students Fellowship Bulletin* 10 (March-April 1987): 25.

———. "Chaos in European Theology: The Deterioration of Barth's Defenses." *Christianity Today*, October 9, 1964, 15–19.

———. "The Christian Pursuit of Higher Education." *Southern Baptist Journal of Theology* 1, no. 3 (1997): 6–18.

———. "Christological Neglect by a Mission-Minded Church." In *Scripture, Tradition, and Interpretation*, edited by W. Ward Gasque and William S. La Sor, 216–33. Grand Rapids: Eerdmans, 1978.

———. "Christ's Resurrection and Human Destiny." *Christianity Today*, April 27, 1973, 8–11.

———. "The Church in the World or the World in the Church? A Review Article." *Journal of the Evangelical Theological Society* 34, no. 3 (1991): 381–83.

———. "The Crisis of Modern Learning." *This World* 7 (Winter 1984): 95–105.

———. "Does Genesis 9 Justify Capital Punishment: Yes." In *Genesis Debate*, edited by Ronald Youngblood, 230–50. Nashville: Nelson, 1986.

———. "Doing Your Own Thing." *Theology Today* 32 (January 1976): 403–10.

———. "Evangelical." In *The New International Dictionary of the Christian Church*, edited by J. D. Douglas, 358–59. Exeter: Paternoster, 1974.

———. "Evangelical Profits and Losses." *Christianity Today*, January 25, 1978, 69–70.

———. "Evangelicals and Biblical Authority: A Review Article." *Journal of the Evangelical Theological Society* 23, no. 2 (1980): 139–42.

———. "Evangelicals and Fundamentals." *Christianity Today*, September 16, 1957, 20–21.

———. "Evangelicals and the Bible." *Christianity Today*, March 3, 1972, 35–36.

———. "Evangelical Summertime?" *Christianity Today*, April 1, 1977, 38–40.

———. "Fortunes of the Christian World View." *Trinity Journal* 19, no. 2 (1998): 163–76.

———. "Further Thoughts about Women." *Christianity Today*, June 6, 1975, 36–37.

———. "Inerrancy and the Bible in Modern Conservative Evangelical Thought." In *Introduction to Christian Theology*, edited by Roger A. Badham, 53–56. Louisville, KY: Westminster John Knox, 1998.

———. "Interpretation of the Scriptures: Are We Doomed to Hermeneutical Nihilism?" *Review & Expositor* 71 (Spring 1974): 197–215.

———. "Jesus and Political Justice." *Christianity Today*, December 6, 1974, 34–35.

———. "Justification: A Doctrine in Crisis." *Journal of the Evangelical Theological Society* 38, no. 1 (1995): 57–65.

———. "Justification by Ignorance: Neo-Protestant Motif?" *Journal of the Evangelical Theological Society* 13, no. 1 (1970): 3–13.

———. "The Living God of the Bible." *Southern Baptist Journal of Theology* 1, no. 1 (1997): 16–31.

———. "Making Political Decisions: An Evangelical Perspective." In *Piety and Politics: Evangelicals and Fundamentalists Confront the World*, edited by Richard John Neuhaus and Michael Cromartie, 99–108. Washington, DC: Ethics and Public Policy Center, 1987.

———. "Man's Dilemma: Sin." In *The Word for This Century*, edited by Merrill C. Tenney, 3–20. New York: Oxford Press, 1960.

———. "Narrative Theology: An Evangelical Appraisal." *Trinity Journal* 8, no. 1 (1987): 3–19.

———. "The Nature of God." In *Christian Faith and Modern Theology*, edited by Carl F. H. Henry, 89–90. Grand Rapids: Baker, 1964.

———. "The Priority of Divine Revelation: A Review Article." *Journal of the Evangelical Theological Society* 27, no. 1 (1984): 77–92.

———. "Prophetic Hope." *Christianity Today*, September 10, 1971, 40–41.

———. "Reality and Identity of God: A Critique of Process-Theology." *Christianity Today*, March 14, 1969, 3–6.

———. "Reality and Identity of God: A Critique of Process-Theology." *Christianity Today*, March 28, 1969, 12–16.

———. "Reflections on Death and Suicide." *Ethics & Medicine* 14, no. 3 (1998): 66–69.

———. "A Response to 'The Bible under Spirit and Church.'" *Touchstone* (US) 4 (Spring 1991): 11–14.

———. "Revelation and the Bible." *Christianity Today*, June 9, 1958, 5–7.

———. "Revelation and the Bible." *Christianity Today*, June 23, 1958, 5–17.

———. "Science and God's Revelation in Nature." *Bulletin of the Evangelical Theological Society* 3, no. 2 (1960): 25–36.

———. "The Spirit and the Written Word." *Bibliotheca Sacra* 111, no. 444 (1954): 302–16.

———. "Stewardship of the Environment." In *Applying the Scriptures*, edited by K. S. Kantzer, 473–88. Grand Rapids: Zondervan, 1987.

———. "Theological Situation in Europe: Decline of the Bultmann Era?" *Christianity Today*, September 11, 1964, 3–6.

————. "Theological Situation in Europe: Decline of the Bultmann Era?" *Christianity Today*, September 25, 1964, 12–14.

————. "Theology and Biblical Authority: A Review Article of *The Uses of Scripture in Recent Theology*, by D. H. Kelsey." *Journal of the Evangelical Theological Society* 19, no. 4 (1976): 315–23.

————. "Theology of Mission and Changing Political Situations." In *Theology and Mission*, edited by David J. Hesselgrave, 275–91. Grand Rapids: Baker, 1978.

————. "Where Is Modern Theology Going?" *Bulletin of the Evangelical Theological Society* 11, no. 1 (1968): 3–12.

————. "Who Are the Evangelicals?" In *Evangelical Affirmations*, edited by Kenneth S. Kantzer and Carl F. H. Henry, 69–94. Grand Rapids: Zondervan, 1990.

————. "Wintertime in European Theology." *Christianity Today*, November 21, 1960, 3–5.

————. "Yea, Hath God Said." *Christianity Today*, April 26, 1963, 26–28, 45–47.

# General Index

reconciliation, 65
redemptive message, of evangelicalism, 175–76
Reformation, 43, 172
    epistemology of, 41, 57
    as over, 58
    and rise of modernity, 44–51
Reimarus, Hermann Samuel, 88
relativism, 130, 187
religion, and cultural authority, 183
religionless age, 39–40, 193
*Remaking the Modern Mind* (Henry), 32, 52
Renaissance, 50, 180
repentance, 64
retrieval, 32
revelation, 53–56, 61, 63–68
    Barth on, 76–77
    and history, 79–80
    Moltmann on, 77
    and narrative, 94–95
    as personal, 77
    unity of, 68–69
revivalism, 17
revolution, 82
Reymond, Robert, 35
Ricoeur, Paul, 108, 109, 154
Ritschl, Albrecht, 29, 88, 89
Rogers, Jack, 119
Roman Catholic Church, 19, 189, 202, 206
    converts to, 42
    Thomism of, 72
Roman mystery cults, 62
Russell, Bertrand, 73n49
Ryle, Gilbert, 113

salvation, 65
Savonarola, 180
Schaeffer, Francis, 20, 32, 109, 119, 155, 202
Schaeffer, Frank, 20, 42
Schleiermacher, Friedrich, 73, 88, 144, 145–46
Schmidt, Wilhelm, 68
Schneider, John, 122
Schopenhauer, Arthur, 73n49
scientific theology, 37
scientism, 71, 144, 185
Scripture. *See* Bible

Searle, John, 22, 103–5, 107, 113–14
second naiveté, 35, 154
secularization, 180
self-transcendence, 67
Semler, Johann, 88
*semper ecclesia reformanda*, 17
Shea, Michael P., 42
show and tell, as strategy for cultural engagement, 198
Silva, Moisés, 95
skepticism, 37, 73, 132, 144, 147–48, 204
Smith, Barry, 113
Smith, James K. A., 123–24, 156
social evils, 166–67, 172
social gospel, 169, 175
social justice, 152, 163
social reform, 152, 166–67, 170
*Southern Baptist Journal of Theology*, 15
Southern Baptist Theological Seminary, 25, 203
special revelation, 69, 70
speech-act theory, 21, 103–5, 107, 112–14
Spinoza, Baruch, 80
Spong, John Shelby, 153
Sproul, R. C., 55, 119
Stalin, Joseph, 185
Stark, Rodney, 195–96
St. Bartholomew's Day massacre, 181
Stein, Gordon, 38
Steiner, George, 185
Stott, John R. W., 19–20, 121
Strachan, Owen, 14
Strauss, David Friedrich, 88, 89, 153
Strauss, Leo, 188
Strawson, P. F., 113
Strong, Augustus Hopkins, 26
supernaturalism, 167–68

tacit knowledge, 190–91
Talbert, Charles, 124
Taubes, Jacob, 163
teleological argument, 72
teleology, 44–45, 51
theodrama, 106, 111
theo-logic, 157
theology, as second-order activity, 92, 111
theophanies of Scripture, 77
*theopneustos*, 133

# Scripture Index